Economic Analysis of
Industrial Policy

This is a volume in
ECONOMIC THEORY, ECONOMETRICS, AND MATHEMATICAL
ECONOMICS

Edited by Karl Schell, *Cornell University*

A list of recent volumes in this series appears at the end of this volume.

Economic Analysis of Industrial Policy

Motoshige Itoh
Faculty of Economics
The University of Tokyo
Tokyo, Japan

Kazuharu Kiyono
Institute of Social and Economic Research
Osaka University
Osaka, Japan

Masahiro Okuno-Fugiwara
Faculty of Economics
The University of Tokyo
Tokyo, Japan

Kotaro Suzumura
The Institute of Economic Research
Hitotsubashi University
Tokyo, Japan

Translated by

Anil Khosla
Centre for Japanese Studies
Sheffield University
Sheffield, United Kingdom

Academic Press, Inc.
Harcourt Brace Jovanovich, Publishers
San Diego   New York   Boston   London   Sydney   Tokyo   Toronto

Translation was financially supported by the Suntory Foundation.

This book is printed on acid-free paper. ∞

Academic Press, Inc.
San Diego, California 92101

United Kingdom Edition published by
Academic Press Limited
24–28 Oval Road, London NW1 7DX

Library of Congress Cataloging-in-Publication Data

Economic analysis of industrial policy / edited by Motoshige Itoh ...
[et al.].
    p.   cm. -- (Economic theory, econometrics, and mathematical
economics series)
    Includes bibliographical references and index.
    ISBN 0-12-375735-5
    1. Industry and state--Japan.   I. Itō, Motoshige,
II. Series.
HD3616.J33E36   1991
338.952--dc20   90-24386
                                                        CIP

PRINTED IN THE UNITED STATES OF AMERICA
91 92 93 94   9 8 7 6 5 4 3 2 1

Contents

Part III. Oligopolistic Control of an International Market

Part IV. Welfare Implications of Strategic Competition in Oligopolistic Industries

I

Introduction

1

What Is Industrial Policy?

1.1 INTRODUCTION

Since the beginning of the 1980s, industrial policy has suddenly attracted tremendous attention, both in Japan as well as abroad. At the same time, historical, political, and economic ramifications of industrial policies have become the focus of empirical analyses and a substantial amount of literature has accumulated on these aspects. Two main factors account for this explosion of interest in industrial policies in general, and Japanese industrial policies in particular.

First, Japanese economic growth, including the high-growth period in the 1960s, has been historically unparalleled and has improved the Japanese position in terms of its share in the world markets. This rapid growth has given rise to frictions—trade and economic—between Japan and other countries, especially the developed countries led by the United States. That Japan, in the course of rapid economic growth and industrialization, did adopt various industrial and other policy measures to protect domestic industry is an undeniable fact although we defer, for the moment, the question of whether or not such policies were effective. That is why most of the other advanced countries suspect that unfair policy intervention, in the form of industrial policies, has been a major factor in the rapid economic development of Japan. These suspicions and a rising sentiment that Japanese growth needs to be countered by the adoption of similar industrial policies explains the recent surge of interest in industrial policy in these developed economies.

Second, chalking out a strategy to promote economic development has been a crucial problem for the developing countries, especially the newly industrializing countries (NICs). From their point of view, interest in industrial policies that seem to have played a major role in the economic development of Japan makes perfect sense. A number of NICs have, in fact, adopted industrial (commercial) policies quite similar to those followed in Japan.

Reflecting these developments, it is not surprising that interest in industrial policies tends to have political undertones. The developed countries are highly critical of Japanese government intervention in free markets to defend its domestic industry. The Japanese government and the developing countries, on the other

3

hand, justify use of interventionist industrial policies that benefit their own economies. As a result, investigation of "policy rationality," indispensable for economic negotiations among the countries, and even the process of rational negotiations, has been severely impeded. It is in this backdrop that the present volume attempts an economic analysis of the industrial policies from an objective and rational point of view.

It goes without saying that industrial policies cover a wide variety of objectives and policy measures. But the available studies on industrial policies are limited only to a restricted number of aspects. It is precisely this lack of comprehensive analyses that makes an investigation into the content and effects of industrial policies both interesting and worthwhile from the viewpoint of economic theory.

The research reported in the subsequent pages deals mainly with the following questions: (1) How are industrial policies analyzed in terms of economic theory? (2) What sort of framework is suitable for evaluating these industrial policies in an objective manner? (3) What policy measures are appropriate if an industrial policy is to be implemented? Thus, this work is a preliminary step for building a general theoretical framework for analyzing industrial policies. It is only through a gradual cumulation of objective analyses, however fragmentary, that a reasonable assessment of industrial policies can be made.

Leaving details to the next section, industrial policy is defined, for our purposes, as a policy which affects the economic welfare of a country by intervening in the allocation of resources between industries (or sectors), or in industrial organization of specific industries (or sectors). In more concrete terms, industrial policies in this sense can be summed up in the following four points:

1. Policies affecting the industrial structure of a country: These policies nurture and protect upcoming industries or regulate and assist the shift of resources away from the declining industries by intervening in transactions with foreign countries, such as trade and direct investment, or through such pecuniary incentives as subsidies and taxes.

2. Various policies designed to correct the market failures associated with technology development and imperfect information: These policies encourage moves toward a more desirable allocation of resources by providing accurate information or through subsidies and tax measures.

3. Policies seeking to raise economic welfare through administrative intervention in the industrial organization of individual industries: More concretely, these policies, such as depression cartels and investment cartels, intervene directly in either the competitive structure of industries, or in allocation of resources.

4. Policies based on political demands rather than economic considerations: Voluntary export restraints and multilateral agreements to deal with problems like trade friction are some examples.

A wide spectrum of economic policies—the fiscal and monetary policies designed to control swings in such macroeconomic variables as GNP and employment over the course of the business cycle, policies aimed at equitable income distribution or pollution control, region-specific policies, policies for small- and medium-sized businesses, and so on—are often included under the umbrella head of industrial policies. Such policies, though closely related to industrial policies, do not find an explicit treatment in this book.

A number of works, including *Industrial Policy of Japan* and publications of the Ministry of International Trade and Industry (MITI),[1] discussing the workings of Japanese industrial policy, are already available. It may be sufficient to follow this literature to get an idea about the objectives and means of industrial policies in concrete terms. But there is a startling lack of studies analyzing the economic mechanisms through which industrial policies affect the Japanese or other economies, or with evaluation of industrial policies from the viewpoint of economic welfare. One reason for the dearth of such studies is the fact that a direct application of traditional Western theories of economic policy (theory of trade policy, analyses of subsidies and taxes, and traditional theory of industrial organization) is insufficient to bring out the essence of Japanese industrial policies. This is because, in many respects, the Japanese industrial policies differ substantially from the conceptual framework of the standard Western theories of economic policy. An analysis of the Japanese industrial policies must take these aspects explicitly into account. That statements by policy authorities and the economists' analyses have tended to diverge in the past is an undeniable fact. How to interpret the statements by policy authorities in economic terms is a significant question in its own right and forms one of the subjects of this book.

Thus the present study aims at providing a theoretical analysis of Japanese industrial policies and their effect on economic welfare, taking into consideration, to the greatest extent possible, their distinctive features. Although details regarding the functioning of Japanese industrial policies and concrete data needed to support our arguments are provided as and when required, our main objective is to explain industrial policies within the framework of economic theory. As stated earlier, the framework of traditional Western theories of economic policy is inadequate for an analysis of Japanese industrial policies. However, recent theories of industrial organization, based on applied microeconomics, may prove fruitful for this purpose. We use this approach frequently in our analysis.

1.2 THE ORGANIZATION OF THE STUDY

This study is organized as follows. In the remainder of this chapter, we present an economic definition of industrial policy and define several other concepts needed for subsequent discussion. Chapter 2 provides a minimal historical backdrop necessary to our discussion. These two chapters constitute Part I, an introduction to this study.

Part II uses the traditional competitive market model to discuss industrial promotion and trade. For a proper understanding of the relationship between Japanese heavy and chemical industrialization and industrial policies and how it affected economic development and income distribution in Japan and the world, it is necessary, first, to fully grasp the importance of the concept of industrial promotion and the choice of industrial structure—an aspect which has been, traditionally, more or less neglected. Furthermore, the diminishing cost phenomenon is also discussed in detail.

Parts III and IV focus attention mainly on analyzing the economic ramifications of the fact that most manufacturing industries targeted for industrial policies were, far from being perfectly competitive, highly oligopolistic. That is, we analyze how competition among individual firms belonging to the same industry affects resource allocation and economic welfare as well as industrial policies that can raise economic welfare in such a situation.

Part III deals with the problems associated with oligopolistic control of an international market by a group of firms belonging to a different country—that is, we undertake an analysis of international oligopoly. To get to the bottom of trade frictions, it is necessary, first, to have a proper grasp of which groups in which countries gain or lose from the adoption of particular policies. An analysis grounded in the theory of international oligopoly, in addition to the traditional trade theory, seems to be the most effective way to deal with such problems.

Part IV discusses the welfare implications of the strategic competition in oligopolistic industries on the domestic economy of a country. Our main purpose here is to provide fresh insights into the concept of "excessive competition," a phrase which is frequently referred to in discussions of Japanese industrial policies.

Part V is devoted to an economic analysis of research and development (R & D) investment, an indispensable element in any discussion of future industrial policies. Research and development activities differ from normal economic activities on at least three counts. As a result, policies directed at R & D tend to be more complicated and subtle.

First, there is problem of low "appropriability" of the fruits of R & D, i.e., technical knowledge. It is difficult for the inventing firm to exclude other firms, which did not play any role in the invention process, from the use of the results of its efforts. As a result, there is no guarantee that the inventing firm can realize the full benefits of its R & D activity. Second, since a multiple number of firms engage in R & D activities with the same objective, it gives rise to the problem of duplicated investments. This feature is referred to as the problem of "common pool" and gives rise to negative externalities. Third, only a small number of large firms are, normally, associated with R & D activities. As a result, strategic interactions among these firms tend to play an important role. Part V considers the desirable form of industrial policies for R & D activities, such as R & D associations or intellectual property rights, by analyzing the above-mentioned aspects along with the role of uncertainty in R & D activities.

Part VI addresses some problems, not included in the above analysis, but nevertheless considered important from the viewpoint of formulating future industrial policies. The problems of industrial adjustment arising from a change in the external environment surrounding a country, various types of economic and political problems related to trade frictions, and the future of international trading system are some of the problems forming the subject matter of discussion in this part of the book.

1.3 INDUSTRIAL POLICY—THE CONCEPT

Japan's postwar industrial policy has been the focus of countless and often heated debates between government authorities and the business community, between the Japanese government and foreign governments, and between government officials and economists. The many policy measures adopted in the name of industrial policy have had an enormous impact on the Japanese society and economy, touching all social classes and many different industries and firms. Looking back at the history of industrial policies, it is somewhat strange to find that there is not even a single accepted and unified interpretation of the concept of industrial policy available and, what is more, the term even lacks a clear definition.

In the 1970s, Kaizuka wrote about this fuzziness surrounding the concept of industrial policy:

It is surprising to note that the term "industrial policy," to the best of this author's knowledge, has never been clearly defined. For example, even Yoshihiko Morozumi's *Sangyo Seisaku no Riron* (Theory of Industrial Policy) (1966), which is considered to be a comprehensive work on industrial policy, does not contain any definition of industrial policy. Numerous other works related to industrial policies are available but none gives a clear definition of this term.

Examining the Morozumi work, carried out at a time when industrial policies were at their zenith, Kaizuka reaches the following conclusions: "If the author is forced to give a definition of industrial policy, he will have to (with some irony) reply as follows. That is, industrial policy is the policy implemented by the MITI" (Kaizuka, 1973, p. 167).

In the 1980s, Hindley also emphasized the political significance of a lack of conceptual guidelines for what constitutes industrial policy:

Yet the truth is that the term "industrial policy" has an entirely spurious sound of precision. Over the past ten or fifteen years, the term has become a portmanteau catchword for that broad range of governmental actions which directly affect the structure of production in an economy. . . . From a political point of view, this very lack of precision in definition is a major attraction of support for industrial policy (Hindley, 1984, pp. 277–278).

Taking note of these points, an analysis of industrial policies within the framework of economic theory and an evaluation of their policy implications, the main objectives of the present study, require a precise and objective definition of an industrial policy. In this study, the phrase "industrial policy" is used in the following sense: Industrial policies refer to

the policies implemented for raising welfare level of a given economy when the defects of a competitive market system—market failures—create problems for resource allocation and income distribution through free competition. Moreover, it includes the totality of policies that are designed to attain this objective through intervention in the allocation of resources between industries or sectors, or in the industrial organization of individual industries.[2]

The "totality of policies" here implies the combination of policy goals and measures. In the subsequent discussion, policy includes both policy goals and policy measures unless otherwise specified.

1.4 POLICY GOALS

Two points need to be noted in the context of this definition of industrial policy. First, we defined industrial policies as policies which are necessary only when market failures prevent the market mechanism from attaining the most desirable resource allocation and income distribution. Thus, according to this definition, industrial policies are intended to complement rather than supplant the market mechanism. The policies unrelated to market failures, for instance, policies that pursue merit wants such as "enhancement of national glory," etc., are excluded from this definition. (The strong suspicions that a substantial proportion of the policies implemented in the name of industrial policy in the postwar period were actually such policies, resulted in a futile debate among the economists and the MITI during the 1960s and 1970s. We prefer to avoid such unproductive debate by taking a normative stand, that is, investigating desirable forms of industrial policies.)

Second, it may be emphasized that the rationale for adopting an industrial policy, as defined here, lies in the fact that it in some way improves the economic welfare of a country. Thus, all policies designed to increase the economic welfare of a country (even at the cost of lower welfare in other countries) are, whether good or bad, the subject matter of the present study.

To analyze the abstract concept of industrial policy, as defined above in the real world economy, it is necessary to determine the nature and causes of market failures. Besides, in considering national economic welfare, it is also necessary to delimit the scope of welfare judgments. This is necessary since the economy of a country is constituted of groups with often conflicting interests—consumers and producers, the present and the future generations, and so on. Policy measures employed in pursuit of industrial policies in a country vary, depending on which interest groups receive priority and which interest groups get only a cursory treatment, and justifications of such measures also differ. It goes without saying that in actually implementing a policy, it is impossible to touch upon the distributive problems explicitly. It is more common to find emphasis on abstract concepts such as "industrial rationalization," "economic independence," "stable growth," "international competitiveness," and "improvement of work and living conditions," which obscure the conflict of interests that lurks behind the policy decisions. An economic analysis of industrial policy, however, should not lose sight of the implications of the policy for distribution besides the total welfare level, i.e., the efficiency problem.

1.5 FEASIBILITY OF POLICY MEASURES

For a policy to be actually implemented, it must be feasible. A feasible policy must satisfy two basic conditions.

First, the government must possess the policy tools to implement the policy effectively. Generally speaking, the tools of industrial policy can be classified on the basis of following criteria[3]:

1. Applicability: On the basis of applicability, policy tools can be classified as discretionary or universal. The discretionary policy tools are those that can be used to confer differential benefits on different firms or firm groups within the same industry. Universal policy tools, on the other hand, are uniformly applied to all firms in an industry.

2. Rights of administrative authorities: In terms of rights of administrative authorities, the policy measures can be divided into incentivist policy measures, which induce the private firms to voluntarily adopt a behavior pattern in conformity with the policy objectives by providing pecuniary or nonpecuniary incentives, and regulatory policy measures such as the right to grant licenses and administrative guidance, with a legal basis used to force private firms to comply.

The second factor that affects the feasibility and effectiveness of a particular industrial policy is its effect on domestic and global economies and the image it projects. In other words, feasibility of adopting a particular policy depends on whether a national consensus can or cannot be built up and whether the policy is acceptable at an international level or not. It should be noted that since implementation of discretionary and regulatory policy measures is left to the discretion of the administrative authorities there is much room for arbitrariness.

For a competitive market mechanism to sustain a desirable level of economic activity over the long run, free and equitable access to economic opportunities is required (as detailed in Chapter 16). It is obvious that industrial policies, intervening in interindustry and intraindustry resource allocation, have an inherent tendency to hinder free and equitable access of economic opportunities. If the policy measure does not have an equitable effect on the firms belonging to an industry and those wishing to enter it, the desired competitive conditions cannot be maintained. In this sense, it is difficult to characterize the discretionary or regulatory policy measures as desirable.

For an industrial policy to be domestically acceptable, a national consensus must first be built on policy objectives and implications, including the distributional aspects such as which firms or industries are to be favored and which to be sacrificed. Moreover, some policy measures simply cannot be implemented just on the basis of private motives of individual economic agents. For instance, organization of a research and development association, or gathering, exchange, and diffusion of information, requires individual private sector firms to offer voluntary cooperation and in turn to be assured the participation and cooperation of other firms. In this sense, a majority support for a policy is not enough and a consensus among the parties concerned is also often necessary.

In considering the feasibility of a policy, the degree of maturity of the economy concerned and its size in relation to the world economy must also be taken into account. Some of the policies, feasible in a small economy, may be rendered infeasible in the case of an economy with strong international competitiveness and with a large share of the world economy since the spillover effects on the international economy may be substantial. For example, there is a strong possibility that protectionist industrial and commercial policies, based on the infant industry protection argument, may be acceptable at the international level. But if the same policy is adopted by a country which has shown sufficient economic growth and has attained a high level of national income, it is bound to face sharp international criticism. Whether other countries are willing to accept a particular industrial policy (or put up with it) is another determinant of the feasibility of an industrial policy.

The discussion above, however, does not imply that a policy is inappropriate just because the domestic economic policy has been criticized by other countries. The point being made here, instead, is that the policy authorities should adopt policies whose appropriateness can be rationally and convincingly put across to other countries. If policies are limited to only those that can be objectively justified, a country can distinguish between the feasible and infeasible policies by itself and can respond to criticism by other countries.

1.6 First-Best and Second-Best Industrial Policies

As noted earlier, we use the term industrial policy to imply the policies implemented to affect the economic welfare of a country through intervention in inter-industry (sector) resource allocation or in the industrial organization of a specific industry (sector) in circumstances where defects of competitive market system—market failures—hinder, in some way, resource allocation and income distribution through free competition. This interpretation of industrial policy poses the following question: Is industrial policy intervention always justified whenever there is a market failure? Let us clarify our stance in response to this question.

In fact, there is no assurance that an industrial policy intervention can invariably raise economic welfare even if a market failure has occurred. This is because quite often the policies, just like markets, tend to fail. Let us dwell on this point further.

Let us assume that a functional impediment has emerged in the market system. What are the conditions necessary for the government or the central planning board—hereafter, simply government—to be able to remove this impediment at a stroke and improve economic welfare?

First, the government must have accurate information regarding the segment of the economy in which the functional impediment appears as well as the cause and the extent of distortion. This is necessary for a proper diagnosis of the functional distortions. Second, the government must have sufficient administrative authority to take effective and efficient measures to deal with each individual distortion diagnosed. This is a necessary condition for appropriate treatment of the functional distortions. Third, the government must be equipped with capabilities to look beyond the direct and immediate effects of a policy, capture its indirect and long-term effects, and make policy decisions to deal with any side effects of the measures on other segments of the economy, and the future of the economy as a whole. This is a necessary condition for aftercare for any side effects of the treatment.

These conditions are clearly very strong. The first condition implies that the government is in a position to accurately grasp the information related to the private economic activities—technical knowledge of the producers, consumer preferences, the placement conditions of resources, etc. All this knowledge and information is dispersed in the form of individually held private information among producers, consumers, and resource owners. Besides, it is difficult to believe that even holders of such information have all this information in a well-sorted and consistent format for accurate and quick transmission to other economic entitites. Therefore, it is practically impossible for the government, and for that matter for any economic agent, to make original holders of such private information divulge it accurately and quickly and to centrally manage and use it.[4]

The second condition relates to the feasibility problem discussed in the previous section. The structure of administrative rights necessary for implementing an effective and efficient policy measure to deal with a market failure may infringe upon basic economic freedoms like freedom to do business and freedom to choose one's occupation, and may also contradict the competition policies like antimonopoly laws.

The third condition requires the government to anticipate the complex and subtle causal linkages and to see through the future shrouded with uncertainties. Let us call the all-knowing and all-powerful government that satisfies all stringent conditions mentioned above as the "first-best government" and industrial policies implementable by such a government as the "first-best industrial policies." Obviously, the first-best industrial policies, attainable by a strong government with perfect, all-pervasive information on all aspects of the economy as well as with regulatory powers, are the ideal way to deal with market failures.

However, from the viewpoint of formulation of appropriate industrial policies by evaluating the real world industrial policies, our main objective here, the first-best industrial policies do not necessarily serve as an interesting reference point. Since the real world government is hardly ever a first-best government, it is not possible to use the same arguments to justify intervention by such an imperfect government as may be used to justify intervention by the first-best government. It is important to note that a policy intervention, intended to correct market failure, may in fact result in deterioration of economic welfare due to imperfectness of the government. This may be compared to a situation where an ideal arbitrator may satisfy all the parties to a dispute but an inconsiderate arbitrator may worsen rather than solve the dispute.

The reasons why a real-world government cannot implement a first-best policy include the limits to which basic private information can be collected and analyzed, the insufficient capability to accurately predict the indirect and long-term effects of a policy, the physical impossibility to implement ideal policy measures, such as a lump sum tax, that do not distort the economy, and so on. The political, historical, institutional, and economic environment of liberal democracy, which prevents the drastic use of coercive policy intervention, and limitations placed on feasible policy measures available to the government by international institutions and practices, etc., are some of the other factors accounting for the failure to implement first-best policies.

We refer to a government that must follow the dictates of physical, capability, institutional, political, and international constraints—not an all-knowing, all-capable government in this sense—as the "second-best government." The industrial policies implementable by such a second-best government, therefore, are referred to as the "second-best industrial policies." While the first-best industrial policy tries to implement drastic and comprehensive measures at one stroke to deal with market failure, the second-best industrial policy takes the constraints on the government as given and attempts to make gradual, piecemeal improvements. The discussion in this book is limited to second-best industrial policies thus defined. As pointed out earlier, we believe this to be the best approach to meet the objectives of this study. From this standpoint, industrial policy interventions by a real-world government in the face of market failure may not necessarily be theoretically justified even though a correction by first-best industrial policy may raise economic welfare. It is only when the second-best industrial policy, formulated on the basis of institutional and other constraints which the real-world government must take as given, leads to improved welfare that the industrial policy is justified.

NOTES

1. For example, see "A Quarter Century of Trade and Industry Administration" (Tsusho Sangyo Chosakai, 1975) or "Industrial Policy of Japan" (Nihon Keizai Shinbun, October–November, 1984). The latter is a series of 38 newspaper articles contributed by a MITI research group on industrial policy.

2. See Okuno and Suzumura (1986, p. 31) and Suzumura and Okuno-Fujiwara (1987, p. 3). This definition is basically the same as used in Komiya, Okuno, and Suzumura (1984).

3. See Okuno and Suzumura (1986, pp. 3–4) on this point.

4. For important implications of this fact, see Suzumura (1982).

2

Postwar Japanese Industrial Policy:
A Historical Overview*

Who were the originators of postwar Japanese industrial policy, what were its objectives, and how was it implemented? What role did this policy play in promoting or hindering the recovery of the Japanese economy in the immediate postwar period, in sustaining postwar rapid growth, and, finally, in the development of the Japanese economy since the 1970s? A thorough examination of this problem would require much more space than is available to us. Fortunately, many objective, critical, and conscientious histories of postwar Japanese industrial policy are already available [for example, Tsuruta (1982); Tsusho Sangyo Gyosei Kenkyu Kai (Commerce and Industry Administration Research Association) (1983); and Komiya, Okuno, and Suzumura (1984, Chapters 2–4)]. Therefore we limit our presentation here to the minimum number of historical facts required to guide the reader through this book.

2.1 POSTWAR ECONOMIC REFORMS:
FORMULATING A COMPETITIVE FRAMEWORK

Upon its defeat in August, 1945, Japan came under the control of the Occupation forces, mainly the United States Army, and a program of direct and strict economic reforms was imposed aimed at the "democratization" of Japan. There is no direct relationship between these reforms and the Japanese industrial policy which was developed later, but there is no doubt these reforms were responsible for creating an extremely competitive economic environment in Japan. As argued below, one of the recurring themes in the history of postwar Japanese industrial policy has been the attempt by government authorities to revive the system of prewar and wartime controls to counter the freely competitive economic environment established by the postwar reforms. For this reason, too, it is impossible to discuss Japanese industrial policies without referring to the Occupation policies.

---

*This chapter is a revised version of a part of Suzumura and Okuno-Fujiwara (1987).

14

Dissolution of the family-dominated zaibatsu (financial groupings), land reforms, and labor democratization were some of the major economic reforms introduced by the Occupation forces.

Dissolution of zaibatsu, which wielded extensive economic power in the prewar period, began with the disintegration of the holding companies, the nucleus of the group, and the splitting up of major zaibatsu firms. But the Occupation reforms went beyond zaibatsu dissolution and aimed at removing the excessive concentration in the production system by putting limits on private ownership. These reforms were made concrete in the Antimonopoly Law (April, 1947) and the Law to Eliminate Excessive Concentration of Economic Power (December, 1947). It is, however, doubtful that these laws achieved much by way of removing concentration in the production system or economic domination, given the fact that the provisions of these laws were later diluted and revised in various ways.[1] But there is no doubt that dissolution of the zaibatsu, along with the purge of prewar business leaders, gave an impetus to the process of separation of ownership and management, and created an economic environment conducive to the vigorous interfirm competition that has characterized the postwar Japanese economy.

Land reforms, on the other hand, resulted in a transfer of property rights to the land owned by absentee landlords and a major portion of the land owned by resident landlords to tenant farmers. This transfer of property rights to those who actually tilled the land resulted in incentives for widespread land improvement and a sharp increase in agricultural productivity. The resulting increase in farm income and the expansion of the domestic market was crucial in sustaining high economic growth in Japan on the demand side. Ironically, however, the revolutionary land reforms made the farmers more conservative by giving them a vested interest in their land ownership and created a bastion of support for the conservative party government.

The labor reform consisted of three laws: the Trade Union Law (December, 1945), the Labor Relations Adjustment Law (September, 1946), and the Labor Standards Law (April, 1947). All the laws were enacted by Occupation authorities and succeeded in establishing an institutional framework for democratic labor relations in the postwar Japan. The three laws led to a rapid increase in the percentage of unionized work force, and working conditions and wages improved substantially. Improved working conditions and an increase in workers' buying power supported postwar Japanese economic growth from the demand as well as the supply side.

2.2 THE RECOVERY PHASE:
FROM RATIONALIZATION TO ECONOMIC INDEPENDENCE

The industrial policy in the immediate postwar period was heavily influenced by the economic principles that guided the wartime system of economic controls.

The priority production system (1946–1948) is representative of such policies. With an objective to achieve a quick recovery of mining and manufacturing production, the meager government funds, imported raw materials, and foreign exchange were placed under strict government controls for priority distribution to a handful of strategic industries considered essential to Japan's economic reconstruction. Since coal was, at that time, the major energy source and energy was considered to be the most important factor for restarting production, coal mining (the major source of energy) and the iron and steel industry (which provided a major input for the coal industry) accordingly were given the top priority.

The coal and iron and steel industries were given priority in the allocation of resources in the sense that almost all the imported heavy oil was allocated to the iron and steel industry, the output of which was invested in the coal industry or back into steel, while the increase in coal output went into the iron and steel industry. The priority production system was supplemented by priority financing of the coal industry by the Reconstruction Finance Corporation, established in January, 1947, for the purpose of providing government and Bank of Japan funds to the industrial sector. In the meantime a strict rationing system for foodstuffs and consumer necessities, a continuation of wartime controls, was in force.[2]

The steady increase in coal output, resulting from the priority production system, made it possible to allocate coal to other industries as well. Few people will disagree with the assertion that economic reconstruction of Japan would have been impossible without the priority production system. Nevertheless, such command economy allocation of resources did not ensure economic efficiency. In fact, expanded production of coal and iron and steel (and later of "stabilization goods" such as chemical fertilizers, soda, and gas) entailed substantial economic costs. The government was forced to subsidize these goods in order to make up the difference between high production costs and low official prices. The Reconstruction Finance Corporation, through which these subsidies were made, used an unorthodox method of financing by issuing reconstruction finance bonds underwritten by the Bank of Japan. This method of financing the priority production system was bound to put serious inflationary pressures on the economy and the wholesale price index, in fact, shot up 13-fold between 1946 and 1949.

Due to the intensification of the Cold War between the East and West Blocks toward the end of 1948, the policies of Occupation forces, especially those of the United States, toward Japan changed swiftly. Assisting the reconstruction of the Japanese economy became the basic policy to turn Japan into the Asian bulwark against communism. In line with this, Joseph Dodge, financial adviser to the Supreme Commander of the Allied Powers, implemented a series of measures, the "Dodge Line," to do away with the system of postwar controls characterizing the Japanese economy, putting more reliance of market mechanisms to bring about economic recovery. As a result, new loans from the Reconstruction Finance Corporation, the main source of inflation, were suspended from 1949. Various types of subsidies, including the price subsidies, were also abolished and a surplus budget appeared. The multiple exchange rate system, which sustained the controlled economy, was also abolished and replaced with a single rate system of ¥360 to the dollar which was to last until 1971.[3]

Most observers considered the yen to be overvalued at an exchange rate of ¥360 to the dollar.[4] Besides, most of the government administrators believed that, given high domestic cost of basic goods, it was essential to embark on a comprehensive policy for rationalization of production, by making a more efficient use of resources and fostering new industries, in order to improve Japan's international competitiveness. In response to this, MITI set up an Industrial Rationalization Deliberation Council in December, 1949 (renamed Industrial Structure Deliberation Council in 1964 after merging it with the Industrial Structure Commission set up in 1961), to build a consensus among government, businesses, and the workers on rationalization promotion policies. What was important about this deliberation council was that it provided an opportunity to private bodies to participate informally in the government's policy-making process through the exchange of ideas with bureaucrats on major industrial policies before they were finalized. The finance subcommittee of this council, in particular, played an important role in reviewing the consistency of investment plans of the major manufacturing industries in terms of demand prospects and availability of finances. The policy authorities often used consistency at the macroeconomic level as a pretext to intervene in the investment plans of private firms. It may be noted, however, that these attempts resulted in dissemination of information about the prevailing conditions in other industries and the economy as a whole to individual firms and industries that became the target of investment plans. Moreover, the Foreign Exchange and Foreign Trade Control Law (Foreign Exchange Law for short) and the Law concerning Foreign Capital (Foreign Capital Law for short) were also enacted. These laws gave the government direct regulatory power to impose import quotas and manage foreign capital flows. These powers made it easier for the government to undertake policy interventions in a number of different ways.

The industrial rationalization policies, equipped with approval systems based on the Foreign Exchange and Foreign Capital Laws and rationalization legislation formulated in the Industrial Rationalization Deliberation Council, showed progress during this period. In contrast to the priority production system, which conferred preferential treatment on the important strategic industries as a whole, the industrial rationalization policies picked up the most technologically advanced firms in a targeted industry for preferential treatment. The increase in productivity, partly based on such rationalization policies, along with the Dodge Line measures, resulted in serious deflation, which pushed many inefficient firms into bankruptcy and raised the unemployment rate.

The black clouds of economic recession were ultimately dispersed by the outbreak of the Korean War in 1950. Exports, production, profits, and employment rose rapidly in a number of industries such as textiles, chemicals, machinery, lumber and wood, and iron and steel. And the foreign exchange earnings from the extraordinary demand (the expenditures by the United States Army and its allied forces) removed Japan from the international balance-of-payments constraint on the expansion of domestic economic activities at one stroke. A more important effect of this war, from the long-run perspective, was that it promoted investment and technological progress in the heavy and chemical industries in Japan. The expansion of the heavy and chemical industries stimulated by the extraordinary demand, along with the technology supplied by the United States Army, made introduction of the latest technology in most of the industries possible and promoted a sharp increase in and renovation of productive capacity. Thus, the basic structure of the postwar Japanese industrial policies, riding with such a tide, took a definitive shape.

Unlike the priority production system, showing strong traces of direct controls used in the prewar controlled economy, the main policy instruments of the industrial policy during this period gradually took on an incentivist and advisory character. The Japan Development Bank (established in 1951) took over the assets and liabilities of the Reconstruction Finance Corporation and encouraged plant investments by providing de facto subsidies in the form of below-market interest rates on investment loans to key industries. Export industries were also subsidized in effect by similar lending policies adopted by the Japan Export–Import Bank for export promotion. In addition, a number of special tax measures were introduced to promote investment and exports. A system of accelerated depreciation for important machinery introduced to facilitate plant investment under the Enterprise Rationalization Promotion Law is one such example. The MITI, already engaging in administrative guidance to encourage firms to cut back on operations, legalized depression cartels and rationalization cartels as well as the revision of the Antimonopoly Law in 1953. Finally, it may be important to note the lapse, in 1952, of the Law on Temporary Emergency Adjustment of Demand and Supply of Goods, which had given the government a direct control over allocation of principal commodities. From this time on, strict domestic controls on industrial goods ceased to be important. In this sense, the lapse of this law symbolizes the transition away from the system of direct controls on the economy, which had held sway both during and after the war, toward a reliance on competitive market mechanisms based on a mixed economy.

The rapid growth of the Japanese economy was already under way in the late 1950s, as is evident from the Jimmu Boom starting in 1956 and the slogan "it is no more the postwar era" in the *Keizai Hakusho* (Annual Report on the Japanese Economy) of the same year. Along with this, objectives of industrial policy also changed. Although still enjoying trade protection, some of the industries, including the automobile industry, that had been targeted for nurturing and promotion were able to stand on their own without any dependence on preferential tax treatment or low interest via the fiscal investment and loan program. A number of industries, such as iron and steel and electrical machinery, characterized by diminishing costs, grew steadily. On the other hand, the rationalization of increasing cost industries, represented by the coal industry, failed ultimately because of the availability of cheap and stable supplies of imported oil. The focus of the industrial promotion policies, under these circumstances, shifted toward new growth industries like synthetic fibers, plastics, petroleum refining, petrochemicals, electronics, and general machinery. While preferential measures were adopted to encourage investment in the petroleum industry to promote a shift from coal to imported oil, adjustment assistance to the coal industry, where production was plummeting at a fast pace, became a serious policy problem. Some domestic industries like the automobile and heavy electrical industries, on the other hand, received heavy trade policy protection in the form of high tariff rates and import quotas which played an important role in the growth of these industries. Introduction of foreign technology, however, was strongly encouraged and, given the big technological gap that had developed between Japan and the developed countries during the war and in the immediate postwar period, technological progress proceeded at a fast rate.

As noted earlier, the rapid growth era began in the late 1950s. Throughout this period, rapid growth was experienced not only by the industries that were already in the process of developing but also by a number of other industries that had just been targeted for fostering. One is tempted to jump to the conclusion that this is proof enough to show that the industrial policies were indeed effective. However, it is not clear whether it is appropriate to attribute to industrial policies either the unprecedented high growth since this period or the fact that a large number of industries targeted for nurturing did indeed develop. This is because a number of other factors—an extremely competitive market environment based on vigorous entrepreneurial spirit, rapid and steady expansion of domestic as well as foreign markets, an abundant supply of imported foreign technology, and superior adaptability of Japanese firms to such technology—were also responsible for bringing about rapid economic growth in this and the subsequent periods. Although it is certain that industrial policies did not place any major obstacle in the way of economic development, it may be pointed out here that, barring a few, most of the scholars working on the Japanese economic history of this period have emphasized the importance of factors other than the industrial policies.[5] In any case, an empirical evaluation of the effectiveness of industrial policies demands a much more detailed investigation of the facts than is currently available and, here, we refrain from drawing any hasty conclusions.

2.3 HIGH-GROWTH ERA: INDUSTRIAL POLICY AT ITS ZENITH

Investments by private sector firms continued to accelerate stimulated by technological progress. The Income Doubling Plan (announced in December, 1960) was considered overly optimistic initially but it soon became evident that the plan had actually greatly underestimated the latent potential of Japan for economic growth. As a result of the rapid increase in investment, the heavy and chemical industries steadily increased their share of both production and exports. Various government institutions involved with industrial policy did their best to support this increase in investment. The Japanese labor market, for the first time in its history, experienced a tightening which further strenghened the incentives for investment in equipment embodying capital-intensive technological progress. Besides, the gap between the advanced manufacturing sector and the more backward sector, composed of agricultural and small- and medium-scale firms, widened further. Policies to modernize agriculture and small- and medium-scale firms through the use of modern equipment and mechanization of agriculture were adopted to correct such imbalances in development.

The rapid increase in Japanese exports of manufactured goods came at a time when the European countries were in the process of dismantling export restrictions on a wide range of products. This led to a strong demand for liberalization of Japanese trade as well. The Japanese government responded by deciding to promote trade liberalization in principle in the 1960s. In terms of the proportion of goods liberalized, trade liberalization was more or less completed by 1964. However, the Japanese government withheld certain key items from this liberalization process for as long as possible. Automobiles, for instance, were not liberalized until 1965; in the case of computers, only peripherals were liberalized in 1972, with full liberalization being put off until 1976. Besides, a number of key agricultural products are still awaiting to be liberalized. The foreign countries, when they point out that Japan has relied on import restrictions to develop its domestic industry, are partially correct.

The year 1964 was a landmark year for Japan as it joined the International Monetary Fund (IMF) as an Article 8 country (which are forbidden to restrict payments and transfers for international transactions on current account) and also became a member of the OECD (the Organization for Economic Cooperation and Development), regaining its stature as a member of the international community at least economically. In doing so, as a responsible member of the international community, Japan was duty bound to gradually liberalize the inflow of foreign direct investment.[6] Faced with pressures to liberalize and internationalize, the goals of Japanese industrial policy shifted away from reconstruction and economic independence toward strengthening the international competitiveness of the Japanese industries. It must be noted that liberalization of trade and capital flows also resulted in a gradual decrease in the number of effective policy measures available to the MITI for intervening in the activities of the private sector firms. The powers that guaranteed the effectiveness of the MITI's administrative guidance and policy intervention—allocation of import quotas, approval of individual licenses or technology import contracts, verification and approval of joint ventures between Japanese and foreign firms—were gradually disappearing with trade and capital liberalization.

Capacity coordination was one of the major industrial policy objectives during the 1960s. It was believed that severe and "excessive competition" led to the emergence of excess capacity in the industry as a whole through the establishment of a large number of "excessively small firms" resulting in weakened international competitiveness. Based on this understanding, the MITI intervened directly in the investment plans of individual firms in industries like steel, synthetic fibers, petroleum refining, petrochemicals, and paper and pulp. Production specialization by coordinating fields of production and establishment of large-scale production systems through industrial complexes was also carried out at the urging of the MITI in order to exploit scale economies. In order to acquire the authority to implement these direct intervention measures, the MITI tabled the Law on Temporary Measures Promoting Specified Industries (tokushinho) in the Diet in March, 1962. This law aimed to increase and improve the international competitiveness of the heavy and chemical industries by promoting standardization of and specialization in production, tie-ups among the firms, formation of industrial complexes, capacity rationalization, mergers, and changes in business forms to reorganize and fine-tune the industrial structure. The bill, if passed, would have given the MITI extensive powers. But the bill was finally withdrawn after repeated tries due to staunch opposition by financial institutions and other private sector interests.

The 1960s are often referred to as the zenith of Japanese industrial policy. In reality, however, there was a clash between two viewpoints, one stressing direct government controls, and the other stressing incentives and pump priming as the tools of industrial policy.[3] By the end of the 1960s limitations of regulatory policies had become clear and the incentivist approach became dominant, bringing with it the increasing use of "soft" industrial policy tools.

For example, the MITI promoted mergers in the chemical, petroleum, metals, and machinery industries to enable them to realize latent economies of scale and strengthening their international competitiveness. Mitsubishi Heavy Industries came into existence in March, 1964, Nissan and Prince merged in August, 1966, and Yahata Steel and Fuji Steel merged to create the steel giant, Nippon Steel Corporation, in March, 1970. These mergers did not come about through administrative guidance by the MITI alone. It is more likely that the MITI intervention was sought and used because the firms may have found that their interests coincided.

This point comes out clearly if we look at the case of the automobile industry. In spite of aggressive promotion by the government authorities, the idea of grouping the automobile firms (July, 1961), by limiting new entry to enable existing firms to expand production and exploit economies of scale, failed to materialize due to a total opposition by the private sector firms. What these and numerous other cases in this period make clear is that private firms willingly offer to cooperate with intervention in the form of regulatory measures by administrative authorities only if the policies happen to coincide with their own private interests. Thus, not even the MITI could force unwilling horses to drink.[7]

Despite the efforts by the administrative authorities to revive discretionary policies, the influence of private incentives of the private sector firms on effectiveness and feasibility of the policies became decisive with the loss of legal and administrative powers of the MITI as a result of trade and capital liberalization.

A new era of industrial policy was dawning in which the role of the MITI was to persuade, advise, and indicate the direction to the private firms.

Symbolizing the end of the high-growth era, destruction of the environment and pollution surfaced as serious problems around 1970 and a good deal of self-criticism ensued. The bizarre proportions of pollution and destruction of natural environment were the inevitable result of the headlong pursuit of rapid economic growth on heavy and chemical industries in a country as small as Japan without any regard to the environmental consequences. Criticism of pollution became heated in the late 1960s, and anti-pollution regulations became a pillar of the industrial policy. The Basic Law to Deal with Pollution was enacted in 1967 and, by 1970, the Water Pollution Prevention Law (1966), Noise Pollution Regulations Law (1968), and Air Pollution Prevention Law (1968) were in force. These laws imposed the burden of proof on the polluter and, thereby, went against the traditional thinking in civil law, which placed burden of proof on the victim and does not recognize the right to compensation until there is definitive proof of malfeasance. Thus, in contrast to the weakening power of economic regulations, the new social regulations, based on direct and regulatory intervention, were quite stringent. Since then, however, the antipollution and environmental protection regulations have lost teeth and strict application of these is on a decline. The social regulations were a devil's child for industrial policy.

2.4 OIL CRISIS AND AFTER: FROM DIRECT INTERVENTION TO INCENTIVIST POLICIES

The year 1973 will long be remembered as a watershed in the postwar Japanese economy. In February of that year the flexible exchange rate system was adopted, and in October the first oil crisis hit. The price of crude oil quadrupled due to a partial oil embargo by the Middle East oil-producing countries. International prices of agricultural and other primary goods also shot up. The rate of inflation rose sharply, reflecting mainly the effect of excess liquidity stemming from yen-buying operations to support the yen in the aftermath of the Nixon shock 2 years earlier, and land speculation triggered by the plans to restructure the Japanese Archipelago. Real economic growth dropped sharply and Japan ran an enormous balance-of-payments deficit.

The quadrupling of the price of Japan's primary source of energy in the wake of the oil crisis dealt a tremendous blow to the Japanese economy since its success was based primarily on the growth of energy-intensive heavy and chemical industries. Thanks to an intensive energy conservation program, especially of oil, the Japanese economy managed to absorb the effects of the oil crisis in the space of 3 years. The cost, however, was structural depression in many of the energy-intensive materials industries, such as iron and steel, nonferrous metals, chemicals (except for pharmaceuticals), paper and pulp, and lumber. In contrast, the industries, with less dependency on imported raw materials and with room for further technological progress, experienced rapid growth, the most notable examples being automobiles and electrical appliances.

Many of the structurally depressed industries were still suffering from stagnant demand and were saddled with excess capacity when OPEC hit them with the second oil crisis in April, 1979. The oil crisis hit Japan hard, as the rise in prices spread to other imported raw materials. But Japan had learned some hard lessons from the first oil crisis and, with appropriate policy response, coupled with the willingness of labor to accept temporary real wage cuts, was able to adjust more quickly and efficiently this time around. With the exception of the adjustment period following the two oil crises, Japan ran continuous current account surpluses from 1970 on, provoking a series of trade disputes with other countries.

Reflecting these conditions, the industrial policy since the first oil crisis has come to focus on following three aspects: (1) adjustment assistance to structurally depressed industries, (2) promoting R & D investment in high-technology industries, and (3) dealing with trade friction. Post-oil crisis industrial policy stands in contrast with the industrial policy of the high-growth era on the following two points. First, the MITI powers as the controlling authority have been further curtailed. In 1977 parts of the Antimonopoly Law were strengthened in response to the criticism that cartels had sprouted up after the first oil crisis "like bamboo shoots after a rain." In 1980 a landmark decision by the Tokyo high court decreed that even the cartels formed under the administrative guidance of the MITI were illegal. In other words, it was clear that industrial policy in general and administrative guidance in particular was to be conducted within the limits set by the Antimonopoly Law.

Second, not only did it become difficult to get voluntary cooperation from private sector firms for direct intervention policies and policies to protect domestic industry, but foreign governments also became much less tolerant of such policies. With the rising importance of the Japanese economy in the arena of international competition, international criticism of the patriarchal industrial policies, reminiscent of master–servant relationships of feudal times, became more bitter. For the private sector firms, too, there was no incentive to submit to administrative guidance unless either the cost of noncompliance was too high because of extensive powers of the administrative authorities of compliance, by mere chance, coincided with the self-interests of the firms, giving them no reason to protest. Reflecting such changes in the policy environment—starting in the 1960s—the nature of industrial policy changed from being active, interventionist, and regulatory to being passive, indicative, and mediating.

The depressed industries, struggling against environmental changes in the wake of oil crises, excess capacity, and "catch-up" by the NICs (newly industrializing countries), received the helping hand of industrial policies in the form of adjustment assistance. A law on temporary measures for stabilizing specified depressed industries (Industry Stabilization Law) was enacted in May, 1978, designating some seriously depressed industries, with excessive surplus capacity and with a majority of the firms suffering from chronic losses, as structurally depressed industries. The Industry Stabilization Law provided adjustment assistance in mainly two forms. First, it created a trust fund to guarantee bank financing needed for replacement of outdated equipment and scrapping of excess capacity. Second, it exempted firms in specified industries from the provisions of the Antimonopoly Law to allow the firms, intending to scrap excess capacity, to form legal cartels. The industries designated as structurally depressed under the law included industries like aluminum refining, synthetic fibers, shipbuilding, cardboard, cotton and other spinning, and chemical fertilizers. Despite these efforts, the second oil crisis made adjustment in these specified industries all the more difficult and a new law—the Law on Temporary Measures for Structural Improvement of Specified Industries (the Structural Improvement Law)—was enacted to provide adjustment assistance. The Structural Improvement Law provided subsidies for development of new production process technologies, and assistance for business tie-ups to increase concentration and for investments in new equipment.

The following points related to adjustment assistance policies discussed above need special emphasis. First, the adjustment assistance policies in this period did not take recourse to highly discretionary and regulatory protective measures like import controls, imposition of tariffs, or subsidies to structurally depressed industries. The United States, for example, has a policy whereby a domestic industry harmed by imports can appeal to the International Trade Commission (ITC) for temporary protection through tariffs or import quotas. Since 1975, 53 cases have been brought before the commission and 13 granted protection. Even when the appeals are not granted, some industries (textiles, steel, automobiles) have succeeded in applying political pressure to get exporting countries to adopt voluntary export restraints.[8] In the case of Japan, however, explicit protectionist measures have been limited to a few cases, such as voluntary export restraints on textiles from South Korea and import tariffs for the aluminum industry.

One of the policies actually implemented was to allow cartels for scrapping capacity. Had the Industry Stabilization Law not permitted cartels for scrapping capacity, it is quite possible that required adjustments may have automatically come about via the market mechanism, allowing only the most efficient firms to survive and making for a smoother transfer of resources from declining industries into developing industries. However, no even-handed and objective evaluation of the adjustment assistance policies is as yet available.

The second important feature of industrial policy during this period was the promotion of R & D investment, focusing on R & D associations or large-scale R & D projects. In Japan, the private sector has invested more in R & D than the public sector. In fact, the recent sharp increase in the Japanese R & D expenditure in recent years owes predominantly to the increased R & D outlays in the private sector. According to the White Paper on Science and Technology for 1984, government spending accounted for a smaller proportion of total R & D expenditures in Japan than in any other major advanced industrialized country. Moreover, almost all the government outlays for R & D are directed toward fundamental research being conducted at university, government, or semigovernment research institutes. Thus, government funding plays a minuscule role in R & D in the high-technology industries. As a result Japanese technological development is heavily weighted toward applied and developmental research in the fields of production technology and product improvement. Policy plays very little part in supporting basic research, with the exception of a few large-scale projects.

The role of the government in assisting cooperative R & D in the private sector, however, cannot be ignored. In particular, measures in the form of provision of favorable tax treatment and subsidies for private firms participating in R & D associations have been taken to promote joint research in high-technology industries.[9] The VLSI (very large-scale integrated circuits) Technology Research Association, constituted by five major semiconductor producers (Fujitsu, Hitachi, Mitsubishi Electric, NEC, and Toshiba) to conduct joint research in computer technology between 1976 and 1979, is the best known and most successful example of such research associations. Judging from the number of patents taken out, the VLSI Research Association showed tremendous success. It is beyond dispute that the joint research project was instrumental in closing the big technological gap with the United States and helped lay the foundations for the success of the Japanese computer and semiconductor industries.

In general, however, the government-sponsored joint research projects have a number of drawbacks. First, Otaki's (1983) case studies indicate that, depending on the project, joint research is continued even when the changed external environment reduces the need for such research, due to institutional inflexibility or, in some cases, the research work is begun when the project is still in premature stages. Otaki also found that, in a large number of cases, actual research was carried out by individual firms at their own facilities and their management was not suited to joint research. Second, even if the projects may appear to have been successful on the basis of the number of patents registered or some other such measure, it does not tell us anything about whether the results of joint research were better than if such research had not been undertaken. Wakasugi (1986), in a study of several representative research associations, used research expenditures per patent application made as an index of research efficiency. The results show that research through associations was generally less efficient than private research with research efficiency of some research associations as low as one-fiftieth of private research. This index may not be the best possible index of research efficiency given the differences in the definition of research expenditures and the quality of research being conducted but, nevertheless, it does underline the fact that a large number of patents registered by a research association do not necessarily imply that it is successful.

Looking back at these circumstances, the success of the VLSI project appears to have been an exception to the rule, which may be attributed to the following chance factors: (1) At the time, IBM had an overwhelming technological lead in the computer field and the VLSI research project was guided by a strong desire to catch up with IBM within a specified period of time; (2) the VLSI Research Association had its own research institute where researchers from the participating firms were able to cooperate and exchange information in an efficient manner; (3) the VLSI research project was provided with a relatively generous supply of funds and its experienced research staff was composed of researchers that had been in close competition with one another for years. We must point out here that a research association system can have undesirable effects from the viewpoint of competition policy which, fortunately, have not appeared in the Japanese economy as yet. The possibility that the firms participating in a research association may form production cartels to earn monopoly profits is but one example of such undesirable effects.

It may be pointed out that, in recent years, government subsidies for R & D activities have shifted toward the development of high-technology industries (electronics, new materials, biotechnology, energy). Since such high technologies involve significant risks and require substantial amount of funds, the private firms lack incentives to put in sufficient efforts to conduct such research. Besides, such technologies tend to be development rather than basic technologies.

The third focus of industrial policy in the period under discussion was on policies to deal with trade and economic frictions. Several factors have been responsible for the recent conflict between Japan and other countries, especially the developed western countries: (1) Japan's share of the world economy has risen—for example, the GNP of Japan accounting for 2.4% of the world total in 1955 has risen to account for 10% of the total in the 1980s; (2) barring the periods immediately following the two oil crises, Japan's current account has shown a steady surplus which has risen to 3% of the GNP in recent years; (3) one segment of Japan's manufacturing industries, the machinery industry in particular, recorded much higher productivity gains than other countries, which, in combination with high dollar in the early 1980s, made them highly competitive internationally; (4) in view of its international competitiveness and the intense competition among Japanese firms, Japanese exports of television sets, automobiles, VCRs, and integrated circuits soared, causing grave difficulties for their overseas counterparts in the United States and elsewhere; (5) in contrast to this, protection of the domestic economy and economic and social constraints have been at times quite stringent, which has increased dissatisfaction in foreign countries.

In this light, the policies to deal with trade and economic frictions can be classified into two broad categories—policies to relax controls and open up the domestic economy, and voluntary export restraints to curb a sharp rise in exports.

In response to demands by foreign countries to open the domestic economy, Japan abolished or reduced remaining import restrictions, removed or lowered tariffs and nontariff barriers, and simplified import procedures and standards. Nevertheless, imports have grown sluggishly compared to the spectacular rise in exports. This has led other countries to resent the remaining restrictions on agriculture, finance, and services industries all the more. In fact, a good many of the remaining restrictions on finance or agriculture, particularly on beef and citrus fruit, are difficult to justify on economic grounds. Though these regulations are more appropriately dealt with by agricultural and financial policies rather than by industrial policy, it goes without saying that there is a need to abolish such regulations and promote opening of the Japanese economy at the earliest.

Thus the Japanese response to trade conflicts cannot be considered speedy and to the point and foreign complaints about the restrictive policies of Japan are justified in a large number of cases. Nevertheless, it must be recognized that Japan's domestic adjustment assistance for structurally depressed industries has not relied on protectionist policies such as tariffs or emergency import controls, except in a very few cases. This may be a significant point in arguing that policy measures adopted by the United States to deal with depressed industries (for example, the automobile industry), as mentioned later, may not have been desirable from the point of view of economic welfare of the country as a whole.

As noted earlier, the valid criticism of Japanese nontariff barriers and unfair business practices should be carefully looked into and dealt with speedily and in good faith. However, it is doubtful that all these demands are justified. For example, the criticism that overly strict environmental standards in Japan act as a nontariff barrier to keep foreign automobiles out of the Japanese market is completely unreasonable. Any country has the right to establish whatever level of environmental standards agreed to domestically for the health and safety of its citizens. There is no reason to abrogate this right just because of foreign criticism aimed at promotion of exports. It must be emphasized that principles of reciprocity and free trade should be applied to all but certain particularly justifiable cases, and it is in Japan's interest as a trading nation to do so. The response of the Japanese administration, including the industrial policy authorities, in a wide range of industries such as finance, distribution, and airline services, has often been one sided and is still far from satisfactory.

Most of the measures to deal with sharp increases in exports have taken the form of voluntary export restraints. A large number of Japanese exports, from textiles to steel, automobiles, machine tools, and integrated circuits, have been subject to voluntary export restraints. The policies to deal with trade frictions, especially voluntary export restraint, are often adopted to protect the interests of individual firms. Most of these policies have undesirable effects on global economic welfare (and quite often on welfare levels of the country asking for such restraints). For instance, voluntary export restraints on automobile exports from Japan conferred large benefits on the United States automobile manufacturers and workers at the expense of the United States consumers by stabilizing prices at a high level. The premium on the Japanese automobiles sold in the United States market also benefited Japanese manufacturers and workers. Some even go to the extent of arguing that the voluntary restraints resulted in keeping the number of automobile firms in the Japanese market high, thereby benefiting the Japanese consumer through increased price competition. Therefore, voluntary export restraints on automobiles has not only hurt the United States but has also resulted in a loss of economic welfare by distorting the global allocation of resources.

Due to the political nature of the responses formulated to deal with trade frictions, not only are economic principles violated, but the results are also seldom favorable for the country asking for such measures. In such situations, it is imperative to weigh the facts of each case objectively and scientifically and decide on the best possible policy measures in a rational manner, taking the effects of alternative policy measures into consideration.

NOTES

1. For example, see Shibagaki (1974) and Uekusa (1982).

2. It is surprising that it was possible to implement policies with a heavy emphasis on producer goods and restricting the supply of consumer goods without force at a time when the country was suffering from extreme poverty and hunger. The main reason that such policies could be implemented was that, besides the fact that there was an intense popular desire to rebuild the economy as soon as possible, the reduction in consumption expenditures was brought about indirectly through inflation.

3. Although Japan was reopened for trade under government supervision in the summer of 1947, no unified exchange rate existed until April, 1949, and a complex exchange rates system, with the exchange rate for each commodity determined *post facto*, was in force.

4. Shinohara (1974), however, believes that the yen was undervalued at ¥360 to a dollar exchange rate to begin with and evaluates its impact on subsequent high growth of the Japanese economy.

5. See, for example, Nakamura (1978), Kosai (1981), and Tsuruta (1982).

6. The first step in liberalization of foreign capital inflow was taken in June, 1967, and liberalization was completed by April, 1973.

7. Even in the 1950s, when the regulatory powers of the MITI were the strongest, one can find a number of instances where the government was unable to impose policies conflicting with private incentives. Construction of a plant in Chiba Prefecture by Kawasaki Steel and entry regulations in the petrochemical industry are two well-known cases. For the details of these cases see Tsuruta (1982) and Komiya, Okuno, and Suzumura (1984).

8. For details, see Baldwin (1984) and Lawrence (1988).

9. The beginnings of R & D associations in Japan date to the early 1960s. For a detailed account see Wakasugi (1986).

II

Industrial Promotion and Trade

3

Industrial Policy and Changing Industrial Structure

3.1 INDUSTRIAL POLICY AND INDUSTRIAL STRUCTURE

Because of its small geographical area and lack of natural resources, the development of the Japanese economy is heavily dependent on foreign trade and direct investment. The Japanese policy makers have been keenly aware of this dependence. Policies on trade and foreign direct investment as well as other policies affecting these variables have been the major pillars of the Japanese industrial policy. The 1949 White Paper on International Trade and Industry, for example, begins by stating the following:

> Our country is extremely small. . . . It will be impossible to sustain our economy even for a single day if the shortfall in food and raw materials were not supplemented by imports. Our country must export in order to raise funds to make these imports possible. Our economy . . . being incomplete within the territorial boundaries, must take recourse to the so-called "reproduction across the seas." Domestic production and employment, in the absence of foreign trade, will shrink leading to an extremely short economic cycle. As a result, maintenance of a reasonable national standard of living will become impossible.

The extent of economic benefits for Japan from its trade with other nations is determined by the structure of trade between Japan and its trading partners, that is, by the type and amount of Japanese exports and imports. The structure of trade, in turn, is determined by Japan's industrial structure, which depends on technology, production facilities, and endowment of productive factors. Therefore, a country must create an optimal trade and industrial structure to maximize its gains from trade.

As is well known, Japanese industrial policies have aimed at what policy authorities refer to as advancement of industrial structure, or priority to high value-added industries. More concretely, this implies heavy and chemical industrialization in the 1950s and 1960s and, subsequently, in the 1970s, a shift to

31

high-technology industries. The thinking of policy authorities on this point is made amply clear by quoting, once again, from the White Paper on International Trade and Industry:

> Advancement of industrial structure implies a move closer to an economically optimal industrial structure. In general, an appropriate industry should be decided on the basis of two criteria—an income elasticity criterion on the demand side and a productivity criterion on the supply side. In other words, on the demand side, growth of industries with high income elasticity is desirable from the viewpoint of advancement of the industrial structure, and, on the supply side, the desirable industries should have a high rate of productivity growth or a high potential for technological development. Thus, industrial sectors meeting the above criteria should be fostered to bring about an advanced industrial structure . . . and it may not be an overstatement to say that heavy and chemical industrialization is the most important issue in attainment of an advanced industrial structure. (*White Paper on International Trade and Industry*, 1964, pp. 238–240)

Withholding for the time being an evaluation of the contribution of such a policy stance of the policy authorities to the actual changes in industrial structure, the process of changes in industrial structure in postwar Japanese economy reveals that the advancement in industrial structure, or heavy and chemical industrialization, has progressed at a surprisingly high speed. Figure 3-1 plots the share of individual industries in total production and total exports to reveal the changes in the postwar industrial and trade structure of Japan. It is clear from Fig. 3-1 that expansion of production and exports of heavy and chemical industries was accomplished by a decline in the light industries.

A detailed analysis of heavy and chemical industrialization and advancement of industrial structure from the standpoint of economic theory is carried out in Chapters 5, 6, and 7. At this point, however, it may be useful to summarize some of the points.

The traditional trade theory, represented by the Ricardian and Heckscher-Ohlin theories, took the industrial structure and technological levels of individual countries as a datum and focused attention on a comparison of the level of economic welfare under free trade and autarchy. The effect of changes in trade structure and economic welfare accompanying a change in industrial structure, however, failed to attract much attention. Yet the industrial structure of a country is a major determinant of its gains from trade. Besides, industrial structure changes with time, and policy intervention, historical accidents, and cultural and institutional factors can affect the direction of this change (see Chapters 5 and 6). Technology, in most cases, is acquired through production experience, investments in technology development, and through market interactions rather than exoge-

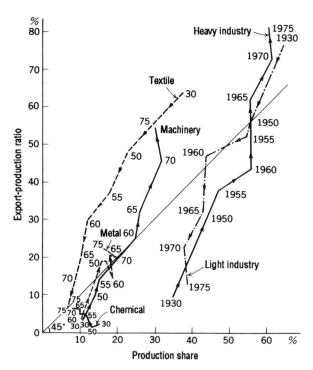

FIG. 3-1. (Source: Environmental Protection Agency, 1978. "Annual Economic Report." U.S. Government Printing Office, Washington, D.C.)

nously obtained. Thus, instead of taking technological level and industrial structure as static, it is imperative to analyze the effect of changes therein on economic welfare. As argued in Chapter 7 at length, the economic welfare of a country generally rises if its industrial and consumption structures conform to a pattern of exports with strong overseas demand, and imports that are cheaply supplied by foreign countries. This can be explained as follows: gains from trade arise from the reallocation of resources and increased efficiency that entails trade. The size of these gains accruing to a particular country, however, differs significantly in accordance with the type of industrial and trade structure of that country. Even if the industrial and trade configuration is the same across the countries, a country that has set up and developed industries with significant scale economies as its export industries benefits more from trade since it can earn a substantial amount of rents by offering a good in the international market that is not supplied by any other country. Even if the gains from trade emerging in the world economy as a whole are taken to be fixed, the industrial and trade structure of a country determines the relative distributive share of these gains accruing to that country.

3.2 INDUSTRIAL PROTECTION AND PROMOTION POLICIES
AND INDUSTRIAL SET-UP COSTS

In what ways does industrial policy contribute to the attainment of a desirable industrial structure? How should one evaluate this contribution in terms of economic theory? The postwar Japanese industrial policies have been quite diverse, ranging from import controls, export promotion, regulation of foreign investment, investment subsidies through the Fiscal Investment Loan Program, tax breaks, and R & D assistance.[1] Each of these policies had some role to play in shaping the industrial structure. Among these, import restrictions and regulations of foreign direct investment were, perhaps, most effective in providing protection to and nurturing domestic industries.

The Japanese government provided extensive protection to a number of domestic industries in the form of import controls and restrictions on inflow of direct investment with a view to protect and foster the fledgling domestic industries. Initially, import restrictions consisted of strict import quotas, but with the entry of Japan into the General Agreement on Tariffs and Trade (GATT) and the IMF in the 1960s, the quotas were gradually removed and replaced with high tariff rates (the effective rate of protection was much higher). Itoh and Kiyono (1984) argue that the Japanese domestic industry during this period was heavily protected by import controls and restrictions on direct investments. Moreover, when Japan was besieged with repeated demands from the foreign countries to dismantle these restrictions, it stalled, delaying the removal of restrictions for as long as possible to allow the domestic industry time to entrench itself firmly.[2]

Figure 3-2 depicts the relationship between a rise in the proportion of exports to total production for some of the major industries and the degree of tariff protection enjoyed by the industry. It is clear from this figure that import restrictions related to the major Japanese industries were removed only after these had been firmly established in the market.

Japan is not the only country to take recourse to strict import restrictions, but there is hardly a country that has been able to match the quick pace of Japanese growth. In this sense, protectionist industrial policies, though definitely one of the factors, cannot provide a full explanation of the Japanese economic development. The main thrust of Japanese economic growth, in fact, was provided by a plentiful and skilled labor force, firms' eagerness to invest, and a high savings rate—the private sector forces. Industrial policies served only to supplement these forces. Nonetheless, if one assumes that Japan could not have exploited the above-mentioned advantages in the absence of heavy protection provided to domestic industry, the role of industrial policy cannot be ignored.

The theoretical analysis presented here makes it amply clear that establishment of an industry is difficult if left to private incentives alone, due to the presence of various types of scale economies, and also leads to social inefficiencies.

In setting up an industry, or starting any economic activity (say, production) in general, the firms usually must bear some costs independent of the scale of the

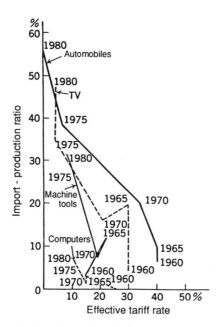

FIG. 3-2. The export–production ratio = (value of exports/value of total production) × 100. In the case of automobiles, however, the figures are in terms of number of units. *Automobiles* include passenger cars, buses, trucks, and three-wheeled vehicles. The effective rate of tariff is for passenger cars only. *Television sets* include both black-and-white and color sets. The effective tariff rate is for color television sets only. Also, the export figure for 1960 is, in fact, for 1962. *Machine tools* include numerically controlled (NC) and miscellaneous machine tools. The effective rate of tariff for 1970 onward is for NC tools only. *Computers* include analog computers. The effective rate of tariff is for digital computers alone. Computers here include the central processing unit (CPU) as well as peripherals and accessories. In principle, the tariffs are applied in the following order: (1) preferential tariffs, (2) GATT-agreed tariffs, (3) temporary tariffs, and (4) basic tariffs. GATT-agreed tariffs are used only if they are lower than temporary or basic tariffs. Finally, since we are concerned here with the effective rate of tariff against the developed countries only, preferential tariffs have been excluded from the calculations.

economic activity. For example, to start a new firm or a shift to a new business area it is necessary to gather more information on market conditions and technology and to construct new production facilities. A large proportion of costs involved become necessary independent of the level of contemplated output.

The difficulties involved in setting up an industry rise as such fixed costs increase. Without a sufficiently large scale of production, it is impossible for the firm to reduce prices to the level acceptable to the consumer and to recover the fixed costs. Now, if the size of the market is limited, the firm cannot operate within costs even with large-scale production. This can impede the establishment of an industry. If establishment of an industry generates a total surplus (producer surplus + consumer surplus) in excess of fixed costs, a failure to start that industry implies a social loss. In such a case, it is socially desirable for the members of the society to shoulder some part of these necessary fixed costs.

Thus, an industry may fail to start in the absence of social sharing (including by the firm actually undertaking the activity) of the costs associated with the establishment of the industry. It is in this sense that we refer to the costs that a society must bear at the time of establishment of an industry, independent of the scale of industrial activity in the postestablishment period, as the industrial set-up costs.

One can think of a number of factors that give rise to industrial set-up costs—the existence of a network of parts makers and subcontractors as seen in many assembly industries such as household electrical appliances and automobiles, technical-scale economies observed in industries with large-scale plants such as iron and steel and petrochemicals, scale economies emerging as a result of learning effects and R & D activities. As discussed at length in Chapter 6, if a number of industries are interlinked and information is imperfect, set-up costs may arise for the industry or a sector as a whole. In such cases, industry is unlikely to be established without government protection.

Whether the government should protect and nurture industries that cannot develop on their own has been debated at length in the discussions on the infant industry protection of international trade theory.[3] The traditional infant industry argument for industrial protection is quite useful in considering the Japanese industrial promotion policies. A brief survey of this field is presented in the next chapter.

The traditional infant industry protection argument, since it uses a partial equilibrium framework and takes global economic welfare as the evaluation standard, is inadequate for a proper evaluation of the role of Japanese industrial policies in industrial promotion. The key to a proper understanding of industrial promotion in Japan is to consider the industrial structure (the "forest") as a whole rather than individual industries (the "trees") and to analyze the effect of the form of industrial structure on economic welfare in the world economy as well as on the Japanese economy.

The changes in the Japanese industrial structure, based on protection and promotion of infant industries, not only affect the Japanese economy, but also restructure the pattern of trade between Japan and its trading partners. This significantly affects the distribution of gains from trade as between Japan and the foreign countries. Such changes in the allocation pattern of gains from trade among individual countries seriously affect economic gains for Japan and for the world as a whole.

3.3 Industrial Promotion and Maturing of the Economy

The above discussion of the relationship between industrial structure and trade has focused mainly on the Japanese economy in its high-growth era. This rela-

TABLE 3-1

Shares of Major Countries in World GNP (%)[a]

	1955	1960	1970	1978	1980	1986
Japan	2.2	2.9	6.0	10.0	9.0	11.8
United States	36.3	33.7	30.2	21.8	21.5	25.2
European common						
market countries	17.5	17.5	19.3	20.2	22.4	18.6
Soviet Union	13.9	15.2	15.9	13.0	11.6	13.2

[a] Taken from United States Government *Presidential Report on the International Economy* and *Presidential Economic Report* (various years). U.S. Government Printing Office, Washington, D.C.

tionship, however, also provides important insights into the frequent trade frictions between Japan and the other developed economies since the 1970s. As pointed out earlier, a part of the economic benefits accruing to Japan, as a result of changes in its industrial structure, arose due to the fact that this structural change made the distribution of gains from trade favorable for Japan, reducing the share of the foreign countries.

Table 3-1 depicts the changes in relative share of the major countries in the world GNP between 1955 and 1986. Japan's share of global production jumped from 2% of global GNP in 1955 to 11.3% in 1986, while that of the United States dropped from over one-third to just over one-fourth over the same period. Any explanation of these changes in GNP shares must take into account not only differences in the rate of capital accumulation and technological progress among countries, but also the changes in the relationship between industrial structure and trade.

In the immediate postwar period, the United States share of the world GNP far outstripped that of other countries due to its overwhelming endowment of productive factors such as capital and labor. Another important factor in this regard is that while the United States industrial structure was inclined toward goods with high-expenditure propensity (heavy and chemical industry at that time), the Japanese industrial structure was weighed heavily toward light industry products with low-expenditure propensity. [Krugman (1979) refers to this as the "technological gap." We will come back to this point in Chapter 7.]

Since the high-growth period, Japan has rapidly closed this technological gap through changes in its industrial structure. As can be seen in Table 3-2, depicting the changing commodity composition of the Japan–United States trade from 1960 to 1980, Japan's exports of such goods as automobiles, machines, and electrical appliances expanded at a rapid pace. As a result, distribution of gains from trade, which had been heavily skewed in favor of the United States, shifted increasingly in favor of Japan.

The changes in the distributive pattern in favor of Japan, a small economy at that time, did not have any serious effect on the United States, a large economy.

TABLE 3-2

Commodity Composition of Japan–United States Trade[a]

	Dollar value (× 10^3)			
	1960	1970	1979	1979/1960
Imports to United States from Japan				
Automobiles	2164	536,039	8,245,727	3,810.4
Watches	584	22,124	188,814	323.3
Televisions	1721	264,838	232,025	134.8
	(1961)			
Tape recorders	6068	256,171	763,375	125.8
Pocket calculators	—	2561	242,827	94.8
		(1967)	(1978)	
Motorcycles	9928	280,076	888,104	89.5
Machines for scientific use	18,923	—	1,327,093	70.1
Metal products	68,624	323,834	910,775	57.4
Synthetic textiles	3542	135,447	152,444	43.0
	(1962)			
Steel	71,684	899,037	2,739,243	38.2
Exports to Japan from the United States				
Lumber	18,337	517,791	2,297,108	125.3
Corn	11,190	75,006	1,018,537	91.0
Iron ore	12,760	48,859	254,059	19.9
Aircraft	40,904	245,174	716,189	17.5
Business machines (including computers)	30,597	—	530,131	17.3
Sorghum	18,566	133,514	259,086	14.0
	(1962)			
Soybeans	102,997	329,610	1,169,288	11.4
Coal	91,561	623,012	1,021,376	11.2
Wheat	62,982	173,698	612,599	9.7
Pulp	27,779	64,197	224,082	8.1
	(1961)			

[a] Source: Industrial Bank of Japan (1981). Survey No. 207–8.

But it is fast becoming the basis of economic conflict with the transformation of Japan into a large economy. A report by the American Semiconductor Industry Association (Wolff, 1983) declared that, by targeting the steel, automobile, home appliances, and integrated circuit industries for development one after the other, Japan has usurped the United States' share of the benefits. Leaving apart the question of whether or not such criticism of Japanese industrial policies is at all justified, it is a fact that the distribution of gains from trade between the United States and Japan has shifted in Japan's favor. The problem of trade frictions is taken up in Chapter 22.

NOTES

1. For the content and evaluation of these policies and for case studies on particular industries, see Komiya, Okuno, and Suzumura (eds.) (1984), and Komiya and Itoh (1986).

2. However, as shown in Chapter 11, the contribution of strong foreign pressures on Japan to open its markets has not been small.

3. See Corden (1974) for a survey of literature in this field.

4

Theories of Infant Industry Protection:
An Overview

4.1 INTRODUCTION

The history of the postwar Japanese economy is the history of development of new industries, such as automobiles, electrical appliances, and steel. These industries share a number of common characteristics. First, most were industries that had already been developed in the West, particularly in the United States, before being started in Japan. Second, since the industrial base of Japan had been completely devastated during World War II, development of these industries without heavy government protection was considered impossible, and such protection was, in fact, provided, at least in the early stages of their development. Even such contemporary leading edge industries as integrated circuits and computers have been heavily protected because of fears that they may, otherwise, not be able to compete against giant foreign firms.

For reasons discussed below, a country with no established firm in an industry can, while a leading group of industries is already in existence in the foreign countries, raise its own level of economic welfare by protecting that industry.

Each national economy has a distinct history of economic development and is therefore endowed with a different economic environment. For example, in countries with a favorable historical environment, new industries may start up and get established without any external help, whereas this is quite unlikely to occur in the follower countries. That is, in the case of the former, dramatic increases in productivity over time give them a competitive edge that follower countries are unable to match, even when their economic environment turns favorable for establishment of that industry. Under such circumstances, an industry cannot develop simply through the private incentives of private firms. However, the fear that a country's firms cannot develop by their own efforts in an industry which has already been established elsewhere does not justify government protection for the industry. A rise in national economic welfare is the minimum condition for justifying protection.

In what situations and for which industries can protection be justified? To an-

40

swer this question, we must establish two points: first, the effects of protecting a domestic industry on the economic welfare of the country concerned and the world as a whole—the economic effects; and second, the effects on international income distribution.

Although many contributions have been made to the analysis of domestic industry protection and promotion policies, the infant industry protection argument is considered especially important in the context of the two points discussed above. In this chapter we present a brief overview of this argument which provides a starting point for the analysis taken up in Chapter 5 and onward.[1]

4.2 INFANT INDUSTRY PROTECTION ARGUMENT AND ITS SCOPE

Infant industry protection policies attempt to establish industries over the long run by giving them temporary protection. The minimum necessary condition that an industry must satisfy to qualify for such policies is that the production activity in the industry improves its cost conditions over time through learning by doing.[2] This feature is referred to as "dynamic economies of scale" or "economies of time."[3] The infant industry protection argument also looks for additional conditions, besides the dynamic scale economies, that justify temporary protection for the industry under consideration.

In considering such additional conditions, two points need to be kept in mind.

First, since the infant industry protection policies are designed to enhance economic welfare, government intervention must be predicated on some sort of market failure. Therefore, it is essential to set up well-defined standards to judge whether a market failure qualifies a given industry to be designated as an infant industry. Besides, it is also important to show why decision making based on private incentives for private firms does not lead to a socially optimal resource allocation.

Second, there is the question of how much weight to attach to change in economic welfare resulting from infant industry protection policy. If the country adopting the protective policy and its share of the world economy are quite small, the effect on the world economy as a whole will be negligible. Therefore, in evaluating the infant industry policies in a small country, it may suffice to consider changes in the home country welfare alone.

On the other hand, in the case of a country with a large share of the world economy, domestic prices in foreign countries are affected through foreign trade and the resulting effect on competing firms in other countries cannot be ignored. Due to this, in the case of a large country, protectionist policies may or may not be justified, depending on whether the effects of the protective policies on economic welfare of the home country alone are taken into account, or whether effects on economic welfare of the world as a whole are also considered.

We begin the next section by examining the infant industry protection argument in detail, paying particular attention to the issues of market failure and the
impact of these policies on the world market. After establishing the additional
conditions under which protection and promotion are justified in the small country case, we turn our attention to protective policies in the large country case.
The infant industry protection argument must deal with issues of a dynamic nature, by necessity. To simplify the analysis, however, we use a partial equilibrium analysis with only two points in time: present and future.

4.3 INFANT INDUSTRIES IN A SMALL COUNTRY AND THE
CONDITIONS NECESSARY FOR PROTECTION AND PROMOTION:
THE MILL AND BASTABLE CRITERIA

Figure 4-1 depicts the conditions obtaining in an industry, characterized by
dynamic scale economies, of a small country (home country hereafter).

Currently, the industry is producing with a high marginal cost represented by a
supply curve S_0. If the current output of the home industry rises above $\bar{x}$, the
dynamic scale economies come into operation, improving its cost conditions
such that the future marginal cost is represented by the supply curve S_1. But if
current production falls short of $\bar{x}$ or zero, dynamic scale economies are not realized and the supply curve stays at S_0. The domestic demand for this industry is
given by curve D, sloping down to the right, and the world price is $\bar{p}$.

The foreign firm's supply curve, if the industry is unprotected and free trade
prevails, is given by the horizontal straight line S^*, and $\bar{p}$ is the equilibrium price
in the domestic market. Protecting the industry by giving the domestic producers
a production subsidy $(p' - \bar{p})$/unit of output, on the other hand, raises the do-

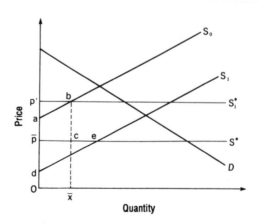

FIG. 4-1

mestic price faced by domestic producers to p'. As a result, current domestic production increases to $\bar{x}$, and the future domestic supply curve shifts to S_1. In other words, temporary protection now makes it possible to realize dynamic scale economies in the future.

Next, let us consider the conditions that must be satisfied for temporary governmental protection for the industry to be justifiable on the grounds of economic welfare of the home country.[4]

First, when the industry is protected and matures, making use of the benefits of dynamic scale economies (at the future point of time), the private firms in the industry must be able to make a profit. Otherwise the industry needs protection forever and a temporary protection fails to produce results. This condition is known as the Mill criterion, after John Stuart Mill, who was the first to point it out. This condition can be interpreted, in terms of Fig. 4-1, as follows.

Let us assume that the government grants the domestic industry a production subsidy (at least) equal to $p' - \bar{p}$ at the present point of time. The domestic industry, which would have been unprofitable otherwise, becomes competitive enough to produce (at least) $\bar{x}$ output. As a result, the future supply curve of the domestic industry shifts to S_1 and the domestic firms earn a profit equivalent to $\bar{p}de$ (the producer surplus) as a whole. Since this value is clearly positive, the firms can operate without government protection in the future, satisfying the Mill criterion.

But satisfying the first condition is not enough to justify government protection for the domestic industry. In addition, the present value of the future social returns from protection, discounted at the social discount rate, must exceed the current social costs of protection and promotion borne by the home country. Failing this, the home country's economic welfare, over time, is higher without protection. This second condition, enunciated by C. F. Bastable, is known as the Bastable criterion.

Since a temporary protection to the domestic industry does not lead to a decline in future consumer prices, the increase in the future economic welfare of the home country is equivalent to the increase in producer surplus $\bar{p}de$ alone. The social cost of protection to the home country (subsidy less producer surplus), on the other hand, results in a loss of (at least) $a\bar{p}cb$ due to subsidy expenditures. An excess of the former, the discounted present value, over the latter implies that Bastable criterion is satisfied.

4.4 DYNAMIC EXTERNAL ECONOMIES AND THE KEMP CRITERION

The above two criteria indicate only that it is in the long-term interests of the home country to establish the domestic industry but do not tell us why government intervention is necessary. To explore this aspect, let us assume that the industry satisfies the Mill and the Bastable criteria and that no industry anywhere in the world is characterized by market failures except for the dynamic scale economies in this industry.

If the industry is currently producing $\bar{x}$ output, the future supply curve shifts to S_1, regardless of whether the present output level results from government protection or the initiative of individual firms within the industry, and the future profits of the industry as a whole are given by $\bar{p}de$. The costs, necessary for producing $\bar{x}$ output at present, are given by $a\bar{p}cb$ in the case of policy protection, and these costs are passed on to the taxpayers by the government. If the production level is achieved through the initiative of individual firms, each firm must bear the costs necessary to produce $\bar{x}$ output. It is important to note that the minimum cost that a firm must bear is exactly $a\bar{p}cb$.

Since there are no other market failures, each firm is fully aware of future profits and all other economic agents (especially the financial institutions supplying funds to the industry) also know the size of future cost reductions accurately.[5] Besides, the capital market is also expected to be perfect and the rate of time preference of the government equals that of the private sector.

Thus, as long as the Bastable criterion is met, private sector firms know that by undertaking production now, even if at a loss, they can turn in profits in excess of the loss over the long run even in the absence of government protection. In other words, the private firms have an incentive to do what the government is trying to make them do even without protection.

Is government protection for such an industry really unnecessary? Or, to put it differently, if the Mill and the Bastable criteria are satisfied, can an industry, characterized by dynamic scale economies, get established simply on the basis of internal incentives?

One can think of several reasons that may prevent such an industry from being established on its own. First, we have the case when capital markets are imperfect. For example, the firm tries to finance its current losses through borrowing but is unable to pay back the loans incurred out of its future profits since the interest rate exceeds the social discount rate due to imperfect capital markets. From a social viewpoint, however, direct intervention in the capital market, the source of market failure, to remove the gap between the social and the private discount rates makes more sense than intervention in the commodity market through production subsidies and trade restrictions. This problem, however, is not intrinsic to the infant industry argument, which is concerned with analyzing the propriety of direct market intervention for the establishment of a specific industry.

The second factor that could prevent the establishment of an industry without protection is imperfect information. If economic agents, especially the firms contemplating entering the industry, are not fully aware of the extent of future cost reductions due to present production activity, they may not have sufficient incentive to enter the industry. Providing accurate information to those concerned with the market and the financiers may be the best policy in this instance. But can the government accurately grasp the information that private economic agents failed to grasp? Even if the government were able to gain access to such information and relay it to the firms, can it induce them to change the behavior of firms which had previously interpreted it differently? Looking at the problem from this angle, imperfect information and the fact that private firm behavior reflects such imperfections do not make government intervention indispensable.

Imperfect information becomes more of a problem, instead, when there are some real difficulties involved in making information the object of market transactions. Generally speaking, information affects the economic agents without passing through the market. As a result, imperfect information generates externalities. In bringing imperfect information into the analysis, it is necessary to reformulate the infant industry argument on the basis of externalities generated in the process, a framework completely different from the one provided by the traditional theory, which looks at the problem of information only in the context of the behavior of individual agents.[6]

A third factor that necessitates government intervention is when the benefits of cost reduction are inappropriable by the firm (group of firms) which bears the initial costs, due to the existence of dynamic externalities. This phenomenon, pointed out by M. C. Kemp, is known as the Kemp criterion in the discussions on the traditional infant industry production argument.[7]

If accumulation of experience and technology improvements that become available at a later date as a recompense for the present losses easily spill over to other firms or industries, the firms are unable to reap future profits and lose an incentive to invest in activities that generate dynamic scale economies. In other words, even if the social benefits from dynamic scale economies, characterizing the industry as a whole, are positive, private incentives alone are insufficient to stimulate investment since private activity, taken separately, results in a loss. Therefore, the social and private valuations differ if current production generates dynamic externalities leading to a dynamic market failure. Government intervention in such a case is justified.[8]

The high-technology industries, where R & D investment is indispensable for new entry, also face a similar problem. This is because the degree of appropriability of technology and knowledge, the fruits of R & D investments, is inherently low, making it difficult for the developer to completely internalize the social benefits of the fruits of R & D. Thus, government subsidies to R & D by domestic industry are justified in situations where R & D results in dynamic externalities, so long as such subsidies assist establishment of an infant industry.[9]

4.5 INFANT INDUSTRY PROTECTION IN A LARGE-COUNTRY CASE AND ENTRY BENEFITS: THE NEGISHI CRITERION

The preceding section dealt with infant industry protection in a small country. It is important to note here that protection and promotion of infant industries does not affect the gains that other countries derive from trade. Thus, policies that raise national economic welfare in the home country also raise welfare of the world economy as a whole. It is in this sense that the traditional infant industry protection argument, in the case of a small country, emphasizes the existence of dynamic externalities as the key factor in determining whether a policy to protect an infant industry is justified from the viewpoint of economic welfare of either that country or the world as a whole.

What happens if the country adopting the protective policy (home country) is large? The Kemp criterion continues to be effective if one is concerned only with the question of whether or not a policy to protect and promote an industry improves global economic welfare. In a large-country case, however, dynamic scale economies may be the result not of externalities, as implied in the Kemp criterion, but of internal economies. Still, infant industry protection may be desirable from the viewpoint of economic welfare of the home country.[10] This is because protection and promotion of domestic industry by a large country significantly affect the economic welfare of not only the home country but also of the world as a whole. In general, these two effects differ.

Our model defines dynamic scale economies as the shift of future production, onto the supply curve represented by the straight line S_1 in Fig. 4-1, made possible by improved cost conditions as a result of current production equivalent to, at least, $\bar{x}$. Two points need to be noted here. First, current production acts as a factor of production, giving rise to future cost reductions. Second, unlike ordinary factors of production, future cost reductions do not materialize if current production drops below $\bar{x}$. The productivity of this factor drops to zero for a production level below $\bar{x}$, giving rise to indivisibilities. The future costs, on the other hand, cannot fall below ad even if production exceeds $\bar{x}$.

Considering these points, the current production level $\bar{x}$ (or level of factor input necessary to reduce future costs) is an indivisible factor of production necessary for realizing future cost reductions, regardless of the future output levels. That is, the (private) loss, which must be borne to produce under the inferior cost conditions prevailing now, may be interpreted as a fixed cost independent of the level of future output produced in the established industry once the cost reductions materialize. This cost, just like the registration fee for setting up a firm, is a fixed cost that must be paid to establish an industry (or firm) regardless of the level of production in the industry. In other words, it is a set-up cost. Such fixed costs generate scale economies insofar as average cost per unit of accumulated production from present to future diminish as future output rises.

Let us consider the changes in the world markets that follow the establishment of an industry, using such indivisible factors of production, in a large country.

If the country is unable to establish the industry in the absence of protection, the domestic output, present as well as future, is zero. In contrast, a protective policy raises current output to at least $\bar{x}$, which generates dynamic scale economies and improves cost conditions as the domestic industry gets firmly established. Thus, the domestic industry is in a position to produce more than its current output. This increase in the current and future output reduces the international price of the product if the country is large. In other words, establishment of an infant industry in a large country raises consumer surplus (not only in the home country but for the world as a whole) by reducing international prices.

Thus, when the benefits from infant industry protection emerge in the form of increased consumer surplus in the home country, private incentives may be insufficient to stimulate entry that is desirable on the grounds of economic welfare (both for the home country as well as for the world as a whole), even in the absence of external economies. The reason is simple. The decision of a private sector firm to enter an industry is guided solely by the present value of the stream of future private profits, the difference between the (discounted present value) increase in profits and the costs it must incur for the indivisible factor of production. In contrast, the social value of establishing the industry includes, in addition to private profits, the increase in consumer surplus. Therefore, the incentives for a private firm to enter the industry fall short of those necessary for socially optimal entry to the extent that consumer surplus rises.

The divergence between private and social incentives due to a change in consumer surplus is unrelated to the Kemp criterion, which selects infant industries on the basis of whether dynamic scale economies produce externalities or are internalized. Besides, even in the absence of dynamic externalities, government protection to establish an industry that may not emerge on the basis of private incentives alone can be justified if the rise in consumer surplus is large enough. A generalized criterion, including the case just discussed, is the Negishi criterion as developed by Negishi (1971).

The Negishi criterion states that infant industry protection and promotion of an industry are justified only if the discounted present value of the stream of net social returns (including the change in consumer surplus) is positive while the discounted present value of the stream of private returns in the absence of such protection and promotion is negative. Thus, the Negishi criterion provides the necessary as well as sufficient condition for justifying infant industry protection and is not predicated on dynamic scale economies taking the form of externalities.

Again, there is no need for the said industry to be perfectly competitive as implicitly assumed here. In fact, since cost reductions result from the use of an indivisible factor of production and the investment undertaken on this account takes on a fixed-cost character as the industry gets established, the industries for which infant industry protection is justified tend to be precisely those where the diminishing cost phenomenon at the firm level is often observed and, hence, are susceptible to oligopolization. Moreover, the Negishi criterion shows that it is necessary for scale economies to emerge as an economic effect with a time dimension. In oligopolistic industries characterized by economies of scale in some form, the private firms, even when they undertake fresh investment to enter the industry, cannot collect the resulting consumer surplus as their own profit. As a result, the incentives for private firms to undertake investments necessary for entering the industry are socially less than optimal, which renders government protection and promotion desirable. Part III of this book examines the policies to protect and promote domestic firms when the industry is internationally oligopolized. The discussion there may be considered as an extension of the infant industry protection argument.

We conclude this chapter by looking into the effect of an infant industry protection policy on global distribution of income.

The protection and promotion of industries in the real world is, more often than not, aimed at raising economic welfare in the home country alone. Let us assume that a large country uses the Negishi criterion, based on economic welfare considerations of the home country alone, to protect and promote an industry. There is a strong possibility, in this case, for protection to result in economic frictions with other countries. The use of a protection and promotion policy by a large country results in a decline in international price of the good and a resulting increase in the consumer surplus in other countries. To that extent such a policy has a positive effect on the world as a whole. But for the developed countries with an already established industry, producer surplus (quasi-rents = profits plus fixed costs), being earned in the short run due to their position as pioneers in the industry, declines. As long as the increase in consumer surplus falls short of the decline in producer surplus, protection and promotion of infant industry by the latecomer subsidy of the infant industry will reduce economic welfare in the pioneering countries.

In the long run, decline in international prices following the entry into the industry by a latecomer country may weaken the competitiveness of the pioneering country in the industry, causing production to decline, workers to be laid off, and driving some of the firms to bankruptcy. The pioneering country industry, faced with such a possibility, takes recourse in government-to-government political pressure to try and block the entry of the latecomer into the industry in order to prevent a decline in quasi-rents and to protect the interests of the entrepreneurs and employees within the industry. This leads to serious economic frictions between the two countries. This encroachment on existing profits, being earned by the industry in the pioneering country, is unavoidable even if the protective policy adopted by the latecomer results in improved overall economic welfare in the pioneer country. Though a protective policy adopted by a large country may, in some cases, improve global economic welfare, it can never result in a Pareto-improving configuration requiring improved welfare for all economic agents in all countries. Thus, even if we grant that a decline in producer surplus in the pioneering country is smaller than a rise in consumer surplus, such that an industrial protection and promotion policy adopted by the latecomer has a positive effect on the overall economic welfare of the pioneering country, the profits being earned by firms in the pioneering country are bound to decline. In such a case, in spite of the fact that protection and promotion policy of the latecomer country improves global economic welfare, difficult political problems arise.

This chapter attempted a critical overview of traditional theories of infant industry protection. It is clear that two phenomena—dynamic externalities or externalities resulting from imperfect information, and the phenomenon of diminishing costs, which may arise for a number of reasons—are extremely important for an analysis of the economic effects of industrial protection and promotion. Leaving a discussion of the role of the second phenomenon in the context of internationally oligopolized industries for Part III, Chapters 5 and 6 examine protective policies based on externality argument in detail.

NOTES

1. Theories justifying industrial protection, within the traditional trade theory, can be divided roughly into (1) economic theories of protection and (2) noneconomic theories of protection. The theory of infant industry protection, developed below, the theory of optimal tariffs, and the theory of distortions fall into the first category. A representative of the second set of theories is Johnson's theory (1965) of industrial preference.

Since we have defined industrial policy as policy which is adopted to compensate for market failures, we will not deal with point (2) above. And, since policies classified under point (1), except for the infant industry protection argument, try to justify permanent rather than temporary protection, they are inappropriate for explaining postwar Japanese trade and industrial policies, which were premised on ultimate liberalization. Therefore, we do not touch on any economic theories of protection other than the infant industry argument, but the interested reader is referred to Corden (1974), Grubel (1966), and Johnson (1970).

2. If this were not the case, the industry will never be able to exist without permanent protection. Therefore, for protection to be justified on grounds of economic welfare, it is necessary that the industry either exert a perpetual distorting effect on the allocation of resources in the economy due to the presence of a semiperpetual market failure, or result in higher welfare for the home country through the beggar-thy-neighbor policies treated in optimal tariff theory. If so, it is not necessary to take recourse to the special framework of infant industry argument.

3. These terms are from Corden (1974, p. 249).

4. The essence of the subsequent analysis is not affected if import restriction measures like tariffs and import quotas are used, instead, as a tool of protective policies.

5. If some economic agents do not possess accurate information on the cost reduction effects, it is a case of imperfect information. Here, as pointed out earlier, since we concern ourselves only with dynamic scale economies characterizing a given industry as the source of market failure, we assume perfect information. For the problems related to imperfect information or incomplete information gathering, see the ensuing discussion and Chapter 6 of this book.

6. See Chapter 6 on this point.

7. See Kemp (1960, 1964, and 1974).

8. The problem is not necessarily solved by providing subsidies (including tariffs) to the industries characterized by dynamic externalities. See Baldwin (1969) on this point.

9. For a discussion of problems related to R & D, see Part V of this book.

10. See Negishi (1971) for the arguments developed below.

5

Industrial Set-up Costs and Marshallian Externalities

The traditional infant industry protection argument, presented in the last chapter, provides the basic framework to discuss the problem of fostering industry. However, it is not possible to apply this traditional argument as such to discuss Japanese industrial policy, especially industrial promotion. Among the various drawbacks of such an approach in the Japanese context, the following two points are the most pertinent.

1. The Japanese industrial promotion policies have been intricately linked with the formation of an ideal industrial structure for the Japanese economy as a whole. This is true whether we look at these from the point of view of attaining the advanced industrial structure that motivated policy formulation or attaining rapid growth and changes in industrial structure. An analysis and evaluation of such industrial promotion policies that covers promotion measures taken in the context of individual industries alone is insufficient. What is required is a general equilibrium approach that explicitly takes into account the changes in the overall industrial structure attained through execution of these policies.

2. The traditional infant industry argument provides a rationale for promotion of individual industries (or sectors). In this context dynamic set-up cost factors, such as learning effects and dynamic economies of scale, were emphasized as is clear from the discussion in the last chapter. However, industrial promotion and industrial development in postwar Japan have been influenced by other factors as well—some equally important or perhaps even more so.

5.1 PROTECTION–PROMOTION POLICIES AND THE NETWORK EFFECTS

In the present chapter, we attempt to clarify the remarks made in point (2) above by using a simple partial equilibrium approach [remarks under point (1) are further developed in Chapter 7]. In the discussion that ensues, we have in mind assembly industries like household electronics and automobiles. In Fig. 5-1,

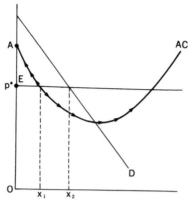

FIG. 5-1

D is the domestic demand curve for a given commodity with p^* as the price of the imported commodity. For simplification, we make the small country assumption such that the foreign supply curve becomes horizontal at p^*.

The long-run average costs for producing this product indigenously are represented by curve AC in Fig. 5-1. What is important for the discussion that ensues is that the AC curve should have a downward sloping segment. The assembly industries are composed of a large number of parts and processes and easily lend themselves to scale merits arising out of division of labor. If the output of these industries is quantitatively small, a single producer will have to set up all the relevant processes, substantially raising unit costs. Large-scale production, on the other hand, gives rise to the possibility of setting up a network of specialized firms producing individual parts. This can result in substantial reduction in unit costs of production. This is nothing but the phenomenon represented in Adam Smith's "needle" production example. Production efficiency rises if a large number of individuals come together and divide up the jobs involved in producing a needle rather than every individual producing the needle in the final form.

For example, the exceptionally low cost of production in the Japanese automobile industry is attributable to the network of a large number of ancillary firms and parts makers. The amount of value added to the automobile as a final product by assemblers like Toyota and Nissan is believed to be about 30% while the remaining 70% is contributed by the ancillary parts and raw materials makers. Expanding scale of production in such assembly industries helps to improve the network of ancillary firms, leading to an effective exploitation of the economies of division of labor. Up to a certain level of output, economies of scale bring down the cost of production, leading to a downward sloping long-run average cost curve for the industry as a whole.

Let us assume the initial output of this commodity in the country is zero and the country depends on imports to meet all its demand, x_2 in Fig. 5-1. In the absence of any form of government intervention, indigenous output of this commodity will stay at zero forever since producers have no incentive to produce as long as average cost of production exceeds price. As shown by the arrowheads on the AC (average cost) curve in Fig. 5-1, a firm will exit the industry if the level of output is below x_1 as the average cost of production for the industry is above the price p^*. As a result, total production in the industry will be zero. If individual producers take a broader view of the industry as a whole and are able to act in unison to raise output beyond x_1, sufficient profits can be earned. For individual producers to see so far ahead in the future and attain output beyond x_1 through collective action, however, is nearly impossible.

One way to help such industries to set up and develop is provision for subsidies by the government. In terms of Fig. 5-1, if production subsidy equivalent to AE/unit of production can be ensured, the price will exceed average cost (cost minus subsidy) and production will expand. If the costs of tax collection and disbursement of subsidies to the government are sufficiently small, such a policy will be an effective policy raising net economic welfare. But, in reality, the Japanese government in the 1955–1975 period did not have enough fiscal resources to engage in such a huge public expenditure program. Furthermore, efforts to raise additional funds for this purpose would have imposed substantial social costs.

An alternative way of doing the same thing would be to develop this industry on the basis of domestic demand by putting temporary restrictions on imports of this commodity. For example, if D is the demand curve for this country in Fig. 5-1, a temporary stoppage of imports through trade restrictions can help raise the total production in the economy above x_1. Once production above x_1 is realized, the industry can stand on its own on the basis of private incentives even if restrictions on imports are removed. For this method to be plausible, domestic demand must be sufficiently high. In terms of Fig. 5-1, if the demand curve and foreign supply curve intersect at a point to the left of x_1, the average cost of production cannot be brought down sufficiently even if the industry is set up under import restrictions. In this case, the industry will vanish as soon as import restrictions are removed. In practice, Japan had a sufficiently big domestic market and, given the fiscal position of the Japanese government at that time, temporary import restraints were perhaps a more practicable policy as compared to a subsidy policy.[1]

Thus, if an industry is characterized by diminishing average costs, private incentives may not be enough to ensure establishment of the industry even when capital markets are perfect. Now, if the industry is established through the process of expansion of domestic production based on domestic demand concomitant with temporary import restrictions imposed by the government, the consumers will be forced to buy this product at higher prices. This imposes a social cost on the economy in the form of lower consumer surplus during the time when import restrictions are in force. Thus, government support for the establishment of an industry with diminishing costs inevitably results in imposition of temporary social costs on the economy. We call these costs the set-up costs of establishing an industry.

5.2 MARSHALLIAN EXTERNALITIES AND THE PRODUCTION–POSSIBILITY FRONTIER

The network effect discussed in Section 5.1 is nothing but the phenomenon referred to as the Marshallian externalities. In the discussion that follows, we model Marshallian externalities in general in a two-commodity world and analyze the benefits conferred by protection and promotion of industries with set-up costs on the national economy as the whole.[2] Marshallian external economies (diseconomies) refer to the phenomenon whereby the cost curves of individual firms in a competitive industry shift downward (upward) due to the emergence of externalities as output of the industry expands, leading to a fall (rise) in prices. As a result, the long-run market supply curve (AC in Fig. 5-1) for the industries with external economies (diseconomies) becomes downward (upward) sloping, giving rise to industrial set-up costs.[3]

Let us visualize an economy producing two commodities (X and Y) using a single factor of production (labor hereafter). Production of commodity X is assumed to be characterized by external economies in the sense discussed above while external diseconomies prevail in the production of commodity Y.[4]

For simplification, we assume that, given the total output of the industry as a whole, production functions of individual firms follow constant returns to scale. If x represents the output of an individual firm and X that of the industry as a whole, the cost function, $C(x; X)$, for an individual firm can be represented as

$$C(x; X) = a(X)x$$

and the average (marginal) cost—that is, private average (marginal) cost—to an individual firm, given X, is fixed at $a(X)$. However, since private average cost to an individual firm, $a(X)$, depends on the total output of the industry, X, due to the presence of external economies, costs fall as X rises, i.e., $a'(X) < 0$. Similarly, if Y is the total output of industry Y, the private cost of production (at firm level) in this industry, $b(Y)$, depends on Y alone and, from our assumptions, $b'(Y) > 0$.

To simplify the matter further, let us assume that the elasticities of private costs to total output in both industries, $\alpha(X) = a'(X)X/a(X)$ and $\beta(Y) = b'(Y)Y/b(Y)$, are constants, independent of the level of production, constrained by $-1 < \alpha < 0$ and $\beta > 0$.

Costs are measured in terms of number of workers. That is, if X is the total output of industry X, $a(X)$ gives the number of workers needed to produce one unit of output. If $A(X)$ is the number of workers employed in industry X and $B(Y)$ the number of workers in industry Y, $A(X) = a(X)X$ and $B(Y) = b(Y)Y$. Here, $A(X)$ and $B(Y)$ represent the total cost of producing X and Y. It can be easily shown that

$$A'(X) = (1 + \alpha)a(X) > 0, B'(Y) = (1 + \beta)b(Y) > 0$$

and

$$A''(X) = (1 + \alpha)a'(X) < 0, B''(Y) = (1 + \beta)b'(Y) > 0$$

Therefore, as output of industry $X(Y)$ expands, employment also rises but at a diminishing (increasing) rate. Now, $A'(X)$ and $B'(Y)$ represent the marginal costs of increased output of the respective industry to the society as a whole and may be termed as social marginal costs. Hence, in this economy, the private and social marginal costs diverge by an amount equal to $(1 + \alpha)$ or $(1 + \beta)$.

The above relationships are depicted in Fig. 5-2. As shown in the second and fourth quadrants, the graphs for numbers of workers employed in each industry are concave and convex to respective employment axes. In the neighborhood of the origin, graph for $A(X)$ becomes vertical while that for $B(Y)$ becomes horizontal. If L is the total amount of labor in this economy, the production frontier is given by a curve satisfying

$$A(X) + B(Y) = L \tag{1}$$

As shown in the first quadrant of Fig. 5-2, the production frontier is convex to the origin when the output of X is small and becomes convex away from the origin as the output of X rises.

The slope of the production frontier gives the social marginal rate of transformation of X for Y (social marginal cost of producing X in terms of Y). As is clear from Fig. 5-2, the marginal rate of transformation of X for Y diminishes initially

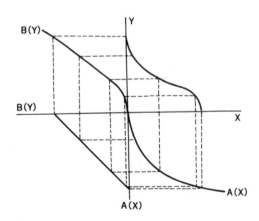

FIG. 5-2

as production of X rises, increasing thereafter. This fact can be interpreted as follows. From Eq. (1), the social marginal rate of transformation can be derived as

$$A'(X)/B'(Y) = (1 + \alpha)a(X)/(1 + \beta)b(Y)$$

As the output in industry X rises, the social marginal cost of producing $X[A'(X)]$ falls due to the operation of external economies. At the same time, since there is a relocation of resources from industry Y, the output of Y declines, leading to a decline in the social cost of producing $Y[B'(Y)]$ due to the presence of external diseconomies. As long as the output of X is sufficiently small, the former effect outweighs the latter, leading to a diminishing social marginal rate of transformation. When the output of X becomes sufficiently large, the latter effect becomes stronger, resulting in an increasing social marginal rate of transformation.[5]

The private marginal cost of production for the two goods is $a(X)$ and $b(Y)$, respectively. Individual firms do not take into account the fact that an increase in their own output can change average costs due to the presence of externalities. As a result, output tends to expand if product price exceeds private marginal cost and contract if the reverse is true. That is to say, if the ratio of private marginal cost in the production of the two commodities is referred to as the private marginal rate of transformation, labor resources will flow out of Y into X if the relative price of X to Y, p, exceeds this private marginal rate of transformation. The output of X will, obviously, expand. Conversely, if p is less than the private marginal rate of transformation, the output of X will decline and that of Y rise. It is clear that the private marginal rate of transformation, $a(X)/b(Y)$, is $(1 + \beta)/(1 + \alpha) \equiv \gamma$ (>1) times the social marginal rate of transformation. Hence, the output of Y or X will rise depending on whether the slope of the production frontier, reflecting the social marginal rate of transformation, is greater or less than p/γ.

5.3 PROTECTION AND PROMOTION POLICIES FOR A SMALL-COUNTRY CASE

Let us assume that the country in question is a small country facing a relative price, p. If $ABCED$ in Fig. 5-3 is the production frontier for the economy, the private marginal rate of transformation exceeds relative price (or social marginal rate of transformation exceeds p/γ) over segments AB and CD. Over these segments, therefore, the output of X will contract. On the other hand, the marginal rate of transformation falls short of relative price over the range BC where the output of X will expand. This implies that this economy can have three long-run equilibrium points, A, B, and C. Of these, A and C are stable while B represents unstable equilibrium. Now, if the economy is in equilibrium at point A, there is no private incentive to move to any other equilibrium.[6]

Now, if production is being carried out at point C, the straight line with slope p passing through this point gives the budget line for the economy as a whole. Similarly, a straight line through point A with slope p represents the total budget

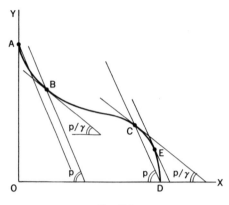

FIG. 5-3

for the economy when production takes place at point A. It is clear from this tha
national welfare (ignoring domestic income distribution) is higher at C than A
although both points represent stable long-run equilibrium. That is to say, poin
C, with a possibility for expanding commodity X, where scale economies can b
exploited due to the presence of external economies, is superior in terms of na
tional economic welfare to point A, which implies specialization in the produc
tion of commodity Y where scale diseconomies prevail on account of externa
diseconomies. From the viewpoint of social welfare of this country, at least, gov
ernment intervention leading the economy to attain equilibrium at a point like C
is desirable.[7]

Assuming that the economy is initially operating at point A, what temporary
policy intervention can help it attain equilibrium at point C? As discussed in Sec
tion 5.1, pecuniary inducements, in the form of subsidies and the like, can als
help in attaining this objective. Provision of subsidies, however, requires in
creased taxation as a revenue source, which leads to inefficiency of resource
allocation. Moreover, tax increases bring the conflict of interests to the fore
making it difficult to settle the issues. Finally, dismantling the subsidies, once
granted, is politically difficult for the government. A policy that is relatively free
of these drawbacks, and which has been put into practice time and again, is tem
porary import controls or imposition of high tariffs.

More concretely, in terms of Fig. 5-4, temporary import restrictions or im
position of tariffs high enough to block imports of commodity X can effectively
insulate the economy from outside influences and a move to point C may be pos
sible. But for this policy to function successfully, the output of X at the equi
librium point for the closed economy, F, should be sufficiently large and should
surpass X_0, the output where (the social and private) marginal rate of transforma
tion is the minimum. If this is not so, the inflow of foreign product, as imports o
X are liberalized, will swamp out the domestic producers.[8] That is, without a

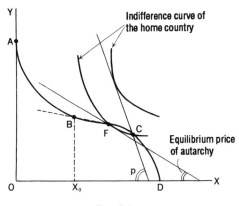

FIG. 5-4

certain minimum level of domestic demand for commodity X, trade restrictions
(unless coupled with other monetary incentives to raise domestic production of
the commodity X above X_0) is useless as a temporary measure and, hence, cannot be effective as a means of interventionist policy for industries characterized
by set-up costs.

5.4 PRODUCTION FRONTIER IN A LARGE-COUNTRY CASE

Let us consider the implications for a large-country case using a two-country
model. For simplification, we assume that the world economy is composed
of two countries having identical production frontiers represented by $CC'C''$ in
Fig. 5-5. Point C' divides the production frontier into two segments, one convex
and the other concave to the origin. Under these circumstances, feasible stable
equilibrium, on the basis of private incentives, for each economy can be attained
at point C or some point on segment $C'C''$ depicted in Fig. 5-5 as a solid line. An
equilibrium point on segment CC' will necessarily be unstable.

What does the locus of total world production (global production frontier), attainable when only private incentives are at work in both the countries, look like?
In fact, two types of global production frontiers can be defined.

The first type of the global production frontier is shown as $AA'A''$ in Fig. 5-5.
This corresponds to the situation when both countries choose the exact same production equilibrium point. For example, if p_w is the world relative price, the (private) marginal rate of transformation is given by p_w/γ and both countries choose
E_C as their respective equilibrium point. The total world output in this case is E_A,
exactly the double of E_C. That is, the first type of the global production frontier,
$AA'A''$, is an exact replica of the production frontier of a single country, $CC'C''$,
enlarged twice parallel to the origin.

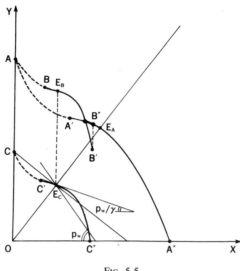

FIG. 5-5

The second type of global production frontier is depicted as $ABB'B''A''$ in Fig. 5-5. With p_w as the relative world price and (private) marginal rate of transformation given by the slope of the production frontier at E_C, one of the countries attains equilibrium at E_C while the other specializes in the production of commodity Y by choosing C as production equilibrium point. The global production frontier in this case is described by the graph ABB' drawn by holding production in one of the countries at C and allowing production in the other country move from C' over $C'C''$. Beyond B', this type of global production frontier overlaps that of the former type as both the countries now produce commodity X. Thus, the overall production frontier is defined by $ABB'B''A''$, that is, the global production frontier is the combination of a segment $B''A''$ when both the countries produce some amount of X and segment AB' when one of the countries specializes in the production of commodity Y.

The point that must be kept in mind about these types of production frontiers is that production of commodity X in both countries is no longer necessary from the viewpoint of efficiency in global production. It is amply clear from Fig. 5-5 that leaving production of commodity X to one country can, in some cases, lead to higher production of both X and Y as compared to the situation when both countries try to produce it. This phenomenon arises due to presence of set-up costs in the production of X. Since production of X entails heavy costs, independent of the volume of output, production of X in a single country shows diminishing average costs. This implies operation of scale economies at the level of single country. Considerations of global efficiency, therefore, dictate concentration of production of X in a single country, rather than in both countries, to make the most of scale economies.

5.5 INTERNATIONAL DISTRIBUTION OF SCALE MERITS

Concentration of production of commodity X in one country may be desirable on the grounds of efficiency but it may raise problems of international distribution of gains. This point has important implications for the concept of industrial set-up costs.

To put the problem in a clear perspective, let us assume that both the countries are not only identical in production but have identical preferences as well. Furthermore, total world demand is assumed to depend on relative prices alone and is not affected by distribution of income among the two countries (that is, we assume that the indifference curves of the two countries are derived from identical homothetic utility functions). Global equilibrium can be represented by a point on the solid segment of the global production frontier. Let point E_B, on segment BB', be such an equilibrium point. At this point, obviously, the private marginal rate of transformation equals relative prices and, therefore, marginal rate of substitution (in consumption).

At this point, one of the countries (say, a foreign country) alone is producing commodity X. The other country (home country hereafter) specializes in the production of Y. As a result, the income of the two countries differs with the budget line for the foreign country lying outside that for the home country, as depicted in Fig. 5-6. The foreign country, producing commodity X with set-up costs, attains a higher level of national welfare as compared to the home country, which does not produce X. It should be noted, however, that production of commodity X in the foreign country is not the result of a difference in resource endowment or

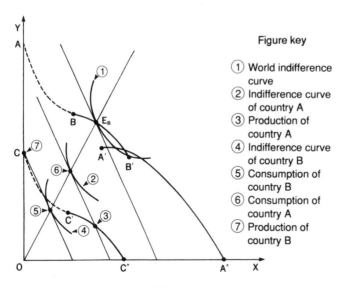

FIG. 5-6

technology, as dictated by the traditional trade theory; instead, it is a matter of pure chance. The total world output will be the same even if the home country produces X and the foreign country specializes in the production of Y (only income and consumption of the two countries is reversed), leading to the same equilibrium point.

Thus, if there are some industries with set-up costs, the industrial structure of individual countries and the structure of international trade is not determined on the basis of the comparative cost principle, that is, the relative resource abundance or technology differences stressed by the traditional trade theory. In such circumstances, factors such as which country takes the lead in setting up the industry, or which country had been producing the product in question historically due to cultural practices, become important. In other words, the noneconomic factors—culture, history, and system—come to determine the pattern of international trade.

One important factor determining the trade pattern in the presence of set-up costs is policy intervention by the government. This is due to the fact that the government can purposefully foster the industry with set-up costs through pecuniary incentives or through protection, as has been discussed in the case of a small country.

Besides, if such an industry is fostered, the home country becomes an exporting country. In terms of Fig. 5-6, the higher the relative price at the equilibrium point (point E_B) attained as a result of fostering this industry (i.e., the greater the global demand for commodity X and the better the terms of trade for the home country), the higher will be the resulting benefits to the nation. Again, since development of an industry is usually time consuming, the industries where marginal costs fall at a faster pace with the passage of time (due to, for example, technological progress) are easier to develop. In this sense, the two criteria for selecting industries for promotion in postwar Japan—the income elasticity criterion, emphasizing promotion of industries where demand was expected to rise as economic growth proceeded, and the productivity growth criterion, stressing the need to foster industries where production was expected to rise faster—can be justified.[9] Whether or not the Policy Bureau took the economic principles propounded above into consideration in setting up the two criteria, however, remains an open question.

Two reservations must be appended to the results presented above. First, there are some problems related to distribution. Even in the context of the small-country case, implementation of various promotion policies invariably gives rise to groups that stand to benefit and groups that stand to lose from those policies. While a subsidy policy leads to redistribution of income from taxpayers to producers, trade control measures redistribute income from consumers to producers (importers). Furthermore, the fact that industrial promotion is possible through temporary measures implies that there is intergenerational transfer of income from the generations when protection policies are in force to future generations.

If this country is a large country competing with other countries, establishment of the industry that generates gains from trade, through governmental policy intervention when, in fact, the industry can develop in any country, is nothing but plundering potential trade gains from the competing countries. In this sense, promoting industries with set-up costs can easily become a source of trade frictions. However, set-up costs may be exhibited by a number of industries. In most of the high-technology industries, cost reductions, based on learning effects or research and development, percolate down to various firms, giving rise to externalities. Given this, respective countries, instead of seeking to monopolize all the industries characterized by scale merits at the country level in pursuit of gains for own country, should explore the possibility for international cooperation in devising ways to allocate and develop these industries among various nations. It is, therefore, necessary to give serious consideration to international cooperation for international distribution of industries and not just for traditional considerations of maintaining free trade.

Second, the two-country model depicted in Figs. 5-5 and 5-6 represents an extreme case. Normally, global welfare considerations will provide a standard to decide upon the country that should develop this industry even if both the countries have identical technology and are of the same size. Except in the case of an economy with labor as the only factor of production, as assumed in this chapter, allowing for multiple factors of production will give rise to differences in resource endowments of the two countries. This implies that the shape of the production frontier in two countries is bound to differ and allowing the country with relatively lower costs will (barring distributional aspects) lead to higher global welfare. The existence of set-up costs shows that trade patterns dictated by the principle of comparative advantage may not come about automatically. In this sense, set-up costs limit the applicability of the traditional Heckscher–Ohlin theory, although not denigrating it completely.

NOTES

1. This phenomenon of diminishing costs can also emerge for the total sectoral supply of industries like iron and steel and petrochemicals, where scale economies operate at the firm (or even plant) level. A detailed discussion of this aspect is taken up in the next chapter.

2. For a discussion of Marshallian externalities, cf. Young (1928) and Chipman (1970).

3. The model presented is based mainly on Panagariya (1981). Herberg and Kemp (1969), Kemp and Negishi (1970), and Ethier (1982) also present similar models.

4. If production of commodity X is characterized by Marshallian external economies, the average cost curve for the industry will be downward sloping. In this sense, the assumption of external diseconomies in the production of commodity Y may seem to be redundant. But nonfulfillment of the assumption of external diseconomies in the production of Y leads to a divergence in economic welfare between a country specializing in production of Y and a country producing both X and Y. This may, in some cases, lead to results contradictory to those derived in this chapter. See Okuno-Fujiwara (1988).

5. Given the assumption of constant elasticity of unit costs, it can be verified that the social marginal rate of transformation will be infinity when output of either X or Y is zero.

6. Since the social marginal rate of transformation is infinity at point A, the economy will be in equilibrium regardless of relative prices (cf. footnote 4).

7. The above argument relates to the second best policy when policy measures are only temporary. The first best point on the production frontier is point E. However, at E, the private marginal rate of transformation is γp and this point cannot be sustained as an equilibrium point unless permanent price intervention measures in the form of subsidizing X and/or taxing Y are resorted to. Since we are concerned here, as pointed out in the beginning, with temporary measures for protection and promotion of industries only, we focus our attention on point C, the second best equilibrium.

8. As pointed out earlier, if the economy faces a relative price p, production of X will fall if the economy is on segment AB and rise if on segment BC. That is, success of this policy hinges on whether or not the domestic production of commodity X has moved to segment BC at the time of import liberalization.

9. *White Paper on International Trade* (1964), Ministry of International Trade and Industry, p. 298.

6

Scale Economies and Information

6.1 MARSHALLIAN EXTERNALITIES AND INDUSTRIAL LINKAGES

As discussed in the previous chapter, the presence of Marshallian externalities is a typical factor giving rise to set-up costs in an industry or a sector of the economy. What are Marshallian externalities and through what mechanism are they generated? The lack of a proper economic explanation of this problem, i.e., the microeconomic underpinnings of Marshallian externalities, is quite surprising. A phenomenon closely resembling Marshallian externalities is quite common in the case of interlinked industries, of which at least some are oligopolistic industries such that strategic behavior is important. In this chapter, we investigate why a sector of the economy, including some oligopolistic industries and satisfying the above criteria, results in the emergence of Marshallian externalities for the sector as a whole.[1]

It is well known that prices, in a perfectly competitive market, automatically provide all the necessary information that is needed by the firms and consumers for making their decisions. The information necessary for profit or utility maximization by individual economic agents is condensed into prices. Prices also convey information related to the supply of factors used in production or to product demand, in fact any information that is of some significance to a firm. This automatically results in a socially optimum (Pareto efficient) resource allocation.

In contrast to this, in the case of an oligopolistic industry, where firms adopt a strategic behavior, prices are not sufficient to convey all the necessary information. In this case, information other than prices, like the shape of the demand curve facing the industry (elasticity of demand, the position of the demand function), for example, is strategically important and is indispensable for profit maximization. Thus, in an oligopolistic industry, the shape of the demand function and supply function of factors of production, factors other than the price variable, determine the nature of the equilibrium as well as pricing and output decisions.

When a number of industries are mutually interlinked (for example, industry A supplies raw materials to industry B, while B provides A with its output, say,

63

equipment) and where strategic oligopolistic behavior has an important role to play, the following problem arises. Since demand for industry A's product is derived demand from industry B, the conditions facing industry A are dependent on what happens in industry B (price and output). Similarly, the demand for industry B's product is derived demand from industry A, and the situation in industry B is dependent on that in industry A.

In short, conditions obtaining in one industry influence the state of affairs in the other. Therefore, changes occurring in one industry affect all related industries. Moreover, such effects are the result neither of changes in technology reflected in the production function nor of changes in market conditions, i.e., prices, but of a change in the strategic environment faced by the affected industry. Such an externality, therefore, can neither be classified as technological externality nor as a pecuniary externality. It is simply an externality. Furthermore, when an industry as a whole shows externalities, due to its linkages with another industry, it affects the strategic environment for all the firms belonging to that industry. This is the mechanism which gives rise to Marshallian externalities.

6.2 Industry Linkages and Limited Information

Whether or not the mutual interdependence among the related industries, as discussed above, generates a market failure, in the sense that the problems arising out of externalities cannot be solved by sole reliance on a free price system, depends on the following points. Let us assume that firms in an industry have correctly grasped the effects on the other industries, described above, and thereby can accurately guess the ultimate effect on their own industry. The market failure, in the sense discussed above, may not emerge in this case since all the direct and indirect effects concomitant on the presence of externalities have already been taken into account by each firm in its decision making process. In this case, the externalities are internalized at the decision-making stages. Next, let us consider what factors, if any, can result in the failure to internalize these externalities by taking a simple example.

Let us visualize a firm considering construction of a large-scale blast furnace to reduce production costs. The high fixed costs (implying scale economies), the construction of the blast furnace, will be unprofitable in the absence of a considerable demand for steel. Yet if the blast furnace is built and steel is supplied at lower prices, demand for steel may increase substantially. First, a drop in steel prices makes the existing industries, like ship building, more competitive on international markets, raising derived demand for steel. The increased demand for steel results not only from higher demand by the shipbuilding industry due to improved cost conditions but also from additional demand generated by an increase in the number of firms in the industry due to new entry. Second, declining steel prices can create entirely new industries, like the automobile industry, which were unviable due to cost considerations. Thus, the automobile industry provides a new source of derived demand for steel and such demand rises further with the development of industries auxiliary to the production of automobiles. Third, a fall in steel prices can result in lower transport costs as industries like ship building, automobiles, and other related industries expand and develop, thereby reducing the raw material cost for the steel industry itself.

But can a steel firm, in deciding whether or not to lower steel prices by constructing a blast furnace, guess all the changes in steel demand, described above, with any degree of accuracy? The various effects of a reduction in steel prices, discussed above, are the general equilibrium effects. In other words, changes in industry A (steel) alter the environmental set up for industry B, resulting in changes in price and demand for that industry's products. This, in turn, affects the environment surrounding industry C, resulting in a change in prices and demand in this industry as well. These chain effects are, ultimately, reflected in changed environment (demand–supply conditions) for the steel industry.

It is extremely unrealistic to assume that the private firms in an oligopolistic industry can acquire the kind of information needed to anticipate all the changes arising out of the general equilibrium effects. A proper understanding of these chain effects requires a complete knowledge of the conditions of demand and supply and their interrelationships for all the industries related to the said oligopolistic firm as well as an accurate calculation of the ensuing quantitative effects. This naturally involves considerable costs. Incentives for information collection depend on the *ex ante* expected profits from such activity. The pace of economic development that follows the construction of a large blast furnace is an unknown not only for the firm in question but also for the society as a whole. Therefore, only a few firms may consider costs of information worth the benefits. Even for firms willing to risk the expense, lenders willing to advance the money may be still fewer.

Let us explain these arguments using the terminology of game theory.[2] Firms in an oligopolistic industry play a strategic game (Γ here). The nature of this game Γ depends on an environmental parameter α consisting of elements such as the price elasticity of the demand function facing the industry and price elasticity of productive factors. The state emerging as the result of this game, the equilibrium state σ (price, total output, etc.), depends on the environmental parameter α governing the strategic behavior of each firm. That is, if the parameter takes a value α and the game is defined by $\Gamma(\alpha)$, equilibrium of the industry is given by $\sigma(\alpha)$.

When two industries, A and B, are interlinked as described above, what happens to the equilibrium of industry A, $\sigma_A(\alpha_A)$, depends on parameter α_A that stipulates the game $\Gamma_A(\alpha_A)$. The equilibrium in industry B, $\sigma_B(\alpha_B)$, on the other hand, depends on parameter $-\alpha_B$ governing the game under play, Γ_B. α_A here is the parameter of the demand for the product of industry A, and depends upon what is happening in industry B, where the demand originates. That is, α_A

depends on $\sigma_B(\alpha_B)$ and industry B is in a position to generate externalities for industry A. The parameter stipulating B's game, on the other hand, depends on the conditions prevailing in industry A, the demand source for its output. That is, α_B depends on $\sigma_A(\alpha_A)$ and industry A also generates externalities for industry B. As a result, equilibrium in industry A, σ_A, the result of the behavior of individual firms, working through σ_B, comes to depend on σ_A itself. This is what is termed as Marshallian externalities.

As already discussed, insofar as individual firms playing the game are ill informed about the above relationships, externalities can bring about a market failure. Firms in industry A must be fully aware of the game being played in industry B and must be able to discern the effect of a change in its own or the rival's behavior on B's game as well as the resulting changes in A's game. Otherwise, Marshallian externalities will result in inefficiencies.

Thus, in contrast to the perfectly competitive firms, taking price as a datum and unfettered with constraints on demand or supply, information is an important problem for the oligopolistic or imperfectly competitive firms, faced with demand and supply constraints and forced to adopt strategic behavior. The market mechanism does not provide any solution to this problem. The limited availability of information in oligopolistic industries leads to externalities and market failures.

6.3 A LINKAGE MODEL WITH TWO INDUSTRIES

In this section, let us try to explain the set-up costs, emerging as the result of factors discussed above, with the help of an extremely simplified model and discuss its implications for the industrial policy. A typical example of set-up costs, as was discussed in the context of set-up costs arising due to the presence of Marshallian externalities, is found in the industries with a forward-falling cost curve. Here, we consider a situation where an oligopolistically organized intermediate goods industry is supplying its product as an input to a perfectly competitive final goods industry. The firms in intermediate goods industry cannot predict changes in the number of firms in the final goods industry. Let us show that the long-run supply curve for the integrated sector consisting of the two industries (in the sense that both the industries are in equilibrium) is forward falling. That is, an increased supply of final goods results in a decline in the long-run equilibrium price.

Let Y be the intermediate good and $Y(q, \alpha)$ be the market demand curve facing the industry producing Y (Y industry). Here q is the price of Y and α is the parameter stipulating market demand for Y industry. As noted above, the technology in Y industry is characterized by large economies of scale (at the firm level) which account for the oligopolistic nature of the industry. We assume that the firms in this industry engaged in Cournot-type competition. The game $\Gamma(\alpha)$ based on α results in a long-run equilibrium $\sigma(\alpha)$ (such that profits are reduced to zero through entry and exit of the firms). Let the long-run equilibrium price be represented by $Q(\alpha)$. A detailed discussion of the relationship between q and α is taken up at a later stage.

For the sake of simplicity, let us assume that X is the only industry using the output of industry Y. Industry X is perfectly competitive with the representative firm in the industry, having the U-shaped average cost function often encountered in textbooks.[3] As is well known, the minimum average cost point (the vertical coordinate) β gives the break-even price. A market price above β results in positive profits for the firm, but if the price falls below β losses result. Thus, β is the long-run equilibrium price for this industry. It is important to note here that the break-even price β is itself a function, $\beta(q)$, of the intermediate product price q. Since a rise in the price of the intermediate product pushes up the average cost curve as a whole, $\beta'(q) > 0$.

Given the cost function as above, let $x(q, p)$ be the individual (firm's) supply curve in industry X, and $y(q, p)$ be the derived demand for the factor of production Y. Here, p is the price of good X and the following conditions obtain

$$\partial x / \partial p > 0. \quad \partial x / \partial q < 0$$
$$\partial y / \partial p > 0. \quad \partial y / \partial q < 0$$

If m is the number of firms in industry X, $X(p; q, m) = mx(p, q)$ gives the supply function for industry X as a whole such that $Y(q; p, m) = my(q, p)$ is its derived demand function for the output of industry Y as a whole. In fact, the parameter α that stipulates market demand, $Y(q; p, m)$ for industry Y, can be written as $\alpha = (p, m)$. To further simplify the analysis, let us postulate that m is the only parameter stipulating the game for industry Y, and p does not affect the environment of industry Y.[4] As a result, the long-run equilibrium price of industry Y can be expressed as $q* = Q(m)$. In this case, the supply function of industry X, $X_S(p; m)$, incorporating the long-run equilibrium condition of industry Y, can be written, with S being the total supply of the entire industry, as

$$S = X_S(p; m) = X[p; Q(m), m]$$

Figure 6-1 plots the market demand curve for industry X, obtained by varying m. In general, since the larger the m value, the larger the scale of industry X, total supply of the industry, S, is higher at a given price. Therefore, the supply curve, $X_S(p; m*)$, corresponding to a smaller number of firms in the industry, $m*$, is drawn to the left of the supply curve $X_S(p; m**)$ with a larger number of firms, $m**$.

Let us now consider how the long-run Cournot equilibrium price $Q(m)$ in industry Y changes as the scale of industry X expands (m increases). A rise in the number of firms operating in industry X amounts to increased derived demand

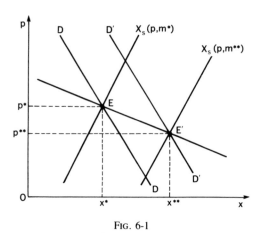

FIG. 6-1

for industry Y. Furthermore, additional demand generated by an increase in the number of firms in industry X, represented by $x(q; p)$ for each new entry, is higher the lower the price of industry Y's output. If the additional derived demand, as m rises, is forward falling with respect to q, the long-run equilibrium price of the output of industry Y declines with a rise in m. That is, $Q'(m) < 0$ holds. Let us demonstrate this below.

Let m be the number of firms in industry X and industry Y be in long-run Cournot equilibrium given the total derived demand $Y(q; m)$. This gives rise to the well-known problem of excess capacity in industry Y as follows. Figure 6-2 depicts the behavior of a representative firm in industry Y. Under Cournot assumptions, the optimal behavior of such a firm is determined by the marginal revenue curve (MR) derived from the residual demand, RD—the difference between the total market demand and the output of all the other firms, and the average cost (AC) and the marginal cost (MC) curves derived from the cost function. Since profits in the long-run oligopolistic equilibrium (E) are zero, price equals average cost (AC $= q$). On the other hand, due to monopoly power held by the firm, the price exceeds marginal revenue $(q > $ MR$)$. Since profit maximization requires marginal revenue to equal marginal cost (MR $=$ MC), equilibrium average cost exceeds marginal cost (AC $>$ MC), and production is carried out at point y^* where average costs are still diminishing and economies of scale operative. Defining the output y^{**} corresponding to minimum average cost point as optimum output, the oligopolistic industry is seen to produce below this level. That is, the oligopolistic industry maximizes its profits at a less than optimum level of output and idle capacity emerges.

Starting with such a state of long-run equilibrium (E), let us consider the case where number of firms in industry X rises from m^* to m^{**}, increasing derived

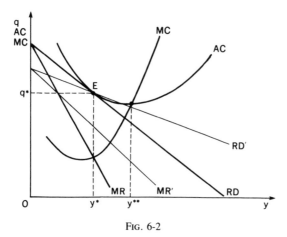

FIG. 6-2

demand for the output of industry Y. In the short run, this results in emergence of profits in industry Y, inducing new entry. Let us assume here, for the sake of argument, that the increase in number of firms in industry Y due to new entry is proportional to the rise in derived demand for its product. Under these conditions, with prices (q^*) staying unchanged, the total demand for Y can be met with each firm producing exactly the same output (y^*) as before. Production by the newly entered firms absorbs the increase in the derived demand.

However, the residual demand curve (RD′) of a representative firm is obtained by subtracting the output of all the other firms (including the new firms) from the new demand curve. Since the additional increase in demand for the output of industry Y is a decreasing function of price q, the new residual demand curve for the entire industry tends to diminish in slope and flatten out as compared to the original residual demand curve RD. As shown in Fig. 6-2, marginal revenue at output level y^* after the change is higher than before and each firm strives to raise its output. As a result, E ceases to be the long-run equilibrium point and each firm produces a higher level of output than y^*. In the new long-run equilibrium, therefore, scale economies are exploited more effectively, average costs drop, and the long-run equilibrium price $Q(m^{**})$ falls.

How can one derive the supply curve for the sector as a whole by putting together the feature of industry Y whereby a rise in m reduces the equilibrium price $Q(m)$ and the supply function $X(p, m)$ for industry X which incorporates equilibrium condition for industry Y, i.e., the supply function of X–Y sector? Let us go back to Fig. 6-1 once again. Let DD represent the demand curve facing industry X and m^* the long-run equilibrium number of firms. The long-run equilibrium price of industry Y, in this case, must be $Q(m^*)$. Since industry X is also the state of long-run equilibrium, profits in X must be zero, and the equilibrium price p^* must equal to the break-even price $\beta\,[Q(m^*)]$. That is, the equilibrium point E, along the curve $X_S(p,\ m^*)$, where price p^* equals $\beta\,[Q(m)]$, must be such as to sustain both industries, X and Y, in a long-run equilibrium simultaneously.

Now, let us assume that the demand for industry X increases to $D'D'$, and the number of firms to m^{**}. As a result, the curve X_S shifts to the right, as shown in Fig. 6-1, while, at the same time, long-run equilibrium price $Q(m^{**})$ in industry Y declines, lowering the break-even point for industry X. As a result, the long-run equilibrium point for the $X-Y$ sector, corresponding to m^{**} firms, shifts to E', representing a higher output level (X^{**}) and a lower equilibrium price (p^{**}) as compared to E. Thus, the long-run supply curve for the $X-Y$ sector is forward falling as depicted by EE' in Fig. 6-1.

For the reasons discussed above, set-up costs emerge in the X industry ($X-Y$ sector to be precise). That is, as explained in Fig. 5-4 of the previous chapter, the industry cannot get established at low levels of output. Once production exceeds a certain level (X_0 in Fig. 5-4), however, not only is the industry established but production also expands at a very fast pace. This phenomenon appears in the model used in this chapter since low output in industry X implies a low level of demand for the output of Y such that the output of individual firms is too low to permit full exploitation of the scale economies[5] and leaves the intermediate goods prices too high. With sufficient demand for intermediate goods, output of the firms in industry Y rises and average costs fall, causing a decline in intermediate goods prices. This decline in raw material costs for industry X (as an export industry) raises its competitive power and, hence, output. This, in turn, raises demand for intermediate goods. The increased demand for intermediate goods once again reduces the price of intermediate product, further raising the competitive power of industry X. This effect is responsible for the emergence of set-up costs in industry X ($X-Y$ sector, to be precise).[6]

As noted above, even if the output level of industry X is low, competitiveness can be enhanced through lower costs if the firms in industry Y expand production and lower their prices. If the firms in industry Y expect the increase in their output to be matched by an increase in demand, set-up costs vanish and private incentives suffice to bring about an optimum resource allocation. However, for firms to make accurate estimates, they must be able to fully grasp all the general equilibrium linkage effects arising out of a reduction in the price of their output.

Thus, set-up costs arising as a result of scale economies or information, discussed above, tend to be more prevalent in (1) oligopolistic industries characterized by considerable scale economies, (2) industries with a greater number of interrelated industries, and (3) (contrary to what our model suggests) related industries which are themselves oligopolistically organized such that prices alone cannot relay all the information required. The possibility is high that set-up costs will emerge, in industries with extensive scale economies, due to the importance of investments in large-scale production plants and technology and due to extensive interindustry linkages (industries with extensive linkage effects and a wide base in the context of Japanese industrial policy). That is why industries like iron and steel, automobiles, and petrochemicals are the usual targets of industrial policies.

6.4 INFORMATION-BASED INDUSTRIAL POLICIES

Before closing this chapter, let us explore the significance of industrial policy intervention for industries where economies of scale and information give rise to set-up costs. As explained in the last chapter, conscious intervention, by way of subsidies, tariffs, or other pecuniary incentives, can help in developing such industries. However, the link between the set-up costs, our major concern here, and information and strategic behavior by the oligopolistic firms, indicates that there is a strong possibility for developing such industries through exchange of information and coordination of behavior among oligopolistic firms—an industrial policy based on information exchange and coordination.

The first point to note here is that set-up costs result in multiple equilibria. In the presence of multiple equilibria, the equilibrium that finally emerges depends on factors such as the collective information shared by the participants of the game and the coordination enforced by those outside the game (referees or the government). Let us illustrate this point with the help of an example.

Figure 6-3 illustrates a game with multiple equilibria. There are two players, A and B, each having two strategies, R and T (represented by rows and columns, respectively). Let us suppose going to Roppongi crossing (in Tokyo) represents strategy R, and going to Tokyo Tower, strategy T. That is, row R indicates that player A goes to Roppongi while column T indicates that player B goes to Tokyo Tower. The benefit that a player derives from the strategy chosen is given by the numbers within the parentheses. For example, if player A goes to Roppongi while B goes off to Tokyo Tower, A gains nothing while B gains 9. The intuitive explanation of such a game is as follows: When two players (say, lovers) meet, both gain a lot. Getting together for a date in Roppongi entails more fun. If they cannot meet, enjoying the view from Tokyo Tower may be a better way to kill time all alone rather than loitering around in Roppongi.

A \ B	R	T
R	(100, 100)	(0, 9)
T	(9, 0)	(10, 10)

Fig. 6-3

This game has two (Nash) equilibria—that is, two strategic combinations in which it is optimal for the player to choose a strategy leading to a Nash equilibrium if the partner also chooses a similar strategy. (R,R) and (T,T) represent these two combinations. For example, if the partner is expected to go to Tokyo Tower, it is desirable for the player to go to Tokyo Tower as well rather than to wander around in Roppongi.

If this game is played without any prior knowledge about how the other player is going to act, what strategy is chosen by each player? The strategy chosen by each player, in this case, depends on what the player thinks that the other will do and also what he thinks that the other player thinks that this player will do. The existence of (R,R) and (T,T) as Nash equilibria implies that whether both players guess that the other will go to Roppongi or both expect the other to go to Tokyo Tower, the expectations are in conformity and self-fulfilling. That is, the available information about which strategy the two players will choose is insufficient. What factors determine the choice of strategy by each individual player and which of the two equilibria obtains? There are two known ways to deal with this problem.

The first way to deal with the problem posed above is the "focal point" approach of Schelling (1960). Let us postulate that both players are university students from Tokyo. In this case, even if the two players are uncertain about one another's destination, they are likely to end up in Roppongi. This is because they both know that Roppongi is much better for dating than Tokyo Tower. What happens if both the players are from way out of Tokyo, say high school students on their school trip? For them, Tokyo Tower is likely to be a more familiar place than Roppongi and quite possibly a more suitable meeting place. If this reasoning is correct, the Tokyo college students will go to Roppongi and the visiting high school students will go to Tokyo Tower. Thus, in a game with multiple equilibria, the resulting equilibrium comes to depend on the environment in which the players of the game (unrelated to the game itself) are brought up and focal points of the society.

A second way to look at the equilibrium that emerges in a game with multiple equilibria is associated with the concept of preplay communications. In the game depicted by Fig. 6-3, let us assume that the two players involved in the actual game meet in advance and agree to play the game, say (R,R). In this case, there is no incentive to choose a strategy other than the one previously agreed upon. For example, it is obvious that choosing R is the optimal strategy for player A if the partner plays the game as previously agreed upon. Similarly, for B too, the optimal choice of strategy is R if A sticks to the agreement. Thus, there is no reason for either A or B to choose a strategy different from R. Thus, the Nash equilibrium (even if we assume the existence of multiple equilibria), given the existence of preplay communications, is characterized by a self-enforcing power.

How can one apply the concepts of focal points or preplay communications to the problem of information in the context of industrial policies? First, the concept of focal points may be indicative of the effectiveness of the industrial policies and economic plans and future visions used widely in postwar Japan. For example, assuming that both high growth and stable growth are feasible courses for Japan, it is not easy for individual private sector firms to determine which of the two courses (equilibria) to pursue. A plan or a vision does not have any effective coercive power. However, it is not impossible to deduce that the government, by providing a focal point for the private sector firms in the form of one piece of information (corresponding to a given equilibrium), can help in coordinating the behavior of various private sector economic agents.

Such an argument is especially appropriate for explaining the much talked about "pump-priming effect" that resulted from the Japan Development Bank loans. Let us assume that the private banking institutions could not decide which of a wide range of private sector projects to finance. If the Development Bank, at this juncture, chooses a project and announces its intention to finance it, it may as well serve as a focal point for the private banking institutions.

In considering the realities of Japanese industrial policies as a means to solve the problem of set-up costs resulting from strategic behavior and incomplete information, as discussed in this chapter, the role of preplay communications, or communications in general, is perhaps more important. If set-up costs, arising due to a lack of information, are the basic cause of market failure, intervention in the form of monetary incentives, like subsidies, tariffs, and trade restrictions, is difficult to justify. If the government is aware of the fact that a given industry or sector can be developed with the help of such policies, the firms involved must also be aware of this and it must be possible for them to establish and develop this industry or sector without any intervention.[7]

If the actual industrial policies had any significance for such industries or sectors at all (except for any accidental effects of ad hoc protective policies adopted by the MITI), it must have been in the form of information exchanges through various deliberation councils or committees. In formulating the industrial policies, the MITI drew up several plans and proposals in various deliberation councils and committees like the Industrial Structure Deliberation Council, bringing together a large number of representatives from private sector firms, financial institutions, and the government. As a result, future domestic and foreign demand for a number of commodities was projected, new technology was introduced, and estimates of required capacity, funds, and raw material supplies were drawn up. Based on these estimates, efforts were made to coordinate and adjust investment, production, and supply of funds in a macroeconomic perspective. It goes without saying that such efforts, at times, resulted in government intervention in the private sector economy which inhibited the normal functioning of the free market economic activity. At the same time, however, the activities of these committees resulted in information exchanges that led to discovery of more desirable equilibria. Indicating the strategies to attain such an equilibrium to the private sector economic agents resulted in the establishment of a self-enforcing equilibrium. Whatever way one considers it, activities of the deliberation councils and committees or government visions and medium- and long-term plans served to provide information, free of charge, about demand and price forecasts of various industries to the private sector firms. Besides, information provided was accurate and of high quality as these estimates were repeatedly updated.

The existence of industrial set-up costs, as discussed above, shows that whether an industry becomes established on its own or not is not determined only by the demand conditions and technological constraints as stressed by the neoclassical economists. That is, the problem of choosing an industrial and trade structure for a country—which industries to develop and which to pass over—is an important policy problem especially in the context of the group of industries characterized by substantial set-up costs. The subsequent chapters focus attention on the problem of optimum industrial and trade structures.

NOTES

1. For details of the argument developed hereafter, see Okuno-Fujiwara (1988).

2. For example, see Suzuki (1981) on game theory.

3. What we are assuming here is that the long-run average cost curve of the firm is U-shaped. It must be noted that all the concepts used here, like the break-even price of the firm and supply functions, are long-run concepts.

4. It is easy to show that this assumption is not essential. See Okuno-Fujiwara (1988) for a rigorous treatment.

5. This provides a microeconomic foundation for the Smithian notion that "division of labor is limited by the extent of the market."

6. Such set-up costs have traditionally been defined as "pecuniary externalities" (cf. Scitovsky, 1954). This view has, however, been criticized since on theoretical grounds pecuniary externalities are not expected to result in market failure [cf., for example, Heller and Starrett (1976)]. The argument developed in this chapter can be interpreted as an attempt to explain the phenomenon that has traditionally been treated as a pecuniary externality in terms of economic theory.

7. This problem is not specific to the case of set-up costs of a sector, as considered in this chapter, where information has an important role to play, but is common to industrial set-up costs in general arising from external economies.

7

Choice of Industrial Structure
and Economic Welfare

In Chapter 3 of this book, we mentioned that choice of industrial structure formed an important tenet of the postwar Japanese industrial policy. The concepts of heavy and chemical industrialization and advancement of industrial structure came up for repeated discussions. All this debate, however, was merely an effort to get at the form that an ideal industrial structure should take. The analysis in Chapters 5 and 6 indicates that it is possible for the government to establish and expand industries using appropriate policy intervention measures. As a result, choice of industries to be targeted for promotion, depending on how far these industries could benefit Japan the most, was a major policy problem.

As will be shown below, gains from trade that a country can appropriate depend heavily on the industrial structure of that country. The advancement of industrial structure pursued by the Japanese policy makers, in fact, played an extremely important role in raising the Japanese gains from trade.

7.1 External Income Position and Pattern of Trade

We take recourse to a two-country framework, to bring out the major features of the argument. The two countries are Japan and a foreign country, and it is assumed that Japan is in the process of catching up with the foreign country. The appendix to this chapter and Itoh and Kiyono (1987) discuss the details of this type of model. In what ensues, we limit our discussion to the intuitive arguments underlying the model. We allow for three goods, referred to as good 1, good 2, and good 3. Production of good 1 is assumed to require simple technology while that of good 3 requires fairly advanced technology. Technology required for producing good 2 is assumed to lie somewhere in between that for good 1 and good 3. This concept of "level of technology" required, however, does not have any analytical significance in the discussion that follows.

We assume Japan to have a comparative advantage in the production of good 1 while the foreign country enjoys cost advantage in good 3. Both Japan as well as

75

the foreign country are assumed to be equally competitive in the production of good 2. As a result, Japan produces goods 1 and 2 while the foreign country produces goods 2 and 3. This classification of goods, although extremely simplified, is useful for grasping the essence of the effects of changes in industrial structure on economic welfare.

The discussion hereafter assumes balanced trade between Japan and the foreign country.[1] That is, the trade balance equation

$$\text{Japanese imports} = \text{foreign imports from Japan} \qquad (1)$$

is satisfied. If average propensity to import for Japan and the foreign country is defined as

$$\text{Average propensity to import} = \text{imports}/\text{GNP} \qquad (2)$$

Eq. (1) yields

$$\frac{\text{Japanese GNP}}{\text{Foreign GNP}} = \frac{\text{foreign average propensity to import Japanese goods}}{\text{Japan's average propensity to import foreign goods}} \qquad (3)$$

Equation (3) can be obtained simply by rewriting the trade balance equation using the concept of average propensity to import and does not imply any causal relationship between the two sides of the equation. It does, however, provide a useful yardstick to measure relative levels of GNP attainable by the two countries given the complex trade relationships. Equation (3) states that the GNP for Japan will be relatively higher, the lower the Japanese and the higher the foreign propensities to import.

Keeping these relationships in mind, let us try to analyze how the changes in the Japanese industrial structure could affect economic welfare. The Japanese industrial structure can change in two different ways. First, there is a pattern of industrial development based on raising productivity and lowering costs in the already established industry (good 1 here). A second pattern of industrial development aims at making the marginal industry (good 2 here) more competitive.

One of the major points of contention in the debate over the postwar industrial protection policy in Japan was the choice of the pattern of industrial development that Japan should follow. In the early postwar period two opposing viewpoints, on whether to protect internationally uncompetitive industries like automobiles and steel or not, were in vogue. One of these stressed the inefficiencies in resource allocation resulting from the protection of industries where Japan did not have any comparative advantage. The supporters of this line of reasoning argued that it was cheaper to import these products from abroad and the resources thus saved could be diverted to textiles and light industry products, where Japan held a comparative advantage.

The second line of reasoning emphasized that Japan could register a fast pace of growth only if it could develop the industries like automobiles and steel successfully as export industries. Export of textiles and light industry products only, according to the advocates of this viewpoint, would result in keeping Japanese income at low levels for a long time. It was stressed that since the pattern of comparative advantage could shift dynamically, the industrial promotion policies adopted should be able to anticipate these shifts.[2]

7.2 INDUSTRIAL DEVELOPMENT WITHOUT CHANGES IN INDUSTRIAL STRUCTURE

Had Japan followed a pattern of industrial development based on progressive reduction in the cost of production of good 1, already established in Japan, what difference would it have made to Japanese economic welfare? Let us try to answer this question in terms of Eq. (3), representing relative GNP of Japan and the foreign country. An important factor determining the propensity to import in Japan and the foreign country is the richness of the range of exportables or what may be called the export menu. If the Japanese export menu is limited to textiles and cheap light industry products, the foreign propensity to import Japanese exports can be expected to be low. Only a few consumers can be expected to devote a large proportion of their incomes to such goods. Besides, a large number of countries could supply these products.

As a result, the foreign and Japanese propensities to import cannot be expected to change appreciably just because Japanese industrial development has been able to reduce costs of production in good 1. In a three-good model being discussed here, the following results can be derived:

1. If the price elasticity of demand for good 1 is unity, a decline in cost of production of good 1 does not have any effect on the relative GNP of the two countries.

2. If the price elasticity of demand for good 1 is less than unity, a reduction in production cost of good 1 leads to a relative decline in Japanese GNP.

3. If the price elasticity of demand for good 1 is greater than unity, lowering the cost of production in good 1 will result in a higher relative GNP for Japan.

These results can be interpreted as follows. If the price elasticity of demand for good 1 is high and the prices fall due to a decline in costs, the rise in demand would be greater than the fall in price. This implies that the foreign propensity to import from Japan will rise. In general, however, the price elasticity of demand for technologically simple good 1 cannot be expected to be very high. That is, occurrence of result 3 is less likely.

Result 1 follows from a Cobb–Douglas utility function. In this case, price changes are not accompanied by a shift in propensity to spend on various goods. Therefore, even if the price of good 1 falls, propensity to spend on respective goods does not change. As a result, propensity to import in two countries also stays constant and there is no shift in relative GNP levels of the two countries. In this case, when the relative GNP of the two countries does not change, reduction in cost of production of good 1 in Japan benefits not only Japan but the foreign country as well in the form of lower prices.

Economic development of the home country, when price elasticity of demand is less than 1, gives rise to the possibility of lower, rather than higher, economic welfare. This is what has been termed as "immiserizing growth" by Bhagwati (1958) and others. In this case, Japan's terms of trade worsen due to a fall in good 1 prices, resulting in a lower relative GNP for Japan. As the foreign factor prices, determining the price of Japanese imports from abroad, are proportional to foreign GNP, a lower relative GNP for Japan implies higher real price of imports from abroad. If this effect outweighs the welfare-raising effect of a fall in good 1 price, Japanese economic welfare can decline.

7.3 Industrial Growth Accompanied by Changes in Industrial Structure

A Japanese pattern of industrial development based on increasing competitiveness in the marginal industry (good 2) leads to substantially different welfare effects as compared to the case discussed above. Let us consider this case now.

As Japan gets more competitive in the production of good 2, the supply source for a part of this good shifts from the foreign to the home country. As a result, the Japanese export menu expands while that of the foreign country contracts compared to the initial situation.[3] How do these developments affect the propensity to import in the two countries?

Let us first consider the case when the price elasticity of demand for each good is unity. In this case, propensity to spend on each good does not change even if productivity change leads to a change in prices. Therefore, in order to find out how this affects propensity to import in Japan and the foreign country, it will be enough to look at the level of exports of this commodity by the foreign and the home countries. Propensity to import is expected to rise for the country importing products with higher expenditure propensity.

Now if Japan increases its competitiveness in good 2 and is able to replace a part of the foreign country exports, its propensity to import will decline in proportion to propensity to spend on this good. At the same time, the propensity to import will rise in the foreign country. The reason for this is that Japan no longer needs to import this commodity while the foreign country will have to begin importing.

The size of the change in propensity to import in the two countries will determine the extent of change in relative income levels as well. In general, the greater the propensity to spend on the good that becomes a Japanese export replacing the foreign country, the greater will be the change in the relative GNP levels. We derive this result mathematically in the Appendix to this chapter. One can, however, also interpret it intuitively as follows.

A nonunit price elasticity of demand for the marginal good (good 2) calls for, in a manner similar to that discussed in the previous section, a closer look at changes in expenditure shares as price falls. If this elasticity for good 2 is greater than 1, a fall in price leads to an increase in the share of expenditure allocated to this good, raising the relative GNP for Japan proportionately. The exact opposite will result if the elasticity of demand is less than unity.

The postwar pattern of Japanese industrial development increased the weight of marginal industries in the industrial structure. In the process, industries like iron and steel, automobiles, and household electronics developed into new export industries. Since the propensity to spend on these goods is normally high, development of these industries into export industries may have considerably raised the relative GNP level.

In the immediate postwar period, Japan exported only low-priced textiles and other light industry products and the foreign propensity to import Japanese products is believed to have been quite low. At the same time, potential Japanese propensity to import from abroad was, probably, substantially high given its dependence on imports of machinery, fuels, and a host of other commodities. In reality, however, severe import controls let only a part of this potential import propensity to materialize. Subsequently, the Japanese industrial structure underwent substantial changes with shipbuilding, iron and steel, electrical machinery, automobiles, machine tools, and semiconductor industries developing into new export industries one after the other. In the process, the foreign propensity to import Japanese products rose steeply while increase in Japanese propensity to import from abroad slowed down. Such a change in industrial structure could have been one of the factors behind the fast pace of increase in Japanese relative income.

Thus, industrial development accompanied by a substantial change in industrial structure contributes significantly to the economic welfare of the nation. Not only does the country reap the benefits of falling product prices as productivity rises but the benefits of changes in relative GNP also come into play. The impact of such a process on economic welfare of the trading partner, however, is not clear.

The foreign country benefits from the lower price of good 2 but loses due to a fall in its relative GNP level. The price of good 1, being imported by the foreign country from Japan, fluctuates in direct proportion to changes in Japan's relative GNP. This follows from the assumption of the model that Japanese factor prices are proportional to its GNP. As the result of a rise in Japanese relative GNP, the price of imports of good 1 from Japan rises. There are no *a priori* grounds to determine which of the two opposing effects is stronger. In the Ricardian type of model developed in the Appendix to this chapter, industrial development in Japan is seen to result in lowering economic welfare in the foreign country.

Thus, we find that industrial development accompanied by changing industrial structure strongly affects relative income position of the home country and its trading partner. The trade friction between Japan and the foreign countries, especially the United States, in the postwar period was, more often than not, related to the marginal industries at respective junctures. Sustained development, in Japan as well as in any underdeveloped country, requires increasing the weight of marginal industries along with lowering the costs in the already established industries. Such a process of economic development, however, can easily lead to economic frictions with the foreign countries.

7.4 RESPONSE OF ADVANCED COUNTRIES

How should the developed industrial countries (foreign country) respond to economic development in an underdeveloped country, such as that achieved by Japan through expansion of its marginal industry?[4] One response could be a recourse to protective trade policies or production subsidies by the foreign country to help its own firms in the marginal industry to retain competitiveness. There is no certainty as to whether or not such a policy can raise economic welfare in the foreign country. The reasons are similar to the ones that account for the uncertain effect of changes in Japanese industrial structure on foreign economic welfare.

If the foreign country does adopt such a policy and Japan retaliates in the same vein, world trade will contract and all the countries involved will be adversely affected. Furthermore, such a stance by the foreign country will bring Japanese economic development to a halt, which is also undesirable.

The foreign country can, however, react in a different way without taking recourse to a defensive posture on the marginal industry. This is by promoting development of the advanced industry. The very fact that the foreign country does not defend the marginal industry implies that resources will move into the advanced industry on the margin. It is not possible, here, to present any definitive argument for or against an active promotion policy for development of the advanced industry. One can visualize various types of market failures in development of technology, technology transactions, and diffusion. Therefore, active government intervention for establishment of advanced industries can be justified in some cases. We will come back to the discussion of this aspect in Part IV of this book.

If the foreign country shifts to the advanced industry (good 3 in this case) and comes up with ever new products, a part of the demand for goods 1 and 2 will shift to the new products. As a result, propensity to spend on goods 1 and 2 will decline while that on good 3 will rise. It follows that propensity to import foreign product will rise, raising the relative GNP in the foreign country.

The expansion of the advanced industry in the foreign country will produce effects similar to those created by expansion of marginal industry in Japan. In both cases, the relative GNP position moves favorably for the country with changing industrial structure. Some aspects of the former, however, are not observed in the latter.

First, expansion by the foreign country into new fields diversifies the variety of goods and services. This benefits the foreign country as well as Japan. Second, expansion into new areas not only raises the foreign GNP but also factor prices. As a result, competitiveness of foreign firms in the marginal industry declines, making it easier for Japanese firms to expand in this industry. The benefits of expansion into new areas by the industrially developed countries, given these two considerations, can be much more pervasive.

7.5 INDUSTRIAL POLICY AND INDUSTRIAL STRUCTURE

In the above discussion, we have focused our attention on the effect that changes in the industrial structure of an economy can have on economic welfare and neglected the role of industrial policy in the whole process. It is, however, clear from the arguments presented in all the previous chapters in this book that industrial policy can have far-reaching effects on industrial structure.

Industries with dynamic economies of scale and Marshallian externalities show characteristics of an infant industry. That is, these industries cannot be established in the absence of governmental protection but can flourish if provided with transitory protection. In the terminology adopted in this book, we may say that the industrial set-up costs in these industries can be overcome only through governmental protection.

Of these, Marshallian externalities have already been discussed in detail. Here we briefly discuss the concept of dynamic economies of scale. Technology and know-how accumulated within a firm or industry have a significant effect on costs of production. Of special importance are (1) accumulated experience in the production process (learning by doing) and (2) investment in technology and product development. Both of these have strong characteristics of dynamic economies of scale.

The long-established firms, in the industries where learning effects result in substantial cost reductions, are in an advantageous position due to a long history of production. With their lower production costs, these firms can corner a larger share of the market than the newly established firms. Large-scale production due to large market share, once again, facilitates learning effects, giving these firms a further advantage. The entry barriers in these industries become higher and new entry becomes difficult. But if the government provides protection to these industries in the initial phases, even the latecomers have a fair chance of becoming established.

Similar dynamic economies of scale can be observed in the industries where technology and product development play an important part. The costs involved in these activities are as good as fixed. Therefore, the unit costs of technology or product development decline in firms supplying the product in large quantities. As in the case of learning effects, government protection, in most cases, becomes necessary for latecomers to overcome entry barriers arising out of dynamic economies of scale.

Most of the marginal industries, like those producing good 2 in the above analysis, are characterized by industrial set-up costs in an underdeveloped economy like Japan. This gives rise to the problem of infant industry protection. Since it is impossible to treat all the infant industries equitably for promotion, it becomes imperative to set up priorities. This is referred to in the literature as industrial targeting.

As revealed in the above analysis, promotion of industries supplying goods and services on which propensity to spend is high helps raise the foreign propensity to import. This, in turn, raises the GNP. Promotion of such industries, therefore, becomes the basic guideline for targeting.

Direct subsidies for promoting infant industries is one possible policy instrument in the hands of the government. Subsidization can take the form of production subsidies, export subsidies, subsidies for technology development and equipment investments, and so on. Import controls can also promote domestic industry if the domestic market is large enough. In the case of Japan, import control measures provied to be quite effective. Of greater interest is the fact that import control measures, in the industries characterized by scale economies, also act as export promotion measures.[5] Large domestic demand brings the scale economies into play, making it easier to export to foreign markets.

Finally, the analysis of this chapter also puts export promotion in a new perspective.[6] In the received trade theory, export subsidies do not benefit the country taking recourse to such subsidies under the conditions of perfect competition. In the model presented in this chapter, export subsidies to the marginal industry raise economic welfare in the country adopting such a policy. This comes about since a rise in foreign propensity to import raises relative income, as was discussed earlier.

7.6 APPENDIX: ANALYSIS OF A MULTISECTOR RICARDIAN FRAMEWORK

This Appendix uses a simplified multisector Ricardian model to take a closer look at the points discussed in the main text.[7]

7.6.1 THE SUPPLY SIDE

Let us first examine the structure of production, that is, the supply side. For simplicity, we assume that the number of goods is infinite, indexed by a number n lying in the interval $[0, N]$. We assume only one factor of production, which we call labor. We also assume that there are only two trading countries, the home and the foreign countries. Production technology for each of the goods in each country is characterized by a fixed input requirement coefficient, i.e., the input of the productive factor needed to produce one unit of a good. We use a_n and a_n^* to represent, respectively, the home and foreign labor input coefficients for producing a good n. In other words, a_n and a_n^* completely summarize all supply-side conditions, including technological levels and the industrial structure of the two countries.

The domestic and foreign wages, in terms of the home currency, are represented by w and w^*.[8] The model presented here is a real model, abstracting from all monetary considerations, so that the relative wage rate w/w^* is the only endogenous variable. The individual wage levels cannot be determined within the model. The pattern of trade under the conditions of perfect competition and free trade is then determined, with the country having a cost advantage being the exporter, as follows[9]:

The home country exports the good if $a_n w \leqq a_n^* w^*$
The foreign country exports the good if $a_n w > a_n^* w^*$

Given these conditions, the home country exports goods for which a_n^*/a_n is greater than w/w^*, and imports goods for which a_n^*/a_n is smaller.

The forward-falling curve a_n^*/a_n in Fig. 7-1 represents this relationship and is referred to as the supply-wage schedule in the ensuing discussion. The curve is forward falling due to the fact that the goods are indexed such that a_n^*/a_n is a declining function of n. This is equivalent to the assumption that the smaller the value of n, the greater is the comparative advantage of the home country. The

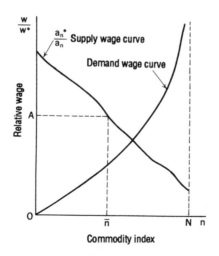

FIG. 7-1

supply-wage schedule also depicts the relationship between the trade pattern and relative wage rate $w/w*$ in the two countries. For example, if the relative wages are given by point A on the vertical axis, the goods indexed by 0 to $\bar{n}$ will be home country exports, and those by $\bar{n}$ to N will be foreign country exports. In this situation, good n is termed as the marginal good.

7.6.2 THE DEMAND SIDE

Next we set forth the demand side. The home and foreign countries are assumed to have fixed labor endowments at L and $L*$, so that wL and $w*L*$ represent the home and foreign country incomes, respectively, expressed in the currency of the home country. The proportion of expenditure on each good (expenditure share) is the most crucial demand variable in our model. The proportion of expenditure on a good n in the foreign and domestic countries is defined by δ_n and δ_n^*, respectively. The proportion of income spent on all goods, as long as all income is spent, must sum (or, more precisely, integrate) to unity, such that

$$\int_0^N \delta_n \, dn = \int_0^N \delta_n^* \, dn = 1$$

The expenditure ratio, in general, is a function of relative prices, but we assume it to be fixed in this analysis for the sake of expository simplicity (in other words, we assume a Cobb–Douglas type of utility function).

Let the marginal good n represent the boundary between exports and imports. For trade to be balanced, the value of home country imports must equal the value of foreign country imports, or

$$(\int_{\bar{n}}^N \delta_n \, dn) \, wL = (\int_0^{\bar{n}} \delta_n^* \, dn) w*L*$$

(the left side gives home country imports, and the right side represents foreign country imports). Rearranging, we get

$$(wL)/(w*L*) = (\int_0^{\bar{n}} \delta_n^* \, dn)/(\int_{\bar{n}}^N \delta_n \, dn)$$

or, equivalently,

$$w/w* = [(\int_0^{\bar{n}} \delta_n^* \, dn)/(\int_{\bar{n}}^N \delta_n \, dn)](L*/L)$$

The upward-rising curve in Fig. 7-1 represents the relationship between the relative wage $w/w*$ and the trade pattern (given $\bar{n}$ as the marginal good) given by the above equation. Hereafter, this curve is referred to as the demand-wage schedule. The demand-wage schedule is always upward rising. This is evident from the fact that the larger the share of foreign expenditure on the home country goods (or the smaller the share of home country expenditure on imported goods), the higher is the relative wage, $w/w*$, and relative income ratio $wL/w*L*$ for the home country.[10]

The home country relative wage rises, in our model, due to diversification of the home country export menu accompanying a rise in the index of marginal good $\bar{n}$ and a corresponding contraction of the import menu. If the range of home country exports expands, the proportion of foreign country expenditures on home country goods will increase, to that extent raising relative income.[11] [More generally, national incomes (or national factor incomes) are determined by the strength of demand for productive factors. If diversification of the home country export menu leads to greater demand, derived demand for the home country's factors of production will also rise, pulling up incomes in the home country.]

7.6.3 EQUILIBRIUM

Trade equilibrium for the two countries is given by the point of intersection between the supply-wage schedule, representing the supply side, and the demand-wage schedule, representing the demand side. In this model, the index of the marginal good n, representing the trade pattern, and w/w^*, the relative wage, are determined by $\{a_n\}$ and $\{a_n^*\}$, the technology and industry structure parameters, and $\{\delta_n\}$ and $\{\delta_n^*\}$, the parameters representing the pattern of demand.

7.6.4 "TECHNOLOGY GAP": INDUSTRIAL DEVELOPMENT AND GAINS FROM TRADE

To investigate the relationship between the pattern of trade and gains from trade within the framework of the model presented above, we introduce the concept of a "technology gap."[12] A_1A_2 in Fig. 7-2 represents the supply-wage schedule at the initial stage of industrial development of the home country. This intersects the horizontal axis at A_2 since the home country does not have the industry or technology to produce the goods with a greater index. At this initial stage of development, the relative wage of the home country is extremely low (OB_1 in Fig. 7-2) since, given the underdeveloped industrial structure of the

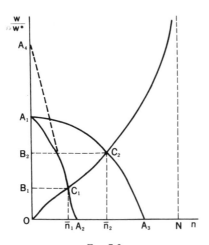

FIG. 7-2

home country, it cannot absorb demand for the goods with an expenditure ratio lying outside the interval $[0, \bar{n}_1]$. The lower the proportion of expenditures on these goods, the lower is the height of the wage-demand schedule in the interval $[0, n_1]$ and the lower is the relative wage w/w^*.

Let us now assume that the home country establishes a number of industries, enabling it to diversify its industrial structure. The supply-wage schedule shifts from A_1A_2 to A_1A_3 as a result of this industrial development. In other words, the industries producing the goods indexed by segment A_2A_3 have been newly incorporated into the home country's technology and industrial structure. With the expansion of domestic industry, trade equilibrium shifts from C_1 to C_2. As a result, the goods indexed by interval $[\bar{n}_1, \bar{n}_2]$ are added to the home country export menu, and the home country relative income (relative wages and wage levels in the home country's currency) rises by the amount of expenditure on these goods, in line with the demand-wage schedule. This increase in the home country relative wage as a result of diversification of the home country export menu follows the mechanism discussed under Section 7.6.2 on demand side.

In the immediate postwar period, the United States GNP far surpassed that of other countries. One main reason for such a situation may have been the structure of world industry resembling more or less Fig. 7-2. In other words, the United States had an overwhelming lead in industries like automobiles, iron and steel, chemicals, and general and electrical machinery, accounting for a substantial proportion of world demand. The proportion of world expenditures on the products of these industries was extremely high, which resulted in United States income levels far in excess of those of other countries. The postwar Japanese economic development can be interpreted as a gradual process of overcoming the technology gap that existed in the initial stages. The industries listed above gradually came to be established as the leading and export industries of Japan. The relative level of Japanese income rose, along the demand-wage schedule, on the basis of the high proportion of expenditures on the goods produced by these industries.[13] This increase in relative income can theoretically occur either in the form of an increase in the wage denominated in the home country currency, or in the form of a decrease in the price of the foreign country currency. During the period when Japan was maintaining its exchange rate at ¥360/United States dollar, the adjustments were carried out mainly through changes in factor prices denominated in the home country currency. Since the 1970s, however, a part of the adjustment has occurred through movements in the exchange rate.

There can be other theoretically possible patterns of industrial development besides the one discussed above. The dotted line A_4A_2 in Fig. 7-2 represents one such alternate pattern. That is to say, R & D or equipment investment in industries where Japan held a comparative advantage to begin with (industries in interval $[0, \bar{n}_1]$ underlying the curve A_1A_2) shifts the supply-wage schedule from A_1A_2 to A_4A_2. If the Japanese economy (the home country in our model) took this path of development, the structure of comparative advantage or the relative wage will hardly change. This is indicated in Fig. 7-2 by the fact that the equilibrium point

C_1 does not shift at all. The factor input coefficient for goods lying in the interval $[0, \bar{n}_1]$ declines for Japan (the home country), and a decline in the relative price of these goods (relative, that is, to other goods) is the only benefit reaped.[14]

In contrast to this, industrial development, accompanied by diversification of the home country export menu by overcoming the technology gap, shifts the equilibrium point along the demand-wage schedule (for example, movement from C_1 to C_2 in Fig. 7-2). This movement raises the relative wage in the home country, and confers benefits not only in the form of lowering the cost of consuming the goods produced by the newly developed industries, but also in the form of higher incomes (or an increase in the value of the yen) that permits imports of more goods than before (goods lying in interval $[\bar{n}_2, N]$ in Fig. 7-2). Thus the pattern of industrial development followed by Japan benefited the home country in terms of pulling up its relative income position (including, of course, changes in the exchange rate).

On the other hand, when the foreign country's industrial development takes the form of reducing the technology gap, the home country is affected in two opposing ways. First, there is a positive effect of industrial development in the foreign country, in that the goods whose production cost declines can now be imported at a lower price. The second effect is negative in the sense that as foreign relative income rises, consumer prices in the home country rise. Let us explain this in terms of Fig. 7-2. Assume that industrial development of the home country results in a shift of the supply-wage schedule from $A_1 A_2$ to $A_1 A_3$. In the process, equilibrium shifts from C_1 to C_2, and the relative wage rises from B_1 to B_2. As a result, the prices of goods in the interval $[0, \bar{n}_1]$ rise for the foreign country, while the prices of goods in the interval $[\bar{n}_1, \bar{n}_2]$ fall in terms of the foreign country's income. Which of the two effects predominates will depend on the degree to which the shift in technological coefficient a_n is concentrated in the marginal industries, and the share of these marginal industries in total demand. The higher the proportion of expenditures on goods of marginal industries, the greater is the slope of the demand-wage schedule at that point. If industrial development centers around marginal industries with high-expenditure shares, the chances that the home country's relative income rises sharply and the foreign country bears losses are greater.

In any case, industrial development of a country that expands the range of industries while lowering the price of goods supplied to the world market, also results in a trade-determined redistribution of income among countries favorable to that country. This pattern of development is extremely beneficial to the country in question, as it involves an international redistribution of income. In the early stages of Japanese industrial development, Japan was a small country and the income redistribution effects may not have been significant. But as industries like iron and steel and automobiles, with a relatively large share in total demand, developed into Japanese export industries, the redistribution of income between Japan and the foreign countries may have become significant, emerging as one of the sources of trade friction.[15]

NOTES

1. This assumption is not far off the mark in the context of economic development in postwar Japan. Japanese economic development did not accompany accumulation of debt to any significant extent. In this sense, the Japanese trade, defined broadly to include trade in services, seems to have been in balance. However, it is possible to develop the arguments that follow, even when trade is not balanced, by manipulating the equations somewhat.

2. The dynamic comparative advantage argument as presented above is, most likely, *ex post* justification. It may be more precise to say that the stance of the then policy authorities was not based on the type of solid arguments presented here.

3. As will be discussed below, the foreign country can expand its export menu by setting up new industries within the technologically most advanced industry, producing good 3.

4. Present-day Japan is included among the developed industrial nations. Hence the problem faced by the foreign country in the above discussion, in fact, applies to Japan. We, however, continue to refer to Japan as an underdeveloped country to keep the narrative consistent with the model where Japan was referred to as an underdeveloped country. This point should not be missed.

5. This fact was pointed out by Krugman (1984).

6. This perspective is discussed in Itoh and Kiyono (1987).

7. For a detailed mathematical exposition of the model in this appendix, see Itoh (1984). Dornbusch, and Samuelson (1977) and Krugman (1979, 1982) present similar models.

8. In reality, since the home and the foreign countries use different currencies, it is possible to develop a model that introduces exchange rate explicitly. Itoh (1985) analyzes this aspect.

9. We assume here that the good is a home country export when the condition is fulfilled with an equality sign. This is purely a simplifying assumption and is not crucial for the subsequent analysis.

10. The above equations can be rewritten in a slightly more general form, as follows:

Value of home country imports = (home country average propensity to import) (home country income level) = value of foreign country imports = (foreign country average propensity to import) (foreign country income level)

Rewriting, we obtain,

Home country income level/foreign country income level = foreign country average propensity to import/home country average propensity to import

11. In our model the goods are indexed in one-dimensional space. A more realistic model would require the goods to be indexed in multidimensional space with dimensions defined by many other characteristics. This will give rise to multiple ways to expand the export menu of the home country. The home country income level will be maximized if the expansion of the menu is such as to maximize the proportion of foreign expenditures on its export goods.

12. This argument is based on Krugman (1979).

13. In fact, during this period, substantial changes were taking place on the demand side as well. This, again, is important for a proper understanding of the modernization of Japanese industry.

14. To be precise, if the elasticity of substitution between the good whose relative price has declined and other goods is greater than unity, the rise in home country relative income will be proportional to the magnitude of this elasticity.

15. On this point, cf. Komiya, Okuno, and Suzumura (1984, Chapter 5) and Itoh (1984).

III

Oligopolistic Control of an International Market

8

Strategic Behavior and Nash Equilibrium

Part II of this book dealt with the problems of industrial promotion, information dissemination, and the choice of industrial and trade structures in the context of the Japanese industrial policy. It was shown that the presence of some form of industry set-up costs, even if the markets were perfectly competitive, could justify government intervention from the viewpoint of economic welfare at least in one of the countries. The market structure in the case of industries like automobiles, computers, robotics, and integrated circuits, which have shown a fast pace of growth in the postwar period, however, is not perfectly competitive.

Production costs in these industries have shown substantial declines on account of technological innovations, learning effects, and economies of scale as the size of plant and equipment became larger. The process of acquisition and mastering the knowledge related to new production technologies and products in industries characterized by such economies of scale entails enormous costs in terms of financial and time resources. These costs are automatically sunk once a firm acquires such knowledge.[1] Application of this new technology, therefore, gives rise to economies of scale resulting in lower average costs of production over a fairly wide range of output. In the case of large-scale production plants, too, the costs involved in setting up large-scale equipment for reaping economies of scale are sunk as soon as the operations begin. This reduces marginal costs to below average costs and, if the firms act simply as price takers, losses cannot be avoided. In this sense, such economies of scale act as entry barriers by themselves resulting in oligopolistic market structure as in the above example.

A model based on perfectly competitive market structure is of no help when industries with such an oligopolistic market structure exist. The latecomer countries where the said industry is yet to be established, therefore, face a completely new set of problems. These problems arise in the internationally oligopolistic industries where the established foreign firms have the advantages of an early start.

The established firms can, by way of making full use of the advantages conferred by an early start, adopt a strategy that checks expansion of market shares by the late entrant firms. In some cases, it may even be possible to erect effective entry barriers. In the 1960s, when liberalization of trade and capital flows was on the rise, the policy authorities in Japan tried to procrastinate on liberalization. One reason for this could have been the fear of losing the domestic market to advantaged foreign firms. The indirect production and export subsidy policies in the form of import controls, deduction of export income for tax purposes, low-interest financing through public financial institutions, and so on may have been instrumental in effectively checking the monopolistic power that the foreign firms could otherwise exercise.[2] By keeping the monopoly power of the established foreign firms under control and promoting growth in the emerging domestic industry by ensuring a market to the budding firms, the government tried to raise long-term economic welfare for the nation as a whole.

Keeping the above considerations in mind, it is important to investigate whether discriminatory intervention policies aimed at manipulating market conditions in favor of the home country are at all desirable from the viewpoint of economic welfare of the country. Even if such policies are found to be desirable in some cases, it is imperative to ask why this socially desirable state cannot be attained through the force of private incentives of the domestic firms. Finally, it is also necessary, assuming that private incentives fail to produce the desired results autonomously and it is possible for the policy authorities to bring about the desired state, to delineate the policy measures desirable from the viewpoint of national economic welfare.

If there is a policy intervention desirable from the point of view of the home country, it is necessary to analyze its international implications. The profits accruing to a firm when it exercises its price-setting powers are generally referred to as "monopoly rents." If the policy authorities can improve the competitive conditions for the domestic firms through some form of discriminatory policy intervention, the competitive conditions for the foreign firms will deteriorate, causing a fall in monopoly rents. Given the fact that firm profits are an important constituent of national economic welfare, the home country intervention in international competition can give rise to serious economic frictions with the foreign countries.

Part III of this book, therefore, is concerned with the problems associated with international oligopolies. The analysis uses Cournot-type oligopolistic markets where the home and foreign countries produce homogeneous goods as the basic frame of reference and addresses the following problems in particular:

1. How does a government subsidy for domestic firms affect economic welfare in the home and foreign countries when the firms of the two countries compete in an internationally oligopolistic market?

2. What sort of effective entry barriers can be erected by the established foreign firms?

3. If the entry barriers erected by the established foreign firms are effective, what are the effects of assistance given to the domestic firms for entering the market on economic welfare?

8.2 Monopoly Rents and Economic Welfare

The present chapter furnishes the basic framework for analyzing oligopolistic markets by discussing Cournot–Nash equilibrium and its properties in the context of international oligopoly. The discussion in Chapters 9 and onward is based on the analytical framework developed in this chapter. Leaving a detailed discussion of such a framework for the subsequent sections, we try to investigate, in this section, the problems peculiar to an oligopolistic market that would arise as a result of policy intervention in the international oligopolistic market. Let us first put the problem in a proper perspective by comparing the effects of policy intervention in an oligopolistic market with those in a perfectly competitive market, the main focus of the traditional trade theory.

In perfectly competitive industries, the market price equals marginal costs, leading to efficient resource allocation. In addition, if all the countries adopt a free trade policy, the international resource allocation is also Pareto efficient and any attempt to raise economic welfare in any one economy will, necessarily, reduce the welfare of some other economy. An optimal tariff policy, improving the terms of trade for the home country by restricting trade volume, is, therefore, the only available policy measure to raise economic welfare in the home country.[3] Such a policy, however, will result in reduced economic welfare in other economies.

Such a beggar-thy-neighbor policy—raising home country economic welfare at the cost of the trading partners—is also possible in oligopolistic markets. In this case, the process takes the form of a transfer of "monopoly rent" being earned by the foreign firms to the domestic firms as the market share of the domestic firms expands at the cost of the market share of the foreign firms. In a sense, the effect of policy intervention is more perceptible in an oligopolistic setting than in the case of perfectly competitive markets.

The competitive pattern of the firms in the oligopolistic markets is intricately involved in determining the form of transfer of monopoly rent that occurs in the wake of policy intervention in that market. As a result, the effect of policy intervention varies with the competitive strategies adopted by the domestic and foreign firms. This consideration complicates the analysis of the effects of industrial policy in oligopolistic markets.

For example, under perfect competition, production or export subsidies to home country exporters lead to a decline in economic welfare in the home country. In contrast, production or export subsidies to domestic firms, under oligopolistic conditions, can, in some instances, raise economic welfare in the home country. The response of foreign firms plays an important part in this context. In what follows, therefore, an investigation into the relationship between interfirm response and the policy intervention becomes important.

Another important feature of oligopolistic markets is that, since such markets do not satisfy Pareto optimality conditions to begin with, policy intervention does not necessarily imply a beggar-thy-neighbor policy. Strategic policy intervention by the home country government can result in raising economic welfare not only in the home country but also in the foreign country. In this sense, the effects of various policies are more complex than in the case of perfectly competitive markets.

In the rest of this chapter we discuss the properties of equilibrium in oligopolistic markets using the Cournot model, where the firms compete by adjusting quantities produced, and the Bertrand model, in which price becomes the strategic variable. This discussion provides us with a framework within which the monopoly rent transfer effect of strategic intervention in international oligopolistic markets can be analyzed.[4]

8.3 Cournot Oligopoly and Cournot–Nash Equilibrium

In this section, in order to facilitate the analysis undertaken in the subsequent sections, we present a preliminary discussion of free trade equilibrium when the foreign and domestic firms compete by adjusting quantities produced of a homogeneous product.

The international market, where both firms compete, is composed of the domestic and foreign markets. If d represents the size of domestic demand and p the domestic price, home country's demand function $h(\ )$ can be written as

$$d = h(p), \quad h'(p) < 0 \qquad (1a)$$

If the respective variables for the foreign country are represented by upper case letters, the foreign country's demand function can be written as

$$D = H(P), \quad H'(P) < 0 \qquad (1b)$$

Under free trade, ignoring transport costs, domestic price in both the countries equals international price. If p is the international price and $f(\ )$ represents the inverse demand function for the world as a whole, $f(\ )$ must, from (1a) and (1b), satisfy

$$f[h(p) + H(p)] = p \qquad (2)$$

Denoting quantity produced by the domestic firm by x and by the foreign firm by X, the profits of the firms of the two countries are, respectively,

$$\pi(x, X) = f(x + X)x - c(x) \tag{3a}$$
$$\Pi(X, x) = f(X + x)X - C(X) \tag{3b}$$

where π and Π are the profits of the domestic and the foreign firms, respectively. $c(\ )$ is the domestic firm's cost function and $C(\ )$ is the cost function for the foreign firm.

The Nash equilibrium (also referred to as Cournot–Nash equilibrium in the case of Cournot oligopoly) in such an oligopolistic market can be defined as follows. Both the firms set their output (strategic variable) at a level where neither has any incentive to deviate from the equilibrium. In concrete terms, the Cournot–Nash equilibrium, (x_0, X_0), is a combination of outputs that satisfies the following conditions: The output of the domestic firm x_0 satisfies

$$\pi(x_0, X_0) \geqq \pi(x, X_0) \tag{4a}$$

for all attainable levels of output x, and the foreign firm's output X_0 satisfies

$$\pi(X_0, x_0) \geqq \pi(X, x_0) \tag{4b}$$

for all attainable levels of output X.

That is to say, each firm, in equilibrium, sets its output at a level that maximizes its profits, taking the output level of its rival as given.

Cournot–Nash equilibrium can be analyzed using the concept of reaction functions. The reaction function for the domestic firm $x = r(X)$ and that for the foreign firm $X = R(x)$ is defined as a function that gives profits maximizing output for the given firm under Cournot conjecture that its competitor does not alter its output level, whatever the firm does to its own output. The reaction functions for the respective firms must, therefore, satisfy the following conditions.

$$\pi_X[r(X), X] = \mathrm{mr}[r(X), X] - c'[r(X)] = 0 \tag{5a}$$
$$\Pi_X[R(x), x] = \mathrm{MR}[R(x), x] - C'[R(x)] = 0 \tag{5b}$$

where

$$\mathrm{mr}[r(X), X] = f'(x + X)x + f(x + X)$$
$$\mathrm{MR}[R(x), x] = f'(X + x)X + f(X + x)$$

represent marginal revenue functions for the domestic and foreign firms.

Using the reaction function defined above, the equilibrium conditions presented in Eqs. (4a) and (4b) can be easily rewritten in the following form.

$$x_0 = r(X_0) \tag{6a}$$
$$X_0 = R(x_0) \tag{6b}$$

Equations (6a) and (6b) allow us to depict Cournot–Nash equilibrium graphically. That is, if we draw the graphs for reaction functions of the respective firms,

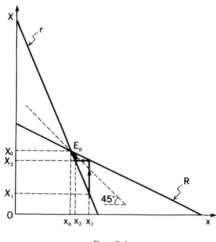

FIG. 8-1

the point of intersection gives the Cournot–Nash equilibrium. Let us now have a look at the nature of reaction functions of the individual firms.

8.4 SHAPE OF THE REACTION FUNCTIONS, STRATEGIC SUBSTITUTES, AND COMPLEMENTS

Figures 8-1 and 8-2 depict typical reaction functions. The reaction functions in Fig. 8-1 is negatively sloped, indicating that the output of the firm falls as rival output rises. In contrast to this, Fig. 8-2 presents the case of positively sloped reaction functions. In both cases, the Cournot–Nash equilibrium is depicted by point E_0, where the two reaction functions of the rival firms intersect. The difference between the two cases lies in the effect that an increase in rival firm output, the strategic variable here, has on marginal revenue and marginal profits (marginal revenue − marginal cost) of those firms.

In Fig. 8-1, the marginal profit of a firm declines as the rival increases its output. Now, if the competitor becomes aggressive and raises its output, other firms become submissive and reduce their output, leading to the negatively sloped reaction function. The strategies followed by the competing firms, when submissive behavior by a firm is the optimal reaction to the aggressive behavior of its rival, are referred to as "strategic substitutes."

Figure 8-2, on the other hand, depicts the case when the profits of a firm rise as competitor output rises. In this case, the firm responds to the aggressive behavior by its rival by becoming aggressive itself. The strategies of the two firms in such a case are termed "strategic complements." [5]

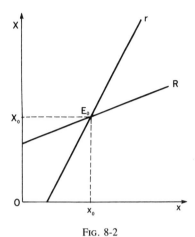

FIG. 8-2

In the following discussion, we assume in both cases that the absolute slope of both firms' reaction functions $|r'(X)|$ and $|R'(x)|$ is less than unity irrespective of the level of competitor output.[6] This assumption is a sufficient condition for the stability of the equilibrium, derived above, in the process of adjustment that follows a disequilibrium. Besides, it also ensures a unique Nash equilibrium. Let us explain these points in terms of Fig. 8-1.

According to Cournot, individual firms adjust their output levels interactively and the equilibrium represents the result of this adjustment process. The individual firms, at any particular time in the adjustment process, presume that the rival will not change its output whatever it does to its own output.

Let us assume that the foreign firm, under such a Cournot conjecture, is initially producing at X_1 in terms of Fig. 8-1. The optimum response of the domestic firm to this is an output level depicted by x_1. The foreign firm now reacts by adjusting its output to X_2, which forces the domestic firm to adjust its own output once again. The result of this adjustment process is, obviously, the convergence of the market to equilibrium E_0. Whatever the initial level of output, the market will converge to point E_0. In this sense E_0 is a stable and unique equilibrium.

The results differ, however, if the reaction functions of the competing firms have a large absolute slope, as in Fig. 8-3, and the conditions regarding the slope of the reaction functions is not satisfied. That is, even if the foreign firm is initially producing at X_1, as before, the output combinations of the two firms will increasingly diverge from the equilibrium point. In this case, the market forces necessary to bring the system back to equilibrium are lacking and equilibrium cannot be attained unless the system is in equilibrium at E_0 to begin with. In this sense, the equilibrium is unstable.

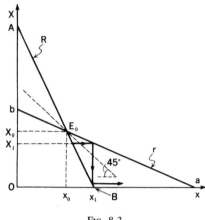

FIG. 8-3

Furthermore, the equilibrium in this case is not unique. In Fig. 8-3, the foreign firm reacts by producing zero output if the domestic firm produces more than OB. The foreign reaction function, therefore, is given by the kinked curve ABx. Similarly, the reaction function for the domestic firm is the kinked curve abX. Therefore, we have multiple equilibria, that is, points of intersection between the reaction functions, at E_0, a, and A. Which of these equilibrium points is attained cannot be determined within the framework of the above analysis.[7]

An analysis of effects of governmental policy intervention in oligopolistic markets requires one to venture some guess about the resulting market structure and the behavior of individual firms. In this sense, nonexistence of a unique Cournot–Nash equilibrium calls for extra caution in the analysis.

As is clear from the above discussion, multiple equilibria cases, as in Fig. 8-3, can be excluded from the analysis by assuming a less than unit absolute slope for the reaction functions of the competing firms. It is easy to verify that exactly similar results occur if the outputs of the competing firms are strategic complements. In the subsequent discussion, therefore, we stay clear of the complexities introduced by the existence of multiple equilibria by assuming the absolute slope of the reaction functions of both the firms to be less than unity.

The stability condition gives rise to an additional property. As long as the output combination is on the reaction function of any one of the firms, the greater the output produced by the rival the higher is the total market output.

Which of the two cases—the case of strategic substitutes or the case of strategic complements—is appropriate for consideration? There is no *a priori* way to determine whether the firm strategies are substitutes or complements. It is believed that assumption of strategic substitutes, as long as Cournot oligopoly with output strategies is being considered, does not pose any significant problem. This is because it is easy to show that, in the case of straight line demand curves or when the sizes of the firms do not differ much due to fixed price elasticity of demand, the most discussed cases in economic analysis, marginal revenue of a firm declines as the output of its rival expands.[8] Hence, the strategic substitutes case (as depicted in Fig. 8-1) should be appropriate as the basis of subsequent analysis.

Finally, let us explain the concept of the isoprofit curve, necessary for the ensuing analysis, in terms of Fig. 8-1. Figure 8-4 represents the same conditions as Fig. 8-1. The set of humped curves represents a set of isoprofit curves. For example, π_0 is the locus of combinations of the output of the two firms that gives the foreign firm the same amount of profit $\pi(x_0, X_0)$ as would be derived by the domestic firm when the domestic firm is producing at x_0 and the foreign firm at X_0. Further, the lower the isoprofit curve is along the reaction function, the higher is the profit level. Let us explain these points briefly.

First, let us consider the reasons for the hump in isoprofit curves depicted in Fig. 8-4. Let us assume that the foreign and domestic firms are initially producing at X_0 and x_0, respectively. If the domestic firm increases (decreases) its output, its profits decline as long as the foreign firm is producing at X_0. This is obvious from the definition of the reaction function, which states that given the output of the foreign firm at X_0, the profit-maximizing output for the domestic firm is x_0. For the domestic firm to earn the same profits as before, the foreign firm must reduce its output. This reduction in foreign firm output tightens the demand–supply balance and domestic firm profits rise due to a rise in market price.

Second, let us consider the relationship between the position of the reaction function and corresponding profits. Let us assume that the domestic firm's output is held constant at x_0 and the foreign firm's output declines to X_1. As output of the foreign firm declines, market price rises. As a result, the domestic firm will

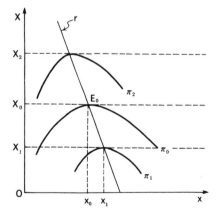

FIG. 8-4

earn higher profits than before, even if it maintains its initial output level. Hence the profit level is higher the lower the isoprofit curve.

8.5 PRICE COMPETITION AND MARKET INTERVENTION POLICY

In the last section we discussed Cournot oligopoly with the competing firms using output as the strategic variable. However, oligopolistic markets are not limited to quantity strategies alone. What are the properties of equilibrium when price, rather than output, is the strategic variable (this is termed Bertrand oligopoly).

Let us assume that the domestic and foreign firms produce differentiated products which are close substitutes. The demand functions facing the domestic and the foreign firms can be represented as follows:

Demand function facing the domestic firm:

$$x = x(p, P) \quad (x_p < 0, x_P > 0) \tag{7a}$$

Demand function facing the foreign firm:

$$X = X(P, p) \quad (X_P < 0, X_p > 0) \tag{7b}$$

where x and p are the output of and the price set by the domestic firm, respectively. Corresponding variables for the foreign firm are represented by upper case letters. Further, $x_p = \partial x(p, P)/\partial p$, $x_P = \partial x(p, P)/\partial P$. Here, $x_p < 0$ indicates that the demand curve faced by the domestic firm is forward falling and $x_P > 0$ indicates that, since the products produced by the domestic and the foreign firms are substitutes, demand for the domestic firm's product increases as price of the foreign firm's product rises. The same holds for the foreign firm.

It is assumed that the demand functions facing respective firms satisfy the following conditions:

$$x_p(p, P) + x_P(p, P) < 0 \tag{8a}$$
$$X_P(P, p) + X_p(P, p) < 0 \tag{8b}$$

This corresponds to the following assumption. Let us envisage a situation where both firms raise their prices simultaneously by the same amount. Since the price of both outputs rises, a part of the consumers will shift to a product other than these two. As a result, demand for the products of both the firms will decline.

The profits for the two firms can be represented as a function of price combination (p, P) set by the two firms.

$$\pi(p, P) = px(p, P) - c[x(p, P)] \tag{9a}$$
$$\Pi(P, p) = PX(P, p) - C[X(P, p)] \tag{9b}$$

where $\pi(\ )$ and $c(\ )$ are the profit and cost functions for the domestic firm and the function represented by upper case letters are corresponding functions for the foreign firm. If $p = r(P)$ and $P = R(p)$ are the reaction functions of the domestic and the foreign firm, respectively, these must satisfy the following conditions:

$$\pi_p[r(P), P] = x[r(P), P] + (r(P) - c'\{x[r(P), P]\})x_p[r(P), P] = 0 \quad (10a)$$
$$\Pi_P[R(p), p] = X[R(p), p] + (R(p) - C'\{X[R(p), p]\})X_P[R(p), p] = 0 \quad (10b)$$

The Bertrand–Nash equilibrium, like the Cournot–Nash equilibrium, is given by the point of intersection of the reaction functions for the two firms, that is the combination of the prices of the two firms (p_0, P_0). Therefore, the Bertrand–Nash equilibrium (p_0, P_0) can be defined by the following two equations:

$$p_0 = r(P_0)$$
$$P_0 = R(p_0)$$

The reaction function under Bertrand competition is normally positively sloped, as depicted in Fig. 8-5. The positive slope of the reaction function here implies that the strategies adopted by the two firms are mutually complementary. The intuitive reasoning behind the assumption of strategic complements rather than strategic substitutes in the case of Bertrand oligopoly is as follows.[9]

Let us consider the domestic firm. As shown in Fig. 8-5, if the foreign firm sets its price at P_0, the domestic firm should choose price p_0 as an optimal strategy. If the foreign firm raises its price to P_1, demand shifts to the domestic product, which has become relatively cheaper. The demand for the domestic product, therefore, will rise even if the domestic firm sticks to its original price. Thus, the domestic firm can increase its profits by raising price. It is due to this factor that a higher price for the domestic product p_1 becomes the optimal reaction of the home firm to the increase in price of the foreign product to P_1.

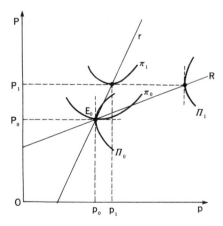

FIG. 8-5

Next, let us consider the properties of isoprofit curves in the case of Bertrand oligopoly using Fig. 8-5. The curves π_0, π_1, and Π_0, Π_1 are the isoprofit curves for the domestic and the foreign firm, respectively. If the firms are producing substitutes, as assumed in this case, the isoprofit curves of the two firms should be convex toward their respective price axes.

If P_0 is the price set by the foreign firm, the domestic firm maximizes its profits at price p_0. Now, if the domestic firm sets a price higher (lower) than p_0, its profits must decline. For the domestic firm to maintain profits it was earning before, the foreign firm must raise its price so that the domestic firm can enjoy higher demand. Thus, we have been able to show that the isoprofit curves for the domestic firm become horizontal on the reaction function and are convex below. Along the reaction function, the higher the isoprofit curve, the higher is the profit level depicted by it. The reason is that, for example, if the foreign firm raises its price from P_0 to P_1, the profits for the domestic firm rise due to higher demand even if the price of the domestic product stays at p_0.

Finally, as in the case of Cournot oligopoly, let us assume that the slope of the reaction function of both the firms ($|r'(P)|$ and $|R'(p)|$) is less than unity and the Bertrand equilibrium is stable and unique. In the case of Cournot oligopoly, the condition corresponding to this assumption was that total output in the market rose as the domestic firm expanded its output along the foreign firm's reaction function. In contrast to this, the stability condition under the Bertrand oligopoly postulates that the demand for domestic (foreign) product declines as the prices charged by the domestic (foreign) firm rises along the foreign (domestic) firm's reaction function. This is because the optimum price response of the foreign firm raises the price of the foreign product as the price of the domestic product rises.[10]

The above discussion has clarified the equilibrium properties of the Cournot and Bertrand oligopolies. In the chapters that follow, we use this framework to analyze the economic impact of discriminatory protection policies by the home government.

NOTES

1. See Part V of this book on technological innovations.
2. See Itoh and Kiyono [Chapter 5 in Komiya, Okuno, and Suzumura (1984)] on this point.
3. On optimal tariff policy, see Komiya and Amano (1972) and Itoh and Ohyama (1985).
4. See Okuguchi (1971), Friedman (1977, 1986), and Shubik (1982) on the Cournot and the Bertrand models of oligopoly developed in the following sections.
5. See Bulow, Geanakoplos, and Klemperer (1985) and Fudenberg and Tirole (1984, 1986) on strategic substitutes and complements and related concepts.
6. An absolute slope of less than unity for the two firms in the neighborhood of equilibrium is a sufficient condition for the ensuing discussion.
7. See Chapter 6, Section 6.3 on problems relating to multiple equilibria.
8. See Bulow, Geanakoplos, and Klemperer (1985) on this point.

9. There is nothing in Bertrand oligopoly that implies positively sloped reaction functions and strategic complementarity relationships. It can, however, be easily shown that in the case of linear demand functions or when cross-elasticity is positive or when marginal cost is not increasing, the reaction functions must be positively sloped.

10. This fact can be rigorously verified as follows. If the domestic firm raises its price by ¥1, the optimum response price for the foreign firm rises by $R'(p)$. The change in demand for domestic product in this case is $dx[p, R(p)]/dp = x_p(p, P)$. Since $0 < R'(p) < 1$, we get $dx[p, R(p)]/dp$ as original $< x_p(p, P) + R'(p)x_p(p, P)$. The right-hand term is negative from Eq. (8). The same holds true for the foreign firm.

9

International Redistribution of Monopoly Rents

In the present chapter, basing ourselves on the analysis presented in the last chapter, we try to analyze the effect of a discriminatory subsidy policy in oligopolistic markets on monopoly rents earned by the oligopolistic firms and on economic welfare in individual countries.[1] The subsequent discussion uses Cournot oligopoly as the basic analytical framework. Bertrand oligopoly is discussed very briefly in the last section.

9.1 REDISTRIBUTION OF RENT THROUGH A PRODUCTION SUBSIDY

Let us assume two firms, one home and one foreign, producing a homogeneous product and engaged in Cournot competition. The home country government is assumed to hand out a production subsidy of s/unit to the home firm in order to protect the industry. How does such government intervention affect competitive conditions between the two firms?

As in Chapter 8, Section 8.3, we assume the market demand function for the world for each firm to be

$$p = f(x + X) \quad [f'(x + X) < 0] \tag{1}$$

Here, x and X represent the output produced by the home firm and the foreign firm, respectively. All the symbols used here have the same interpretation as in Chapter 8.

From Eq. (3a) of the previous chapter, (private) profits for the home firm, in case the home country government grants a discriminatory production subsidy, are given by

$$\pi_s(x, X) = f(x + X)x - c(x) + sx \tag{2a}$$

As a result, the reaction function for the home firm $r_s(X)$ is transformed into the following equation:

$$\pi_{sx}[r_s(X), X] = \text{mr}[r_s(X), X] - \{c'[r_s(X)] - s\} = 0 \tag{3a}$$

As long as the foreign government does not countervail such a discriminatory protection policy, the foreign firm's profit function remains unchanged and can be represented as

$$\Pi(X, x) = f(x + X)X - C(X) \tag{2b}$$

As in Chapter 8, Section 8.3, the foreign firm's reaction function is given by the condition

$$\Pi_x[R(x), x] = MR[R(x), x] - C'[R(x)] = 0 \tag{3b}$$

The reaction functions for the home and foreign firms as derived above, are presented in Fig. 9-1 as r_s and R, respectively. A reaction function r, for the home firm, assuming zero production subsidy, is also drawn to facilitate comparison with free trade equilibrium. As in the last chapter, we assume a less than unit value for absolute slope of the reaction function for each of the firms.

As shown in Fig. 9-1, the new reaction function r_s for the home firm lies to the right of r, the reaction function without production subsidy. This follows from the fact that the home firm has an incentive to produce a larger output than before as its marginal cost declines by the amount of production subsidy.

The introduction of production subsidy shifts the point of Cournot–Nash equilibrium from E_0, the equilibrium under free trade, to E_s in Fig. 9-1. Let us now look into the changes in the market brought about by such a shift in equilibrium.

First, a discriminatory production subsidy to the home firm leads to an increase in output by the home firm and a decrease in output by the foreign firm. Since a production subsidy provides an incentive for expanding production, the output of the home firm will rise. Increased production by the home firm forces the foreign firm to become defensive and, hence, reduce its output.

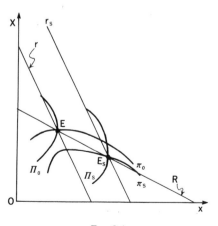

FIG. 9-1

Second, given the assumption of less-than-unit slope of the reaction functions for each country's firm, total production in the world market rises and international price falls. The introduction of a production subsidy shifts the equilibrium along the foreign firm's reaction function from point E_0 to E_s. As was pointed out in the last chapter, the sum of outputs of the two firms—the total world production—rises, if the absolute slope of the foreign firm's reaction function is less than unity. The fall in price level under such conditions is obvious.

Third, foreign firm profits must fall. Subsidy handouts raise the competitiveness of the home firm, resulting in reduced output by the foreign firm. Besides, as international price also falls, the foreign firm profits must fall. This is depicted in Fig. 9-1 by the shift of the foreign firm's isoprofit curve from Π_0 to Π_s.

In the following, we present a detailed analysis of the strategic effects of a production subsidy handout, assuming the change in production subsidy to be infinitesimally small.

Let us represent the changes in output of the home and foreign firms and the international price, as a result of a shift in equilibrium from E_0 to E_s, by Δx, ΔX, and Δp, respectively. With constant international price, a marginal unit change in output changes foreign firm profits, from Eq. (3b), by $[p(x + X) - C'(X)]$. With output level constant, a marginal unit increase in international price increases profits in proportion to the level of output. Therefore, the change in foreign firm's profits $\Delta \Pi$ can be approximated by

$$\Delta \Pi = [p(x + X) - C'(X)]\Delta X + X\Delta p \qquad (4a)$$

Using the inverse demand function as given in Eq. (1), the change in international price Δp can be represented in terms of a change in output of the two firms, Δx and ΔX, as

$$\Delta p = p'(x + X)(\Delta x + \Delta X)$$

Here, $p'(\ )$ represents the slope of the inverse demand function. Substituting this equation into Eq. (4) and using the fact that marginal revenue of the foreign firm is given by $MR(X, x) = p(x + X) + p'(x + X)X$, we get

$$\Delta \Pi = [p(x + X) + p'(x + X)X - C'(X)]\Delta X + Xp'(x + X)\Delta x$$
$$= [MR(X, x) - C'(X)]\Delta X + p'(x + X)X\Delta x$$

Substituting the profit maximization condition for the foreign firm [Eq. (3b)], we get

$$\Delta \Pi = p'(x + X)X\Delta x$$

Given a negatively sloped demand function and the fact that output of the home firm rises due to production subsidy handout, it is easy to see that $\Delta \Pi$ is negative. The change in foreign firm profits, as derived above, is nothing but the strategic effect of a discriminatory production subsidy policy.

Fourth, the home firm profits must rise. This follows, intuitively, from the following two effects. First, a production subsidy raises profits directly. Second, there is a strategic effect resulting in usurpation of foreign firm market share by the home firm as production subsidy makes the home firm relatively more competitive. A rigorous interpretation of these effects is as follows.[2]

If s represents the initial subsidy ratio and Δs represents a change in production subsidy that causes the equilibrium to shift, the change in home firm profits $\Delta \pi_s$ can be decomposed, in a manner similar to that adopted to work out the change in profits of the foreign firm, as

$$\Delta \pi_s = \{p(x + X) - [c'(x) - s]\}\Delta x + x\Delta p + x\Delta s \qquad (4b)$$

Here, it should be noted that private marginal cost to the home firm is given by $[c'(x) - s]$ and a marginal unit increase in production subsidy raises profits in proportion to output produced, just as in the case of a price change. Given this, the change in home firm profits, as in the case of the foreign firm, is given by

$$\Delta \pi_s = \{\mathrm{mr}(x, X) - [c'(x) - s]\}\Delta x + p'(x + X)x\Delta X + x\Delta s$$

The first term on the right-hand side is zero from the first order profit maximization condition [Eq. (3a)]. Therefore, the change in profits for the home firm $\Delta \pi_s$ can be written as

$$\Delta \pi_s = p'(x + X)x\Delta X + x\Delta s$$

The first term in the above equation corresponds to the strategic effect of production subsidy as explained above. The second term represents the direct profit-raising effect of a production subsidy. As output of the foreign firm declines, given a negatively sloped demand curve, the first term must be positive. The second term is clearly positive. Hence, profits of the home firm must rise.

The point to be noted here is that a discriminatory subsidy policy in favor of the home firm promotes redistribution of monopoly rents among the firms. With a discriminatory subsidy policy, the home firm can expand its market share more than could be possible under free trade as such a policy strengthens its relative competitiveness. This implies a reduction in foreign firm market share, making it possible for the home firm to usurp monopoly rents from the foreign firm. By focusing on the redistribution and transfer of rent effects, it is possible to explain the welfare-raising effect of discriminatory protection policies in favor of the home firm, a fact that could not be properly explained by the traditional theory. In the next section, we deal with this aspect inclusive of the effect on foreign country economic welfare.

9.2 Transfer of Monopoly Rents and Economic Welfare

In what follows, we use total surplus generated by the given commodity as a measure of the economic welfare of each country. The home country economic welfare, in this case, is a sum of consumer and producer surpluses obtained from the given commodity less government expenditure on production subsidy. That is, economic welfare for the home country w is given by

$$w = cs[p(x + X)] + \pi_s(x, X) - sx \qquad (5a)$$

where $cs[p(x + X)]$ is the total amount of consumer surplus for the home country when x and X are the output levels of the home and foreign firms, respectively, and $p(x + X)$ is the international price. It is clear that consumer surplus is an inverse function of price, i.e., it rises as price falls.

The sum of the last two terms on the right-hand side of Eq. (5a), following Eq. (3a) of Chapter 8, Section 8.3, represents the total revenue earned by the home country minus the social cost $c(x)$, the value of socially necessary resources for producing the given commodity, with outputs of the home and foreign firms given at x and X, respectively. It should be noted that the sum of these two terms, in the absence of a production subsidy, equals the profit, or the producer surplus, function for the home country firm. Thus, total home country economic welfare can be represented as a sum of consumer surplus and profits net of production subsidy.

Similarly, foreign country economic welfare W can be measured by

$$W = CS[p(x + X)] + \Pi(X, x) \qquad (5b)$$

Let us now try to work out the effect of a production subsidy, granted to the home country firm by the home government, on economic welfare in the two countries. The home country case is considered first.

Let d, x, and p represent the home country consumption, production, and international price in the initial equilibrium. Further, assume that, as a result of a discriminatory production subsidy policy, home production rises by Δx and foreign production declines by $-\Delta X$. As discussed in the previous section, the net change in total world production $\Delta x + \Delta X$ is positive. Hence, total world production rises and international price falls. Let the decline in the international price be represented by $-\Delta p$. It can be easily seen that increase in consumer surplus Δcs nearly equals $(-\Delta p)d$ if the decline in international price is sufficiently small.

We already know that change in private profits for the home country firm can be represented as in Eq. (4b). Moreover, the rise in cost of a production subsidy to the home country government is given by the sum of (1) higher costs, as a result of an increase in the rate of subsidy, proportionate to output of the home country firm Δsx and (2) higher costs due to an increase in output induced by the production subsidy $s\Delta x$. Now, if we use $\Delta \pi$ to represent the change in profits net of production subsidy granted by the government $(\pi = \pi_s - sx)$, we get

$$\Delta \pi = \{[p - c'(x) + s] \Delta x + x\Delta p + x\Delta s\} - (\Delta sx + s\Delta x)$$
$$= [p - c'(x)]\Delta x + x\Delta p$$

Profits, net of production subsidy, thus determined rise as long as the amount of production subsidy granted is not very large. In fact, this profit function may be interpreted as the home firm profit function in the absence of a production subsidy. As a result, the change in profit can be easily determined by comparing the isoprofit curve attainable with a production subsidy with that attainable without a subsidy. Since the equilibrium point, as depicted in Fig. 9-1, shifts from E_0 to E_s, the isoprofit curve, representing the home firm profits net of the subsidy, shifts downward from π_0 to π_s. Clearly, the home firm profits net of subsidy rise.

Using the above results, change in home country economic welfare Δw can be written as

$$\Delta w = \Delta cs + \Delta \pi = d(-\Delta p) + \{x\Delta p + [p - c'(x)]\Delta x\} \quad (6a)$$

Similarly, the change in foreign country economic welfare ΔW can be represented as

$$\Delta W = \Delta CS + \Delta \Pi = D(-\Delta p) + [X\Delta p + \{p - C'(X)\}\Delta X] \quad (6b)$$

Equations (6a) and (6b) can be interpreted as follows. The welfare gains from a discriminatory protective policy in favor of the home firm operating under the oligopolistic international market can be attributed to two factors. The first of these, represented by the first terms on the right-hand side of Eqs. (6a) and (6b), is the "increased consumption effect." The second effect, represented by the second terms on the right-hand side of the respective equations, is the "profit-shifting effect" of a strategic competition intervention policy, as discussed in the last chapter.

The above decomposition of welfare change can be rewritten along the line of traditional trade theory as

$$\Delta w = (d - x)(-\Delta p) + [p - c'(x)]\Delta x \quad (7a)$$
$$\Delta W = (D - X)(-\Delta p) + [p - C'(X)]\Delta X \quad (7b)$$

The first terms on the right-hand side of Eqs. (7a) and (7b) represent the "terms-of-trade effect" while the second terms represent the "allocational effect." It goes without saying that the terms-of-trade effect represents an improvement in terms of trade for the home country as a result of the protection policy and its sign depends on whether the home firm is an exporter or an importer. The allocational effect represents a reduction (increase) in welfare loss, arising due to a divergency between market price and marginal cost, and an increase (decrease) in social efficiency of resource allocation as output of the oligopolistic industry in the given country rises (falls).

A discriminatory protection policy of the type being treated here can be interpreted, if we focus on the rent-shifting effect alone, as a policy improving the home country's economic welfare at the cost of the foreign firm. This comes about as a result of an intervention, in the struggle for monopoly rents among the internationally oligopolistic firms, that raises monopoly profits accruing to the home firm.

This point can be easily clarified by assuming the product under consideration to be a pure exportable in the sense that it is not consumed at all in either of the two countries and is exported to a third country market. Since the consumption of this product is zero in both countries, the effect of a discriminatory subsidy policy on consumer surplus in each country, as is clear from Eqs. (6a) and (6b), is also zero. The change in economic welfare for individual countries, in this case, equals change in profits (net of production subsidy) or producer surplus. Hence, a policy aimed at increasing economic welfare for the home country must raise profits π obtained after deducting the total amount of production subsidy from private profits.

The home firm protection policy of the government raises the value of π, what may perhaps be termed as social profits, by raising private profits accruing to the home firm. Thus, in the context of international oligopolistic markets, it is possible to raise national economic welfare by allowing the oligopolistic firms to earn huge profits. The main factor behind such a result, as pointed out earlier, is the fact that oligopolistic industries (or the presence of entry barriers, assumed implicitly in our discussion) give rise to monopolistic quasi-rents and the government protection puts the home firm in a favorable position in the competition for international rents.

It was pointed out in the last section that such a policy also results in lowering economic welfare in the foreign country at the same time [this corresponds to a minus sign on the rent-shifting effect term for the foreign country in Eq. (6b)]. In this sense, a discriminatory protection policy in favor of the home firm leads directly to a worsening of the foreign country's economic welfare and is, therefore, a beggar-thy-neighbor policy.

It must be pointed out, however, that the beggar-thy-neighbor aspect of a discriminatory subsidy policy should not be overemphasized. In most practical cases, the consumers, in the home as well as the foreign country, are expected to consume the product under consideration. Hence, the terms-of-trade effect referred to above cannot be ignored.

The fall in market price results in benefits for the consumers in individual countries if they do, in fact, consume the given commodity. Not only the home country consumers but consumers in the foreign country also benefit from such a fall in price. Now, taking the existence of consumer surplus for the foreign country into account, the consumption-increasing and terms-of-trade effects are positive if the country is a net importer of the product. Therefore, a possibility for a rise in economic welfare for the foreign country does exist if these effects swamp the negative rent-shifting effect.

The effect on home country economic welfare also deserves a closer look. A discriminatory subsidy policy raises home country economic welfare unequivocally only if the home industry stays relatively uncompetitive against its foreign forerunner. This is obvious from Eq. (7a), which states that both the terms-of-trade and the rent-shifting effects work to raise home country welfare if the country is a net importer of the product. Even if the country is a net exporter, the negative terms-of-trade effect is expected to be quite small compared to the positive rent-shifting effect as long as its share of the world market is sufficiently small. However, if the industry in question is a mature export industry, it is possible that a recourse to discriminatory subsidy policy may result in lowering economic welfare as the negative terms-of-trade effect could swamp the positive rent-shifting effect. Thus, the effectiveness of a subsidy policy is limited to the case of immature industries in the sense that the home industry is relatively far inferior to its foreign forerunner.

Finally, let us consider the economic welfare of the two countries taken together. Ignoring any third country and assuming that the world is composed of only the home and foreign countries, the terms-of-trade effects for the two countries will cancel out. As long as marginal cost in the home country does not exceed that for the foreign country, the rent-shifting effect is definitely positive as the rise in home country output exceeds the fall in foreign output. In other words, home government protective policy increases net economic welfare for the world as a whole by raising consumer surplus in both the countries. This rise in consumer surplus is a reflection of a larger world supply and the resulting decline in international price.

The above discussion focused on production subsidies to the home country firm. Similar results can also be obtained by providing export subsidies to the home firm or imposing tariffs on imports from the foreign firm. Export subsidies to the home firm shift the home firm reaction function outward while imposition of tariffs on imports from the foreign firm shifts the reaction function for the foreign firm inward. Thus, in markets characterized by Cournot oligopoly, it is possible for the government to raise economic welfare for the home country by granting production or export subsidies or by introducing import restrictions.

The above conclusions, however, beg the following question. Why does the home firm, trying to maximize profits, not behave in the same way before the policy intervention by the government? The government intervention raises the profits of the home firm by putting it in an advantaged position in competition for monopoly profits. Is it not possible, then, for the home firm to use the reaction function that increases its profits in the case of intervention before the government actually intervenes?

9.3 CREDIBLE THREAT AND THE ROLE OF THE GOVERNMENT

Let us assume that the home firm tries, in the absence of any protection policy, to increase its profits by moving to the reaction function it would have used had a protection policy been introduced. If such a strategy were to be successful, the home firm's optimal strategy could not have been represented by the usual type of reaction function. Why, then, does the reaction function represent the home firm's optimal strategy? In other words, why is the Cournot–Nash equilibrium, defined by the intersection of reaction functions, meaningful? A proper answer to those questions requires a closer look into the Cournot–Nash equilibrium.[3]

Normally, the Cournot–Nash equilibrium, or its more generalized version, the Nash equilibrium, is interpreted as follows. The individual firms in this market (the players of the game in terms of game theory) are assumed to have full prior knowledge of the market demand function as well as cost conditions prevailing in each firm. Therefore, while deciding on their own output (strategy), each firm knows beforehand the amount of profits (returns) that will accrue to individual firms. Furthermore, each firm (player) also knows that the other firms (players) also have the same information. Moreover, each firm knows that every firm knows the fact that all other firms have this information, and so on. That is, it is assumed that this information, the information regarding information itself, and the information related to this fact itself, and so on, is fully and universally known. In reference to this assumption, it is said that the demand and cost conditions in such a market are common knowledge.

Now, assume that demand and cost conditions in this market, as well as the fact that every firm behaves so as to maximize its profits, are common knowledge. Each firm, before implementing a particular economic strategy (playing the game), tries to make an informed guess about the market outcome of such a move.

An accurate guess, normally, would require information on strategies adopted by the other firms (players) before one's own optimal strategy is determined. This problem does not arise, however, if all information about the market, as well as the fact that profit maximization guides the behavior of each firm, is common knowledge. The reason is that individual firms will not be acting rationally if they choose a strategy that fails to attain a Nash equilibrium.

This argument can be easily understood in the following manner. If the Nash equilibrium is not expected to come about, it implies that at least one of the firms (players) expects that the equilibrium that emerges is such that it can increase its profits by changing its own strategy given the strategies adopted by other firms. But the fact that the said firm has not adopted a strategy that maximizes its profits implies either that the firm is not guided by the profit-maximizing principle or that there is some sort of incomplete information.

However, we have assumed that all information, including the fact that profit maximization is the guiding principle for each of the firms, is common knowledge. No firm is expected to adopt such a strategy and the firm trying to make the guess also knows this fact. Hence, given our assumption that all information is common knowledge, every firm, even before implementing a strategy, expects the Nash equilibrium to materialize. This is one interpretation of the Nash equilibrium. According to this interpretation, the Nash equilibrium is the inevitable result of firm behavior based on ultrarational expectations by the players, hinged on common knowledge about demand–cost conditions and profit maximization behavior, even before the game is actually played.

Argued in this manner, it it obvious why an individual firm cannot, on its own, choose the same reaction function and attain the same level of profits as it would do under a protection policy. By implication, even if the home firm adopts the strategy or chooses a reaction function that is compatible with a protection policy, the foreign firm knows that such a strategy does not follow from the profit maximization behavior by the home firm. In other words, even if the home firm tries to raise its output and usurp monopoly rents being earned by the foreign firm without a protection policy, the foreign firm is able to see through this strategy. In this sense, such a strategy fails to become a credible threat.

As against this, a production subsidy by the government, by changing the shape of the profit function of the firm in question, results in output expansion, in itself becoming a profit-maximizing strategy for the firm. In other words, the market outcome is changed as the empty threat, in the form of expanded output, becomes a credible threat.[4]

9.4 PRICE COMPETITION AND MARKET INTERVENTION POLICY

In the above discussion, we carried out a detailed analysis of welfare effects of a discriminatory subsidy policy within the framework of Cournot oligopoly, where each firm used its output, the quantity variable, as the strategic variable. However, it is not necessary for competition in an internationally oligopolistic industry to be limited to output adjustments alone. How are our conclusions modified if price, rather than output, is the basis of competition?

Let us discuss a model of Bertrand oligopoly as developed in Chapter 8, Section 8.5. That is, the home and foreign firms produce differentiated products that are close substitutes such that the demand functions faced by the respective firms are[5]

$$x = x(p, P) \quad (x_p < 0; x_P > 0) \tag{8a}$$
$$X = X(P, p) \quad (X_P < 0; X_p > 0) \tag{8b}$$

As in case of Eqs. (8a) and (8b) in Chapter 8, we assume that these demand functions satisfy the following conditions:

$$x_p(p, P) + x_P(p, P) < 0 \tag{9a}$$
$$X_P(P, p) + x_p(P, p) < 0 \tag{9b}$$

If the home government provides a subsidy of s/unit of output to the home firm, the profit function for the respective firms can be written as follows:

$$\pi_s(p, P) = px(p, P) - c[x(p, P)] + sx(p, P) \tag{10a}$$
$$\Pi(P, p) = PX(P, p) - C[X(P, p)] \tag{10b}$$

As in case of Cournot oligopoly, the home firm's reaction function $r_s(P)$ and the foreign firm's reaction function $R(p)$ are defined by the following equations:

$$\pi_{sp}[r_s(P), P]$$
$$= x[r_s(P), P] + [r_s(P) - (c'\{x[r_s(P), P]\} - s)]x_p[r_s(P), P]$$
$$= 0 \tag{11a}$$
$$\Pi_P[R(p), p)$$
$$= X[R(p), p] + (R(p) - (C'\{X[R(p), p]\})XP[R(p), p]$$
$$= 0 \tag{11b}$$

It should be noted here that, as shown by Eq. (11a), production subsidy leads to a decline in private marginal cost for the home firm even in the case of private competition.

Figure 9-2 depicts the Bertrand–Nash equilibrium in the presence of production subsidy. Curves r_s and R represent reaction functions for the home and foreign firms, respectively, and the point of intersection E_s represents the Bertrand–Nash equilibrium. Curve r, the reaction function for the home firm in the absence of production subsidy, is drawn in for reference purposes. The Bertrand–Nash equilibrium in this case is given by point E_0.

The home firm's reaction function with a production subsidy r_s lies to the left of its reaction function without a subsidy. The reason for this is that a production subsidy reduces marginal costs and the home firm adopts an aggressive strategy to capture the foreign firm's market share by setting a lower price, whatever the price set by the foreign firm. We continue to assume, as in the last chapter, that the reaction functions of both the firms have a less than unit absolute slope. Therefore, given Eqs. (9a) and (9b), an upward shift of the equilibrium point along the reaction function of one of the firm implies a fall in the output of its rival.

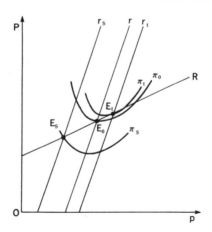

FIG. 9-2

It is possible to show that, even in case of Bertrand oligopoly being discussed here, a discriminatory protection policy in favor of the home firm by the home country government is effective from the viewpoint of economic welfare of the home country. The Bertrand oligopoly, however, differs from the Cournot oligopoly in that a strategic subsidy policy improves economic welfare through terms-of-trade and resource allocation effects and not through the rent-shifting effect, as in the case of the latter. In the remainder of this chapter we discuss this point further.

As a result of production subsidy, the equilibrium point shifts from E_0 to E_s. Since this shift is downward movement along the foreign firm's reaction function, it implies, as pointed out before, that the home firm produces a larger output than under the free trade equilibrium E_0.

It was shown in Section 9.2 that private profits net of subsidy, or what may be called the social profits, can be represented by a free trade profit function, irrespective of the amount of subsidy, as

$$\pi(p, P) = px(p, P) - c[x(p, P]$$

It is clear that this social profit is declining since the isoprofit curve attained with equilibrium at E_s shifts down from π_0 to π_s. In other words, the strategic rent-shifting effect of a discriminatory subsidy policy in this case worsens economic welfare in the home country.

What happens if a production tax is introduced instead? Since a production tax can be interpreted as a negative subsidy, if the home government taxes production at the rate of t $(= -s)$/unit, the home firm's reaction function, as shown in Fig. 9-2, shifts to the right from the free trade reaction function r to r_t. E_t is the new equilibrium point and the home firm moves to the isoprofit curve π_t, representing profits net of production subsidy. This, obviously, raises social profit in the home country. Thus, production tax, rather than production subsidy, will be a welfare-improving policy for the home country if we focus only on the strategic rent-shifting effect.

This interpretation, however, is misleading if we consider the consumption-expansion effect as well. This point can be clarified by decomposing the welfare effect of a production subsidy into terms-of-trade and resource allocation effects, rather than into consumption-expansion and rent-shifting effects.

Following the discussion in Section 9.2, economic welfare in the two countries can be represented as follows:

$$w = cs(p, P) + \pi(p, P) \tag{12a}$$
$$W = CS(P, p) + \Pi(P, p) \tag{12b}$$

It should be noted, however, that consumer surplus in this case is dependent on the set of prices charged by the two firms, since we are discussing oligopoly with differentiated products.

If Δx, ΔX, Δp, and ΔP represent the changes in output and prices of the respective firms as a result of production subsidy, change in welfare in the two countries Δw and ΔW is given by

$$\Delta w = (d_h - x)(-\Delta p) + d_f(-\Delta P) + \{p - c'[x(p, P)] + s\}\Delta x \quad (13a)$$
$$\Delta W = (D_f - X)(-\Delta P) + D_h(-\Delta p) + \{P - C'[X(P, p)]\}\Delta X \quad (13b)$$

where d_h and d_f (D_h and D_f) represent consumption of the home and foreign output by home (foreign) country consumers. The first and second terms on the right-hand side of Eqs. (13a) and (13b), taken together, represent the terms-of-trade (consumption-expansion) effect and the third term represents the resource allocation effect.

As has been discussed earlier, a discriminatory subsidy policy in favor of the home firm results in lower prices being charged by the firms of both countries. At the same time, output of the home firm rises. Keeping this in mind, it is easy to see that although the first term on the right-hand side of Eqs. (13a) and (13b) is negative, the second and third terms are positive. That is to say, the home country does incur a loss in terms of deterioration of terms of trade for the product produced by the home firm, as the result of a production subsidy. At the same time, however, it benefits from an improvement in terms of trade for the product produced by the foreign firm and greater efficiency in production due to expansion of production by the home firm. Therefore, if the home firm is relatively less competitive than the foreign firm and if its exports are not very large, the benefits from the latter two effects outweigh the negative effect of the first term, leading to an improvement in economic welfare for the home country. In this sense, as in the case of Cournot oligopoly, the home country can enjoy a higher level of economic welfare as compared to the free trade situation by taking recourse to a discriminatory production subsidy if the home industry is not highly competitive internationally.[6]

NOTES

1. The analysis here owes heavily to Dixit (1979, 1980, 1982), Eaton and Grossman (1987), Eaton and Lipsey (1981), and Spence (1977).

2. In the case of private profits of the domestic firm, the shape of the isoprofit curves becomes distorted due to production subsidy handout. Therefore, the reader should note that it is not possible to determine the change in domestic firm profits directly from the attainable isoprofit curve as in the case of foreign firm.

3. The three paragraphs that follow are somewhat technical and the reader can safely skip these without losing the main thread of the argument.

4. For the concepts of credible threat, empty threat, and commitment, where the threat is held out not as an empty threat but as a believable threat, see Schelling (1969). Moreover, the existing firms quite often use investment in facilities as well as research and development to prevent new entry. The relationship between these strategies and the empty and credible threats is discussed in Chapter 10. For a detailed discussion, see Kiyono (1987).

5. The symbols in the following discussion are the same as those used in Chapter 8, Section 8.5.

6. Eaton and Grossman (1987) focus on the negative strategic rent-shifting effect of a production subsidy and conclude that a production tax, rather than a production subsidy, is desirable in a Bertrand oligopoly. The discussion here, however, shows that these authors ignore the terms-of-trade improvement and resource allocation effects of a discriminatory subsidy policy.

10

Strategic Entry-Deterring Behavior and Entry-Assistance Policy

10.1 STRATEGIC ENTRY-DETERRING BEHAVIOR
AND CREDIBLE NATURE OF THREAT

A monopolistic or oligopolistic industry, in itself, does not imply the existence of monopoly profits or monopoly rents over and above what are termed normal profits. The reason is that entry by new competitive firms into the market, if possible, lowers prices and, hence, profits may vanish. In the absence of any autonomous entry barriers, a firm or a group of firms earning monopoly profits can defend their profits only by erecting artificial entry barriers by adopting some form of strategic behavior. The theory of limit pricing is one such theory of strategic entry barriers.

The theory of limit pricing states that the established firm or a group of firms can defend its monopoly profits by producing an output large enough to deter potential new entrants. Let us assume that the industry is characterized by a technology giving rise to scale economies so that the cost curve is either forward falling or U-shaped. The established firms can corner a major proportion of the market by producing a sufficiently large output.

If the market share of the established firms is sufficiently large, the share of the market available to a firm contemplating new entry, even if such a firm does exist, will be very small. It will be impossible for this firm to earn profits, even when it succeeds in entering the market, since it cannot reap scale economies if the level of output is small. As a result, the firm contemplating entry loses its incentive and entry does not come about.

The established firms, on the other hand, produce a large output and enjoy scale economies which allow them to produce at lower average cost and hence earn profits. Thus, according to the theory of limit pricing, the established firms can defend their monopoly profits by adopting a large-scale production strategy which results in lower prices and hence effectively blocking new entry.

The theory of limit pricing has been criticized on the following grounds. It has been pointed out that entry is dynamic behavior and it is necessary to distinguish clearly between the firm behavior before and after entry. The key question is

118

whether or not the established firms have an incentive to continue to follow their preentry strategies in the postentry period. The limit-pricing theory, however, fails to take note of this aspect.

Will a firm continue large-scale production once new entry has come about? If a new firm is actually able to enter the market, it will also try to expand its scale of production, and hence market share, in order to exploit economies of scale. As a result, the total output in this industry rises above the level intended by the established firms and prices and profits decline. Therefore, the established firms, instead of sticking to their preentry large-scale production strategy, may reduce their output and raise prices. Such a strategy may be an optimal profit-maximizing strategy, although it involves sharing the market with the new entrant. If the firm contemplating market entry is able to foresee this possibility, the large-scale production strategy cannot function as a limiting strategy.

The large-scale production strategy adopted by the established firms acts as a "threat" to the potential entrant, and the basis of the theory of limit pricing is that a firm contemplating entry abandons all its plans in the face of such a threat. But if the large-scale production strategy is a threat without substance and a firm enters refusing to yield, it is not possible to enforce the contents of the threat. In this sense, large-scale production strategy is no more than an empty threat or a threat without substance.

For the threat to be effective in forcing the rival to change its strategy, it is imperative to convince the rival that the threat in fact will be implemented. A threat that convinces the rival is termed hereafter a "credible threat." What conditions are necessary for a strategy of entry preventing behavior to become a credible threat?

The rival can be convinced about the credible nature of the threat only if he or she believes that the firm or group of firms holding the threat will in fact execute it. In the context of strategic limiting behavior, therefore, it implies that the established firms have an incentive to implement such a strategy. In other words, the threat, to be successful, must be in conformity with equilibrium in case entry actually occurs.

The reason that large-scale production strategy loses its credibility as a threat lies in the fact that in this strategy future scale of production (maybe due to new entry) can be readjusted any time. This is due to the fact that reduction in output, even if large-scale production has led to higher market share, does not entail any cost. Had the established firms adopted an irreversible strategy, before new entry took place, such that large-scale production was the optimal strategy in case new entry did come about, such a strategy could be effective.

10.2 LIMIT-PRICING THEORY RECONSIDERED

First, let us once again explain the received theory of limit pricing in the context of a duopolistic industry. We consider two periods, the present (period 1) and future (period 2). In period 1, it is assumed that the established firm has monopolistic control over the industry. Further, it is assumed that a new firm is contemplating entry into this industry and it is possible for this firm to enter in period 2.

Let us now consider the state of technology and demand conditions in the industry. First, both the firms are assumed to be governed by the same cost conditions, represented by

$$C(x) = cx$$

Here, x represents the output of the given firm and c is the average variable (marginal) cost (independent of the scale of output). The new firm, if it tries to enter the industry in the next period, must pay, over and above the production costs, a set-up cost (for the firm) F needed to enter the industry. The set-up cost, being a fixed cost independent of scale of production, gives rise to scale economies and the average cost curve slopes downward. Both the firms are assumed to produce a homogeneous product and the industry demand is a declining function of price.

We now turn our attention to the representation of postentry equilibrium in this industry assuming that the new firm enters the market. In this discussion, we assume that the two firms compete, using output as the strategic variable, and the postentry equilibrium can be represented as a Cournot–Nash equilibrium. Given this, the reaction functions for the two firms are depicted in Fig. 10.1.

The vertical axis in this figure represents output X of the established firm and the horizontal axis gives the output x of the new entrant. The intercept of the reaction function of the established firm on the vertical axis X_M gives the optimum output of the established firm when the output of the new entrant is zero. This corresponds to the output when the established firm has monopolistic con-

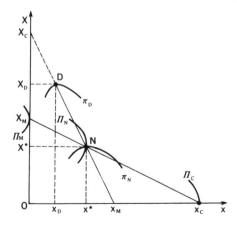

FIG. 10-1

trol over the market. The group of curves centered on this point are the isoprofit curves for the established firm, i.e., the combinations of (x, X) that give the same level of profits to the established firm. The farther away the curve is from point X_M, the lower is the level of profit represented by it. The intercept of the established firm's reaction function on the vertical axis x_C is the point where the established firm does not produce any output. Hence the isoprofit curve passing through this point corresponds to zero profit.

Similarly, the intercept that the reaction function of the new entrant makes on the horizontal axis x_M gives the output when the new entrant monopolizes the industry. The group of curves centered around this point represent isoprofit curves for the new entrant. The curve passing through point X_C corresponds to zero output by the new entrant and indicates a loss equivalent to the set-up cost. The zero profit isoprofit curve for the new entrant passes through D rather than X_C. Alternatively, if the output of the established firm exceeds X_D, the new entrant cannot earn positive profits whatever production strategy it may adopt. Let us term X_D as "limit production."

The essence of the theory of limit pricing is that the firm contemplating entry into the industry loses its incentive to enter if the established firm produces at X_D in period 1, when the output of the new entrant is zero. Let us, however, assume that the firm contemplating entry actually enters in period 2. In this situation, the new entrant has either already incurred or has decided to incur set-up costs. At this time, the set-up costs are not recoverable even if the firm decides against entry. That is, the set-up costs have been sunk.

The discussion that follows assumes that the whole amount of the set-up costs are sunk. Since the sunk costs cannot be recovered, any profits (quasirent) earned on the basis of its production activity are meaningful. As long as the established firm produces below X_C, the quasirent for the new entrant is positive. The whole of the reaction function of the new entrant, from x_M to X_C, therefore, is meaningful.

The established firm, however, will not produce X_D under these circumstances. The reason is that if the established firm chooses X_D, the optimal output for the new entrant is x_D. This can be easily guessed by the established firm since it is familiar with the conditions of the new entrant on account of the limiting behavior adopted by it. If it is possible to make such a guess, the established firm can be expected to adopt the optimal production strategy assuming that the new entrant will choose x_D. It is obvious that X_D is not the optimal output in this case.

When the established and the newly entered firms estimate each others' output levels independently and use it to select an optimal strategy of their own, the estaimtes by the two firms are in mutual conformity only in Nash equilibrium (point N in Fig. 10-1). A new entrant that foresees this situation will gate crash into this industry, even if the established firm produces at X_D in period 1, trying to earn profits that are compatible with Nash equilibrium. That is why the theory of limit pricing fails as an explanation of strategic limiting behavior. This also explains why the threat by the established firm, that it will continue to produce X_D if the new entry actually occurs, is no more than an empty threat.

10.3 INSTALLED PRODUCTION FACILITIES AND CREDIBLE THREAT

The present and following sections try to look into whether or not it is possible for the established firm to prevent new entry effectively by deciding on a strategic installation, in period 1, of production facilities large enough to bring down marginal costs. Such a strategy can prevent new entry by serving as a credible threat. The costs of installing production facilities, once undertaken, are sunk. In this sense, it is an irreversible strategy.

As in the previous section, we once again consider a duopoly and assume that competition in this industry takes place over two periods of time. That is, the established firm can prepare for expected new entry in period 2 by investing in production facilities in period 1 (when the new entry has yet to take place). It is possible for the established firm to add to, but not reduce, its production facilities in period 2. The new entrant, on the other hand, cannot enter the market except in period 2 and it is possible for the firm, within this period, to install production facilities and begin production. All production occurs in period 2 only.

Costs for both firms are composed of costs of installing production facilities and costs involved in actual production. For simplicity, we measure the size of production facilities by the maximum possible output attainable with these facilities. Let by be the cost of installing production facilities y, where b is the cost of an additional unit of production facilities. Production is possible only if output level x is less than or equal to the size of production facilities y. The cost of actual production is assumed to be ax. Thus, the total cost of producing x, $C(x; y)$, for a firm having production facilities y is given by

$$C(x; y) = \begin{cases} ax + by & \text{(when } x < y) \\ (a + b)x & \text{(when } x = y) \\ \infty & \text{(when } x > y) \end{cases}$$

For the new entrant, since it chooses the size of production facilities and output simultaneously, any excess production capacity signifies a total loss. Cost of production for such a firm is given by

$$C(x) = (a + b)x$$

For the home firm that has already invested in production facilities of size Y, the installation cost bY is already sunk. Therefore, cost of producing X is given by

$$C(X; Y) = \begin{cases} aX + bY & \text{(when } X \leq Y) \\ (a + b)X & \text{(when } X > Y) \end{cases}$$

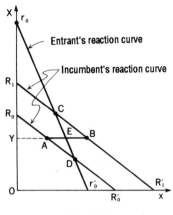

Fig. 10-2

Fig. 10-2

Consequently, as shown in Fig. 10-2, marginal cost for the established firm which has invested in production facilities of size Y and has, thereby, sunk these costs, shows a jump at the point where output equals Y.

Let us now assume that the established firm has already installed production facilities of size Y and has sunk these costs. What sort of (Cournot–Nash) equilibrium will emerge in period 2 in this case? Curves $R_0 R_0'$ and $R_1 R_1'$ are the reaction functions for the established firm when marginal costs are given by $(a + b)$ and a, respectively. The reaction function with marginal costs given by a is drawn to the right of the reaction function when marginal costs are $(a + b)$ because it is advantageous to produce more when marginal costs are declining even if the output and marginal revenue of the new entrant are the same.

As long as output X is below Y, the size of production facilities already installed, the reaction function for the established firm is given by $R_1 R_1'$ since marginal cost is given by a. Once the output exceeds the size of installed production facilities Y, $R_0 R_0'$ becomes the relevant reaction function. Thus, the reaction function for the established firm is given by kinked curve $R_0 ABR_1'$, including the horizontal portion corresponding to $X = Y$. For the new entrant, since its marginal cost is given by $(a + b)$, the reaction function is a straight line represented by $r_0 r_0'$ in Fig. 10-2.

Thus, the Cournot–Nash equilibrium for period 2, when the established firm installs production facilities of size Y in period 1, is given by point E in Fig. 10-2, where reaction functions of the two firms intersect. The established firm, however, tries to choose the optimal size of its production facilities in period 1 expecting such a Cournot–Nash equilibrium to emerge in period 2. It is quite obvious that the established firm can, by choosing an appropriate size of produc-

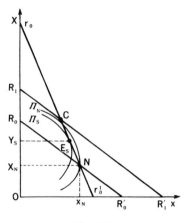

FIG. 10-3

tion facilities Y in period 1, attain period 2 equilibrium as long as it is on segment CD on the reaction function of the new entrant.

In the case of oligopolistic competition, therefore, when it is possible to irreversibly install production facilities, equilibrium is attained at a point on segment CD where the established firm earns highest profits. As shown in Fig. 10-3, let us consider point E_S on segment CN where the period 1 isoprofit curve [taking care of costs of installing production facilities, i.e., when marginal costs are given by $(a + b)$] of the established firm Π_S is tangent to the reaction function of the new entrant. It is clear that equilibrium in this case is attained at point E_S. That is, the established firm chooses the point of Stackelberg equilibrium when the established firm is the leader and the new entrant is the follower.

If, as in the previous section, it is not possible to install marginal cost-reducing production facilities, the marginal cost for the established firm is given by $(a + b)$ and $R_0 R_0'$ is the appropriate reaction function. The Cournot–Nash equilibrium in this case would have been at N, corresponding to output X_N and profits Π_N. However, the established firm, by installing production facilities in period 1 and sinking this cost, is able to increase its profits by successfully making the new entrant believe in its strategy, namely, that it will produce a larger output Y_S and hold a larger share of the market.

The act by which a player of the game (the established firm in this case) makes its rival believe in its future strategy (large-scale production strategy here) by adopting a strategic behavior (choice of irreversible installation of production facilities) is termed as "committing" to that strategy (production facilities). In Fig. 10-3, the established firm is able to attain the Stackelberg equilibrium by committing to production facilities of size Y_S in period 1, giving credibility to its period 2 strategy of undertaking large-scale production at level Y_S.

10.4 STRATEGIC ENTRY BARRIERS USING PRODUCTION FACILITIES

Can an established firm prevent new entry by committing itself to production facilities? To consider this possibility, we introduce a modification into the model presented in the previous section. This relates to set-up costs of entry discussed in Section 10.2.

Let us assume that the new entrant, in an industry with cost and competitive structure as described in the previous section, must incur fixed set-up costs of entry for any positive output level. As shown in Fig. 10-4, the reaction function of the new entrant in this case is kinked twice due to reasons discussed in Section 10.2.

It is possible for the established firm to prevent new entry effectively when the new entrant must incur set-up costs. Let us explain this point with the help of Fig. 10-5. The established firm, in this case, can prevent new entry by installing production facilities of size X_D in period 1. Commitment to production facilities of size X_D in period 1 lends credibility to the threat that the established firm will not reduce its production below X_D even if the new firm does enter.

Another possible choice for the established firm is to allow new entry. This case, due to reasons discussed above, will result in a Stackelberg equilibrium E_S where the established firm acts as a leader. In Fig. 10-5, we present the case where the profits of the established firm are lower when new entry is allowed (Π_S) than when it is not (Π_D). Under these circumstances, the established firm has an incentive to prevent new entry. Further, the new firm cannot enter as long as the established firm is committed to production facilities of size X_D. The new firm can easily foresee that it cannot earn profits even if it enters, since the established firm has an incentive to continue producing X_D. Thus, if conditions as presented

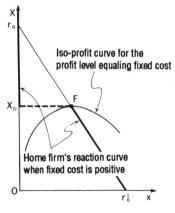

FIG. 10-4

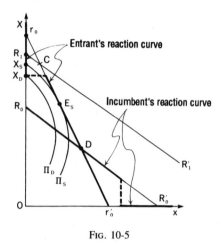

FIG. 10-5

in Fig. 10-5 prevail, entry by a new firm is effectively prevented and the established firm can maintain its profits at Π_D.

10.5 ENTRY ASSISTANCE BY THE HOME COUNTRY GOVERNMENT AND EFFECT ON ECONOMIC WELFARE

Let us consider a situation where the established foreign firm uses production facilities to prevent entry by the home firm. The cost functions for both firms are assumed to be the same as in the previous section so that it is optimal, as in Fig. 10-5, for the foreign firm to prevent the home firm from entering the market.

The home country government, in this case, can use a protective policy to assist the home firm to enter the market. Let us explain this point with reference to a capital subsidy to the home firm that reduces set-up costs of entry.[1]

The government adopts a policy to grant the home firm a fixed amount of subsidy on the condition that it enters the industry in question. This governmental assistance reduces fixed costs for the home firm and changes the shape of its reaction function. In concrete terms, the kink in the home firm reaction function, as shown in Fig. 10-5, shifts upward by the amount of reduction in fixed costs. Consequently, if the kink in the home firm reaction function moves above the point of intersection between the foreign firm isoprofit curve associated with Stackelberg equilibrium and the vertical axis, the home firm will enter this industry.

This follows from the fact that if the home firm eventually enters in period 2, even when the foreign firm chooses to commit to new entry-limiting production capacity X_D' (not depicted in Fig. 10-5 to avoid cluttering), the foreign firm expects its profits to be higher by allowing the home firm to enter and moving to equilibrium at E_S rather than by sticking to output level X_D'. Thus, the threat by the foreign firm—to continue producing output X_D'—is no longer credible and fails to prevent new entry.

How does a policy of capital subsidy to the home firm affect economic welfare in the home country? The change in welfare, in this case, is composed of the change in consumer surplus and social profits. The sign on the effect on economic welfare depends on the direction of change in consumer surplus as social profits, in the Stackelberg equilibrium that comes about once the home firm has successfully entered the industry, take a positive value.

The price under Stackelberg equilibrium is always lower as long as level of output under such an equilibrium exceeds the total output attained in an equilibrium without home firm entry. Hence, the change in consumer surplus, in such a case, is always positive. That is, total change in economic welfare is always positive as long as the condition

Market supply after entry by the home firm
> market supply before entry by the home firm

is satisfied.

On the other hand, it is possible for the foreign country's economic welfare to rise if the decline in prices, following entry by the home firm, is large enough to raise consumer surplus in the foreign country to an extent that it more than compensates the fall in foreign firm profits. Thus, a subsidy policy to assist home firm entry, when the foreign firm is characterized by monopoly rents, can also have a positive effect on overall economic welfare in the foreign country.

NOTES

1. This analysis also applies to the granting of production subsidies to the home firm and to imposition of tariffs and quotas against the foreign firm.

11

Strategic Intervention in International Competition: Significance and Limitations

Let us put the discussion of the previous chapters in a proper perspective. The productive resources invested in an oligopolistic market earn monopoly rents or rewards in excess of what could be earned in their alternative uses. Individual firms, placed in an international oligopolistic environment, compete vigorously for these monopoly rents. A capital or production subsidy, given exclusively to the home firm in such an industry, serves to strengthen international competitiveness of the home firms. This results in a transfer of monopoly rents from the foreign to the home firm, thereby improving economic welfare in the home country. Our discussion in the previous chapters shows that this "monopoly rent-transfer effect" or the "profit-transfer effect" forms the essence of strategic trade and industrial policies.

To what extent is the theory of strategic trade and industrial policies, dependent on the profit-transfer effect, appropriate for discussing real work economic policies? The present chapter tries to determine the extent to which the static Cournot oligopoly framework, discussed heretofore, can be generalized and the limitations involved. In Sections 11.1 to 11.4, below, we discuss the implications of extending the static model to introduce dynamic considerations. From Section 11.5 onward we discuss the limitations of the static framework presented in the previous chapters and suggest some possible improvements.

11.1 A Dynamic Analysis of an International Oligopoly: Protection Policies and Growth of Industry

Industrial policy considerations in an oligopolistic market entail a number of problems which cannot be properly discussed without introducing dynamic factors. To begin with, a rise in technological prowess of a firm over time forms the kernel of infant industry protection and dynamic concepts, like competition over time and firm behavior based on long-term strategies, become important.

Competition among oligopolistic firms takes on more complex and diversified

128

forms in a dynamic rather than a static world. Oligopolistic competition in a static world, as discussed earlier, mostly takes recourse to either price or output strategies. In a dynamic environment, however, competition through investment in production facilities or in technology develoment becomes important. Factors like severity of price competition in the market at the present juncture and expected price trends in the future also determine the degree to which a firm adopts an active investment policy and its incentives for technology and product development. In this sense, setting of the present price level, assuming dynamic investment competition, has important implications for the long-term firm strategy and also determines the long-run performance of the industry as a whole.

One reason for considering dynamic competition is the fact that it allows a detailed analysis of the relationship between the long- and short-run aspects of competition among the firms. The firms do not compete for present-day profits only. Price setting, investment, and accumulation of experience today is significantly related to the long-run strategy of a firm. This is especially important in industries where accumulation of production experience results in substantial cost reductions, or in industries with ample scope for technology development. Part V of this book discusses technology competition in detail. In this chapter we limit the discussion only to the aspects pertinent to dynamic oligopolistic competition.

Another reason for studying dynamic oligopolistic competition lies in the fact that it shows that the contents and effects of industrial policy can differ, depending on the phase of life cycle of an industry. This is because the competitive pattern and principles of firm behavior differ as between growing and stagnating industries.

As will be shown below, the fact that a large number of industries were in a growth phase is an important factor in understanding the mechanism of postwar Japanese industrial promotion policies.

11.2 Principles of Firm Behavior in Growth Phase and Industrial Protection Policies

In dynamic oligopolistic competition, as in a static oligopoly framework, government policy affects distribution of rent between the home and foreign firms, thereby affecting economic welfare in the home country. There is no significant difference between static and dynamic competition in this respect. A dynamic model, however, raises a number of issues for the first time. One such issue, discussed hereunder, is the effect of industrial policy on an industry in its growth phase.[1]

It is normally believed that the content as well as the effect of industrial policy differ depending on whether the relevant industry is a growing or mature industry. It is imperative to note, for a proper understanding of postwar Japanese protection and promotion policies for industries like automobiles, household electronics, and computers, that the period when these industries were protected overlapped with the growth phase of these industries. This fact, however, lacks an economic explanation.

Individual firms in these industries, backed by a steep rise in demand, expanded their capacity at a fast pace. This investment surge was also intricately related to the policy protecting domestic industries at that time. These industries were protected by stringent controls on imports and foreign direct investment, but it was widely believed that these controls would be abolished sooner or later. The rapid expansion of capacity by the firms was, to a large extent, in the form of advanced preparation for severe foreign competition expected in the postliberalization period.

Thus, the long-run firm behavior is characterized not by considerations of short-run but of long-run profit maximization. The reason for this lies in the fact that when the demand for the product of a given industry is rising rapidly, it is rational for the firm to strive for higher and larger profits in the future rather than enlarging their short-run profits.

The ranking of the firms in terms of market shares, once established during the growth phase, does not change easily when the industry becomes stable. The reason is that the firms find themselves committed to their investment in production facilities and technology (irreversible choice) and this dampens the investment urge of new entrants. A new entrant, or a firm contemplating investment in production facilities or technological development in such an industry, places great importance on the installed capacity and technological level of its established rival firms. If new entry or expansion of production facilities occurs in an industry where the installed capacity and technological level of the established firms is low, the possibility of earning large profits is quite high. If, however, the established firms are strong enough, new entry or investment results in severe competition and large profits are also less likely.

Such reasoning by the new entrants, on the other hand, plays right into the hands of the established firms. That is, the established firms, as was discussed in Chapter 10, can invest in production facilities or technological development to smother the desire of new firms to enter the industry or to dampen the will of the existing rival firms to expand their production facilities.

It is this factor that provides an incentive for individual firms to outdo each other in accumulation of capital at a fast pace during the growth period. The ability of a firm to outdo others in holding a high level of production capacity smothers the investment urge of other firms.

Similar behavior by all the firms, however, leads to severe investment competition in the industry as a whole. The stiff investment competition or competition for market shares in the growth phase of an industry can be attributed to such a mechanism.

An interventionist policy by the home country government can have repercussions for interfirm competition when some of the firms, competing for market share using an investment strategy against the home firms, are foreign firms. For example, if the government provides the home firms with investment or production subsidies, the home firms can use these to get an upper hand in investment competition.

A policy to prevent foreign firms from entering the home market temporarily by using import control measures also produces similar results. Such policies are believed to have played an important role in postwar Japanese industrial protection policy. The following section undertakes a somewhat detailed discussion of such policies.

11.3 TIME-BOUND PROTECTION AND THE FORM OF OLIGOPOLISTIC COMPETITION

A large number of industries in postwar Japan were protected by stringent import or foreign investment controls. However, these protective policies in Japan were distinctive in the sense that the private economic agents believed that these import and foreign investment controls would not continue forever. Since its entry into the GATT in 1955, the Japanese government gradually dismantled these trade controls.[2] Dismantling of trade controls was not necessarily considered to be an optimum policy for the Japanese government at that time but was an unavoidable choice in order to be included in the group of industrially advanced nations as a GATT and IMF member country.

External pressures for liberalization were also instrumental in bringing about an awareness about the temporary nature of the protective policies. The pressures, by the United States and other countries, for opening up of markets increased during the 1960s and such external pressure was an important factor determining the pace of market liberalization in Japan.

The effects of a time-bound protective policy can be discussed under the heads of the effects of a protective policy and the effects of a time-bound policy. The protective policy, by limiting the activity of the foreign firms in specific Japanese markets, was aimed at delaying entry by foreign firms into the Japanese market. For the foreign firms this delay in entry during the period of rapid economic growth proved to be lethal. As entry into the Japanese markets became possible with dismantling of import control measures, the foreign firms found themselves face to face with Japanese firms that, in most of the industries, had already attained competitiveness and held a high level of production capacity. It was not easy for the foreign firms to enter such a market and rewards for extra efforts to enter the market may not have been very high.

Being a time-bound policy, on the other hand, implied that the possibility of competition with foreign firms, as and when protection was withdrawn, hung as the sword of Damocles over the Japanese firms. This threat may have been instrumental in increasing the willingness of Japanese firms to expand investment and production at an accelerated pace. Most of the Japanese firms, at that time, were occupied primarily in quickly building up strength to meet expected competition from foreign firms in the postliberalization period. In this sense, time-bound protective policies were responsible for raising the Japanese firms' willingness to invest.

Competition among oligopolistic firms can give rise to various competitive patterns and the time-bound protection policies in Japan are believed to have had a significant effect on the form of competition among the domestic firms. Stiff price competition is one such extreme form of competition. Individual firms, in this case, find it difficult to undertake technology and product development or expansion of production facilities due to the following reasons. A heavy dependence by the firms on internal sources of funds to meet their investment expenditures implies that they must meet it out of their operating profits (sales – production cost). But such investment cannot be undertaken if operating profits are extremely small due to severe price competition. On the other hand, even if the firm is in a position to borrow or raise enough external funds to meet all its investment requirements, these funds will have to be redeemed out of the future operating profits. But there is no guarantee that the firm will be able to repay its loans if price competition is expected to remain stiff and the banks will not be willing to lend to such a firm.

Against this, it is also possible for competition to take a form that allows the firms to set prices at a high level and invest most of the operating profits thus generated. Such a competitive form has a greater potential to contribute to the growth of a firm and development of an industry. For some time in the postwar period, there was a tendency in the automobile industry to avoid price competition. The threat of future competition from the Western firms, however, not only promoted investment in this industry but also helped the firms to choose a strategy to avoid excessive price competition in order to undertake sufficient investments.[3]

The fast pace of industrial growth and time-bound protection policies, as described above, acted as the engine of growth in industries like the automobile industry. It is not clear how far the policy authorities were aware of such a mechanism but protection policies, in effect, raised the speed of industrial growth.

A question as to why, although a number of countries have a protected automobile industry no other country has been as successful as Japan, is posed time and again. This question may have a number of explanations. The mechanism discussed above is, however, one important explanatory factor.

For a time-bound policy to be effective as an intentional policy the firms must be convinced of the credibility of the time limit. It is, however, extremely difficult to implement a time-bound protection policy in a credible form. Once the government introduces a time-bound protection policy, the firms get used to it and it is difficult for the government to retract such a protective measure.[4]

11.4 IMPORT CONTROLS AS AN EXPORT PROMOTION POLICY

Most of the investments are accompanied by declining costs.[5] Besides, accumulation of production experience also lowers the production costs of a firm. We explained this decline in costs, in our earlier discussion, as a part of the phenomenon of decreasing costs. Time-bound import control measures, in an industry where the phenomenon of decreasing costs holds sway, not only have an industry-fostering effect but also have an export-promotion effect.

If the home firms can undertake sufficient investments and accumulate production experience before any foreign firm can do it, the relative competitive position of the home firms improves. This improvement in competitive position is irreversible even if import control measures are withdrawn at a later date. As a result, exports will naturally be promoted as the home firm now holds competitive advantage not only in the home but also in the foreign market. Thus, in cases where a decreasing cost phenomenon dominates, the irreversible effects of time-bound protective measures are strong enough to affect exports as well.

11.5 LIMITATIONS OF THE STRATEGIC TRADE MODEL: ENTRY, EXIT, AND MEASURES TO PROTECT DOMESTIC INDUSTRY

In the rest of this chapter, we consider the assumptions and analytical limitations of the strategic trade model presented in the previous chapters. We also venture some comments on the directions that future research in this field should take.

The first problem with strategic industrial policy in the context of an oligopolistic trade model relates to entry and exit of the firms. The assumption implicit in the discussion up to now has been that firms neither enter nor exit the industry under investigation. Once we allow the possibility of entry and exit, however, uncertainty about effectiveness of strategic trade and industrial policies rises.

Let us consider, following the analysis in Chapter 8, an oligopolistic industry where the firms produce a homogeneous product in a Cournot-competition setting. There are n firms engaged in actual production in the home country and all these firms, including potential entrants, are governed by exactly the same cost conditions. Further, x_n is the output level of a representative firm with profits given by $\pi = px_n - c(x_n)$. The total home country output, obviously, is given by $x = nx_n$ and total profits by $\Pi = n\pi_n$. Now, if we assume that the firms are perfectly free to enter or exit the industry such that the industry is at the free entry equilibrium with the representative firm earning zero profits, how does a production subsidy to home firms affect economic welfare?

Generally, a production subsidy is expected to lower the market price of the product. If we follow the derivation of Eq. (8a) of Section 8.5 of Chapter 8, the change in economic welfare for the home country is given by

$$\Delta W = (x^* - d^*)\Delta p + \pi_n^* \Delta n + n^*[p^* - c'(x_n^*)]\Delta x_n \qquad (1)$$

An asterisk here indicates the presubsidy equilibrium value of the respective variables. The first and third terms on the right-hand side of this equation represent the terms-of-trade and profit-transfer effects, respectively. The newly emerged second term captures the contribution of profits earned by new entrants to economic welfare.

Ignoring the problems related to the condition that the number of firms should be positive, the profits of the new entrants with an infinitesimally small subsidy equal the profits of the established firms in the presubsidy case. In this case, with perfectly free entry and exit, the second term in the above equation is zero. Thus, the implications of Eq. (1) seem to exactly replicate the conclusions drawn in Chapter 8. If entry and exit are factually restricted, the earlier discussion stands. But the conditions differ if there is perfectly free entry and exit. The reason is that the composition of the profit-transfer effect undergoes a change.

A production subsidy to the home firms improves cost conditions of the established firms. At the same time, if firms are free to enter, it also induces new entry.[6] As a result, the established firms face a declining demand and output falls. While the direct effect of a production subsidy raises output of individual firms, the indirect effect leads to a decline in the output of the established firms by way of inducing new entry. One cannot make any generalizations about which of the two effects predominates.[7]

The third term in Eq. (1) is negative if the latter indirect effect dominates the direct effect. In this case, if we keep in mind that production subsidy lowers the market price, economic welfare in the home country must decline as a result of a production subsidy if it exports the product in question. Thus, for an exporting country, production tax is the appropriate policy.

In the case of an importing country also, economic welfare declines if the level of imports is low and the terms-of-trade effects are small or if output of the established firm declines substantially as a result of new entry and the profit-transfer effect is large. In this case too, production tax becomes the appropriate policy measure for the home country. Even when the country is an importer and a production subsidy raises economic welfare, the optimum rate of subsidy is lower as compared to the case where entry and exit are restricted.

The above discussion can be summarized as follows. Ignoring all other problems arising out of competitive structure of the market, a production subsidy can raise economic welfare in the home country only if individual firms expand their output level making full use of scale economies. A production subsidy, under the conditions of free entry and exit, however, induces inefficient entry that hinders exploitation of scale economies and results in lowering economic welfare in the home country.[8]

11.6 LIMITATIONS OF THE STRATEGIC TRADE MODEL: SOCIAL COSTS OF INDUSTRIAL PROTECTION

The second problem of the strategic trade model relates to considerations of social costs of a strategic subsidy policy. The choice of industry to be targeted for subsidy, when there is more than one oligopolistic industry, should be based on a comparison of benefits from adopting the policy and its social costs. Social costs of a strategic subsidy policy require closer attention on this account.[9] The discussion to this point implicitly assumed that there was only one oligopolistic industry in the economy as a whole. However, in general, a number of oligopolistic industries show the characteristics being discussed here. Moreover, since these industries compete for the same productive resources, protecting a specific industry implies negative secondary effects on other oligopolistic industries.

Competition for high-quality technical workers is especially fierce among the technologically advanced industries. In this case, subsidy to any particular advanced industry, by tightening demand and supply in the market for technical workers, raises wages and cost conditions deteriorate for other home country industries using technical workers. Consequently, the rents earned by the home firms decline. The economic welfare for the home country, when these external diseconomies are sufficiently large, declines even though monopoly rents in the industry targeted for subsidy rise.

Thus, a subsidy to home firms just because the industry is an oligopoly does not necessarily raise economic welfare in the home country. The selection of industry for subsidization must be based on considerations of general equilibrium in the economy inclusive of the external diseconomies discussed above.

11.7 LIMITATIONS OF THE STRATEGIC TRADE MODEL: RETALIATORY INDUSTRIAL POLICY BY THE FOREIGN GOVERNMENT

The third problem involving the static model relates to the fact that this analysis does not involve a game setting in the true sense of the word. If the home country can improve its economic welfare by taking recourse to discriminatory measures to protect the home firms, there is no reason why a foreign government cannot adopt similar measures to protect its own firms. In other words, we must imagine a game in which both countries adopt protective policies in favor of their own country firms and analyze the economic implications of the resulting equilibrium to understand properly the effects of a protective policy by the government.

It is not possible here, due to space limitations, to discuss this aspect in detail but we would like to stress the following points.[10] First, a game among governments that involves adoption of retaliatory policy measures can clearly lead to a contractionary trade equilibrium. Not to mention the experience of an interwar period, it goes without saying that such retaliatory measures can have a multitude of adverse political and economic implications.

However, if the governments of the two countries use production subsidies as the only strategy in the subsidy game, it is possible, at least at a theoretical level, to attain an expansionary equilibrium that raises the world economic welfare. The reason is that the output of the oligopolistic firms in both countries, in the equilibrium attained as the result of this game, is higher as compared to the no policy intervention case and international price declines significantly. It is possible in this case for economic welfare in both countries to rise on account of an increase in consumer surplus.[11]

11.8 LIMITATIONS OF THE STRATEGIC TRADE MODEL: STRATEGIC BEHAVIOR OF THE PRIVATE SECTOR AND POLICY FORMATION

A fourth problem of the strategic trade model arises from the fact that the positions of the private sector and the government in the game discussed here are asymmetrical. Our analysis implicitly assumes that the government makes its behavioral decision and is committed to it before the private sector makes any move. The private sector cannot change the policy once adopted and takes it as given in making behavioral decisions. Do these assumptions obtain in the real world?

Private sector support, by the way of voting behavior, is critical in determining whether the party in office can continue to govern the country or not. As a result, the government policy formation is inevitably influenced by private pressure groups. The home industries freely use this influence on the policy formation process to maximize their own profits. Even if production subsidies raise home country economic welfare, the entrepreneurs tend to secure the maximum possible subsidy from the government.[12] The amount of subsidies finally decided upon in this case tend to be excessive from the point of view of maximization of economic welfare, including benefits to the consumer.

A similar problem arises even when the private sector firms do not influence the process of governmental policy formation directly. Let us assume that the government decides on protecting a specific industry through a strategic subsidy policy. The result of our analysis, showing that such a policy improves economic welfare, was based on the implicit assumption that the government has exactly the same amount of information as the private sector. In other words, it was assumed that the government knew precisely about market demand as well as cost conditions obtaining in the home and foreign firms. This assumption assumes that the government can calculate, beforehand, the increase in home firm rent and the decline in market price as a result of a given level of production subsidy and, hence, can determine the rate of subsidy that maximizes home country economic welfare.

It is, however, natural to assume that economic agents in direct touch with the industry concerned (private sector firms) have more precise information about market and cost conditions than the agents lacking such links (government). The government can do no more than make indirect inferences about market and cost conditions obtaining in the firms by observing actual market performance. It is impossible for the government to jointly own the information held by the private sector firms and, in this sense, private sector firms have an informational superiority over the government.

This information asymmetry raises the following problem. Let us envisage a situation where the government takes a low market share of the home firms under free trade as an indicator of home firm cost disadvantage against the foreign firms. This belief leads to an unnecessary increase in subsidy. Now, let us assume that private sector firms know the rule by which the government judges market performance and the policy rule based on this. In such a case, the home firms have an incentive to influence market performance, by deliberately suppressing their output, and to distort government policy. By doing this, the home firms can mislead the government to believe that there is a substantial cost disadvantage and hence can extract a higher amount of subsidy. Again, the foreign firms also have an incentive to signal that the home firms do not have a significant cost disadvantage by purposely holding down their exports. Such signaling reduces the rate of subsidy to the home firms and the foreign firm can avoid a relative decline in competitiveness due to the subsidy policy to a certain extent. If both firms adopt such manipulative behavior, output under a subsidy policy will decline and resource misallocation resulting from an oligopolistic market structure may, in fact, be compounded.[13]

11.9 THREAT BY FOREIGN FIRMS AND THE POSSIBILITY OF IMPLEMENTING STRATEGIC INDUSTRIAL POLICY

The behavior of foreign firms raises a still important problem. It is possible for the foreign firms, even if there is no information asymmetry and even if the foreign firms do not pressure their own governments, to influence the policy decisions of the home firms by adopting certain behavioral patterns.

For example, let us consider the large-sized commercial aircraft industry.[14] Boeing Corporation and Airbus, subsidized by the European Community (EC) governments, are the main competitors in this industry. The most recent market in this industry is for aircraft with seating capacity for 150 passengers. The analysis carried out in the previous sections indicates that the European governments should commit to an extensive assistance program for the home country aircraft industry to prevent entry by Boeing. By doing this, Airbus can ensure a market and can earn a huge amount in monopoly rents. The actual developments, however, are not taking this course.

The Boeing Corporation revealed its intention to enter the new market before the Airbus (EC countries) and has started a worldwide campaign claiming that there is no room for a late entrant and the subsidization of Airbus by the European governments involves considerable costs. This is nothing but threatening strategic behavior aimed at preventing implementation of a protective policy by the European governments. There is no way to tell how effective such a threatening behavior can be. But it does point to the need for serious reservations on implementability of strategic trade and industrial policies as discussed here. This example demonstrates that the private sector (especially the foreign) firms can adopt a strategy to turn the situation in its own favor and enjoy first mover advantages. A necessary condition for strategic trade and industrial policies to be effective is that the government commit itself to the policy before any other economic agent makes a move. The Boeing example shows that this condition is not necessarily satisfied in the real world. If so, implementation of a strategic protection policy by the home government loses its very purpose if the threat by the foreign private firms is credible.

NOTES

1. The discussion below is based largely on Matsuyama and Itoh (1985). Our discussion here is mainly intuitive. For a rigorous treatment the reader is referred to the above article.

2. For a discussion of postwar Japanese trade policy and trade, including this point, see Komiya and Itoh (1986).

3. See Itoh (1987) for a discussion of the relationship between the growth pattern of Japanese automobile industry and protection policies.

4. On the credibility of such trade and industrial policies, see Itoh, Kiyono, and Honda (1986, 1987).

5. The discussion here is based on Krugman (1984).

6. This problem does not arise, however, if the subsidy is granted only to the established firms. It is not difficult to conceive of such a discriminatory subsidy policy. Most of the joint research and development associations established under the guidance of the Ministry of International Trade and Industry (MITI) did, in fact, select the participating firms in a discriminatory fashion. In most instances, however, it is difficult to carry out such discrimination and is undesirable on grounds of fairness.

7. For a detailed discussion of this point, see Kiyono (1986).

8. An oligopolistic market with free entry and exit is beset with a number of economic welfare-related problems other than those discussed above. Chapter 13 of this book takes up these problems in detail.

9. For the arguments that follow, see Dixit and Grossman (1986).

10. Details of arguments presented below can be found in Brander and Spence (1984, 1985). Also see Dixit and Kyle (1985).

11. It must be noted that taxation needed to meet the needs of production subsidy leads to distortions in resource allocation and strategic funneling of subsidies into a particular industry results in social unfairness. Given this, whether a subsidy game is, on balance, advantageous from the viewpoint of national economic welfare, requires a careful analysis.

12. Such private sector behavior is known as "rent seeking" in public economics.

13. If the government perceives the existence of such information asymmetry and also the fact that the firms have an incentive to distort information through manipulative behavior, the market performance indicator will be more sophisticated than considered here. The essence of the discussion in this section, however, still holds. For further details, see Itoh, Kiyono, and Honda (1986, 1987).

14. This example is based on Krugman (1984).

IV

Welfare Implications of Strategic
Competition in Oligopolistic Industries

12

The Concept of Competition: An Evaluation

12.1 TWO ACCEPTED NOTIONS OF COMPETITION AND ECONOMIC WELFARE

The social decision-making process in the modern democracies is governed politically by a decentralized political structure, as reflected in representative democracy, and economically by a decentralized economic structure based on a competitive market system. It is usually believed that forces of free competition, carried out among various social groups in such decentralized social systems, lead to political decisions acceptable to the majority and result in an efficient allocation of resources. The logic of the process, in the economic context, can be described as follows.

A social decision-making process giving rise to inefficient resource allocation unleashes forces of free competition for profit opportunites arising from efforts to remove these inefficiencies. As a result, competition leads to removal of inefficiencies in resource allocation, static as well as dynamic, as long as there are no artificial barriers, institutional or social, hindering the competitive process. Moreover, success of the economic entities in a freely competitive environment is predicated upon development of new and superior products, development and introduction of ever more efficient production processes, new organizational forms, and new incentive structures. It is the existence of such ever-existing pressures for reform that ensures long-run efficiency of resource allocation in a decentralized society.

The "Basic Theorem of Welfare Economics" summarizes this thinking within the framework of formal economic theory.[1] This theorem states that a perfectly competitive market system, that satisfies the sufficient conditions, attains an unwasteful Pareto efficient resource allocation. Since perfect competition refers to a state when the number of competitors is unlimited, this argument naturally leads to the conclusion that increasing competition raises economic welfare (Stiglitz, 1981). The traditional industrial organization theory typically incorporates this notion based on the traditional economic theory. For example, Baumol (1982, p. 2) states that ". . . the standard analysis leaves us with the impression that there is a rough continuum, in terms of desirability of industry performance,

143

ranging from unregulated pure monopoly as the pessimal arrangement to perfect competition as the ideal, with relative efficiency in resource allocation increasing monotonically as the number of firms expands." Following this reasoning, merger prevention measures aimed at restricting market shares of individual firms, or constraints on collusive behavior among firms, have usually been placed at the core of traditional antimonopoly (competition promotion) policies.

If the logic of traditional economic theory is termed as the first accepted notion on competition and economic welfare, there exists a second notion in the Japanese context. This notion implies that competition is bad, cooperation is good. In Japan, particularly, the second notion is widely accepted and provides a strong justification for competition-restricting policies in the form of approving cartels and other government controls. According to Imai *et al.* (1972, Vol. 3, p. 255), ". . . in Japan, there is a traditional belief that 'competition' is bad and 'cooperation' or 'order' is good. In practice, there is a distinction between 'insiders' and 'outsiders'; severe competition among 'outsiders' is quite prevalent."

Those who espouse the second notion on competition and economic welfare, however, do not completely negate the role of competitive pressure as one of the basic conditions for efficient functioning of an economy. Nor do they deny the fact that introduction of new technologies and products, as a means of competition, is indispensable for the long-term progress of the economy. There is no dearth of examples indicating extensive bureaucratic waste and inefficiency when economic activity is placed under controls.

12.2 EXCESSIVE COMPETITION AND ECONOMIC POLICY

For those who encompass the second notion, the adage "doing in excess is as bad as not doing enough" is applicable to competition as well and believe that government intervention in industry organization is proper and justified if competition is so severe that benefits attained from competition in terms of national economic welfare fall short of losses in the form of national economic costs (Morozumi, 1966, p. 62). The concept of excessive competition, frequently referred to in general discussions on industrial and competition policies, is nothing but an extreme expression of such a view of competition. In postwar Japan, various forms of government intervention into the organization of industry and restrictions on the private sector have been affected in the name of excessive competition and are still being implemented.

To those who believe in the first notion, however, the concept of excessive competition is self-contradictory in itself.[2] Competition weans out the winners from the losers and it is impossible, in the process, to avoid some frictions and waste. This friction and waste is a social cost necessary to eliminate inefficient firms from the market and to shift resources from the industries that have become uncompetitive. Government intervention aimed at avoiding these costs preserves inefficiencies and has no effect other than an unnecessary delay in adjustments that are eventually unavoidable. This, in a nutshell, is the argument of adherents to the first notion.

A phenomenon like excessive competition has no place in the first notion of competition and economic welfare and policy intervention for such a purpose serves the interests only of the bureaucratic system itself. Only the competition-promotion policies have a meaning for efficiency in resource allocation and competition-limiting policies generate no social benefits.

The debate over the two notions, however, has not been necessarily dispassionate. Moreover, the theoretical underpinnings of these notions have not been theoretically confirmed. Taking the first notion, for example, there is a big gap between the intuitive reasoning behind the desirability of competition and the concept of perfect competition that sustains the basic theorem of welfare economics. This is because the concept of perfect competition, interpreted as the state in which firms are too small to affect market price, differs substantially from the concept which implies that existence of profitable opportunities give rise to vigorous competition to exploit such opportunities. In reality, it may be impossible for the firms under a certain minimum size to gather information on the existence of profitable opportunities and exploit them to earn profits.

As for the second notion, a plausible explanation of why and how excessive competition develops is as yet lacking. It is not enough just to say that competition is severe. The mechanism by which the severity of competition gives rise to an undesirable state of affairs, from the viewpoint of efficiency and equity of social resource allocation, is still unclear.

In view of the above discussion, formulation of a desirable economic policy, inclusive of social controls on the form of competition, requires an analysis of the effects of a change in the degree of competition, from the standpoint of social welfare interpreting the concept of competition fairly in the context of economic activity, and investigating into the theoretical relevance, if any, of the concept of excessive competition. In other words, decisions regarding whether competition is excessive and needs limitations, or whether it is too low and requires further enhancement, should be based on whether such intervention leads to improvement or deterioration of social welfare. A dispassionate and objective analysis of the concept of excessive competition in terms of the standard analytical tools of economic theory cannot only provide a basis for debate over competition policy but is also meaningful for determining which economic policy should be adopted.

12.3 PERFECT COMPETITION AND EFFICIENCY IN RESOURCE ALLOCATION

Let us consider the first notion. The reasoning behind this notion makes efficiency in resource allocation the standard to evaluate an economic system (or the main standard to evaluate social welfare). It is well known that product price, when perfect competition prevails, equals marginal costs and resource allocation is efficient. Product price, on the other hand, is the monetary representation of marginal benefit attained by the consumer from consumption of that product. The equality of consumer's marginal benefit and marginal cost ensures efficiency in resource allocation. Moreover, in a perfectly competitive industry, there is no hindrance to resource mobility, and free entry and exit lead to a production level that minimizes average costs.

However, a perfectly competitive industry is defined as an industry where individual firms have a negligible share of the overall market. From this point of view, large-sized firms are bad and the smaller the size of the firms, the better it is.

If the number of firms is small and the share of individual firms cannot be neglected, the firms are said to have monopoly power and a deviation between price and marginal cost emerges. The reason is that a profit-maximizing firm equates marginal revenue and marginal costs and there is a divergence between price and marginal revenue. The greater the divergence between prices, reflecting marginal benefit, and marginal costs, the greater the loss in allocational efficiency, and higher inefficiency results. The first notion, thus, is based on the belief that the larger the market share of a firm the higher the rate of divergence between price and marginal cost, and the greater this rate of divergence the greater the loss in social welfare.

For example, marginal revenue of firm i, producing a homogeneous good and engaged in Cournot competition using output strategy, is given by:

$$P(x_i + X_{-i}) + x_i P'(x_i + X_{-i}) = P(x_i + X_{-i})(1 + \theta_i \varepsilon)$$

$P(X)$, here, represents the inverse demand function when the industry output is given by X. x_i represents the output of firm i, X_{-i} is the total output of all firms other than i, θ_i is the share of firm i given as $x_i/(x_i + X_{-i})$, and ε is the inverse of price elasticity of demand $(x_i + X_{-i})P'(x_i + X_{-i})/P(x_i + X_{-i})$. Thus, we find that if the competitive structure is defined by Cournot competition with output strategy, divergence between price and marginal cost and, hence, inefficiency of resource allocation, is higher the higher the θ_i, the market share of firm i. It is the cognizance of this fact that sustains the first notion.

The perception that the rate of divergence is proportional to the market share of a firm, however, is applicable only to Cournot competition with output strategy only. This result cannot be easily extended to a different competitive form. This becomes quite clear if we consider Bertrand competition with price strategy, or the contestability theory that has drawn much attention recently.[3] Especially in the contestability theory, costless entry and exit and existence of potential entrants and hence potential competitive pressures lead to the most efficient resource allocation (Ramsey optimal) even when there is only a single firm in the market.

Thus, a case for desirability of smaller market shares for individual firms cannot be rested even on grounds of efficiency. This is because smaller firm size does not necessarily imply existence of competitive pressures. It is possible to visualize instances where sufficient competitive pressures develop only when firms are large sized.

Thus, for a proper understanding of competition and industrial policies from the standpoint of interfirm competition and for analyzing the concept of excessive competition within the framework of economic theory, it is necessary to take note of all aspects of these policies, in addition to the efficiency in resource allocation, that affect social welfare. The effects of productive efficiency and strategic factors on social welfare and the implications of dynamic competition are some of these aspects. The next section considers the implications of these factors in a framework where the assumption that a reduction in firm size lowers monopoly power and improves efficiency in resource allocation is granted.

12.4 SCALE ECONOMIES AND THE CONCEPT OF EFFICIENCY

First, it is not necessarily true that the firms increase their scale of production just because a higher market share gives them greater monopoly power. That is to say, economies of scale may be operative in industries where large-scale production facilities are an absolute necessity or where experience helps acquire ever-advanced technological levels. The implications of an increase in the scale of production intended to realize these economies are absolutely different from the increase in scale to acquire monopoly power.

It is easier to consider the role of scale economies by breaking up the criterion of efficiency in resource allocation into two subcriteria—(1) efficiency of resource allocation in a narrow sense and (2) production efficiency. As discussed earlier, monopoly power of a firm causes prices and marginal costs to diverge and gives rise to a dead weight loss. The traditional theory has implicitly assumed that existence of such divergence by itself gives rise to inefficiency in resource allocation. In the subsequent discussion, the problems rooted in divergence between price and marginal cost are referred to as "efficiency in resource allocation in the narrow sense."

First, the size of fixed costs is independent of marginal costs. This is because producing the same level of output in some industries may require investment in fixed costs equivalent to that of a number of firms taken together in another industry. If this industry has a large number of firms, the total resource requirements would be enormous. Thus, a small number of firms in this industry may, in fact, raise efficiency. Efficiency in this sense is reflected not in marginal but in average costs since average costs fall as the output of each firm rises. This is what we refer to as "production efficiency" in the ensuing discussion.

In the presence of scale economies, the higher the level of output of a firm (plant), the greater is the decline in average cost and the higher the production efficiency. Since the same output can be produced at a lower cost, the surplus productive resources can now be utilized in the production of other commodities, raising social welfare.

Thus, there exists a trade-off between an increase in efficiency in resource allocation in the narrow sense and a decline in production efficiency resulting from a rise in average cost of production as firm size is reduced. Whether or not the degree of competition in an industry, as reflected in market shares or firm size, is excessive from the viewpoint of the social welfare criterion depends on this trade-off. It is not easy, therefore, to make generalizations about whether to promote or restrict competition, at least in the industries where scale economies are important. It is only on the basis of economic theory that one can determine the conditions under which competition policies raise social welfare or when competition restriction policies are desirable.

Second, unlike the perfectly competitive industries where individual firms have only a negligible share in the market and hence do not affect the economic environment for other firms through their own behavior, oligopolistic industries show a high degree of interdependence and strategic behavior becomes important. The behavior of a firm in an oligopolistic industry is determined by the way it expects its rival to react to the change in its own behavior. It is, therefore, important for the firm to determine a behavioral strategy that forces the rival to adopt a behavioral pattern conforming to the interests of this firm.

These strategic considerations throw up postulates that are quite different from what has been proposed by the traditional economic theory. It is not obvious whether the firm behavior based on such strategic considerations leads the oligopolistic firms toward excessive or too little competition. In this context, too, a proper policy prescription requires a careful theoretical analysis.

Third, competition in the real world and the theoretical notion of competition (especially the static equilibrium theory that gives credence to the basic theorem of welfare economics) are, in some respects, as close to one another as water and oil. This is because in the economic world visualized by the static equilibrium theory, a profitable opportunity arises only at a certain given time. That is, the firms can use only price and cost variables to compete for such a profitable opportunity. The concept of dynamic competition over time, where the firms vie to gobble up the profitable opportunities before any one else can get to it, has no place in this interpretation.

In the real world, however, interfirm competition takes the form of marketing the products before the rivals can do it and at a lower price. Once the market has been lost to a rival, it is not easy to recoup it just by supplying the same commodity at a slightly lower price. In this sense, the economy visualized by the static equilibrium theory describes a state where "a state of affairs into which so many competing participants have already entered that no room remains for additional entry (or other modification of existing market conditions)." (Kirzner, 1973, p. 28). The concept of competition in the static equilibrium framework, thus, is the culmination of the process of competition among the firms and hence cannot deal with the dynamic path that the competitive process takes. That is why, in stressing the importance of the process of "constructive destruction," i.e., the process of dynamic competition based on breakthroughs in new products, development of new technology, discovery of new supply sources of productive factors, establishment of new forms of industrial organization—"sudden transformation of industry-revolutionizing economic structure from within"—over competition by way of "production processes, especially competition within the fixed classification determined by the assumption of unchanging form of industrial organization." Schumpeter, in fact, is pointing to the dynamic phenomena that cannot be fully handled within the framework of static equilibrium theory (Schumpeter, 1950, p. 153).

12.5 ORGANIZATION OF PART IV

In the background of the above discussion, Part IV attempts a piecemeal theoretical analysis of competition and economic welfare.

Chapter 13 considers whether promoting new entry into an oligopolistic industry improves economic welfare by itself or not. Promotion of new entry may lead to rising efficiency in resource allocation. At the same time, however, it also leads to a decline in output of each firm. If, as a result, average production cost rises, production efficiency deteriorates. In such a case, competition-restricting policy may raise economic welfare.

Chapter 14 discusses an extremely simplified case of strategic competition. When firms compete, knowing that an increase in investment leads to cost reductions, their investment activities are not undertaken just for reduction in costs. Since by increasing investment the firms can attain an advantage over their rivals, the firms tend to make investment decisions based on such strategic considerations.

The results of the analysis in these two chapters indicate that, given certain conditions, there is a tendency for entry and hence investment to become excessive. We, however, are not interested in emphasizing these results as such. The message we intend to put across to the reader through these results is that neither of the two notions mentioned earlier—that competition, especially perfect competition, leads the economy to the desired state or that competition is bad and subjugation of competition leads to the desired state—can be taken for granted. The reality lies somewhere in between. There is no clear-cut way to say whether competition should be promoted or restricted.

Taking its cue from these analyses, Chapter 15 deals not only with the question of whether competition should be promoted or restricted, but also tries to look into the form of competition that is desirable. The essence of competition is a fair and free competition for all profit and economic opportunities that arise. In this sense, policies concerning whether to promote or to restrict competition, by intervening in competition being conducted in a free and fair manner, have exactly the same competition-restricting effects. A proper competition policy should aim at avoiding social waste from excessive or too little competition while ensuring free and fair competition for profit and economic opportunities (equal opportunity principle). One of the major objectives of this chapter is to show that efforts to directly intervene in the process of competition and putting controls on the free and fair use of economic opportunities can, in itself, induce excessive competition.

Dynamic competition over time is also briefly discussed in Chapter 15 but we leave the details for Chapter 18 in Part V of this book.

NOTES

1. For more details of the basic theorem on welfare economics, see, for example, Okuno and Suzumura (1988, Part IV).

2. For example, Bronfenbrenner (1966, p. 114) writes: "To an economist raised, like myself, in an orthodox tradition, the visceral reaction to *kato kyoso* talk is 'Impossible!' and the subsequent intellectual reaction is extreme suspicion."

3. For contestability theory, see Bauoml, Panzar, and Willig (1982) or Okuno and Suzumura (1988, Part V).

13

Economic Implications of Entry-Restriction Policies

This chapter critically analyzes the accepted notion that increasing competition raises economic welfare, by analyzing the effect on economic welfare of new entry in an oligopolistic industry.

To do this, we take recourse to a Cournot oligopoly setting with a homogeneous product and where the new (old) firms can enter (exit) freely. The potential entrants into the industry can be visualized as, first, making a decision on whether to enter or not and then, if they decide to enter, considering the level of output they want to produce. Each player in this two-stage game, where the decision to enter constitutes stage 1 and the decision on the level of output to produce is stage 2, needs to make an informed guess about equilibrium profits that are likely to emerge in stage 2 in case the firm decides to enter, before choosing its strategy for stage 1. Keeping this point in mind, we begin by inquiring into the nature of equilibrium emerging at stage 2 of the game.

13.1 EQUILIBRIUM IN A COURNOT OLIGOPOLY WITH N FIRMS

Let us assume that there are n firms, with an identical technology represented by the cost function $C(x)$, contemplating to enter this industry. Here, x is the output of the homogeneous product. The average costs, defined as $AC(x) = C(x)/x$ for the cost function $C(x)$, are assumed to be decreasing such that

$$AC'(x) < 0 \tag{1}$$

holds. This assumption can be justified if we assume that the industry in question has high fixed costs due to large-scale production equipment required and, hence, is characterized by substantial economies of scale.

The inverse demand function for the product in question, with industry output at X and market price p, is given by $P(\ )$ as follows.

$$p = P(X) \qquad [P'(X) < 0] \tag{2}$$

Now, the profit function $\pi_i(\ )$ for firm i $(i = 1 \ldots n)$ can be defined as

$$\pi_i(x_i, X_{-i}) = P(x_i + X_{-i})x_i - C(x_i) \tag{3}$$

151

Here, x_i is the level of output produced by firm i and $X_{-i} = \Sigma_{j \neq i} x_j$ is the combined output of all firms other than i.

It is clear that profits of firm i decline as output of its rivals rises. If the output level of the rival firms X_{-i} is large enough, firm i necessarily faces a loss whatever the level of output it chooses. In practice, this result can be easily verified if scale economies, as defined in Eq. (1), result from high fixed costs. Noting this, we assume that the following condition holds:

$$\text{If } X_{-i} > (X_{-i})_0, \text{ max } _{x_i} \pi_i(x_i, X_{-i}) < 0 \tag{4}$$

That is, if the rival firms are already producing at a level above $(X_{-i})_0$, firm i necessarily earns a negative profit.

Now, assume that individual firms maximize profits using Cournot conjectures. Since all firms are symmetric, the reaction functions $r_i(X_{-i})$ thus determined must be the same for all the firms. This allows us to use the same notation $r( )$ for the reaction functions of individual firms. By definition, these reaction functions must satisfy[1]

$$\text{For } X_{-i} \leq (X_{-i})_0, \qquad r(X_{-i}) = x_i \tag{5a}$$

[note that x_i satisfies $\partial \pi_i(x_i, X_{-i}) / \partial x_i = P(x_i + X_{-i}) + P'(x_i + X_{-i})x_i - C'(x_i) = 0$]

$$\text{For } X_{-i} > (X_{-i})_0, \qquad r(X_{-i}) = 0 \tag{5b}$$

We continue to assume, as has been done previously in this book, that the firm strategies are strategic substitutes and the slope of reaction functions for individual firms is less than unity. That is, we assume that following condition holds[2]:

$$\text{For } X_{-i} \leq (X_{-i})_0, \qquad 0 > r'(X_{-i}) > -1 \tag{6}$$

This ensures that the Cournot–Nash equilibrium configuration $(x_1^*, \ldots, x_n^*)$, as defined below, is stable for the process of Cournot adjustments. Under these assumptions, the reaction function for a firm i, as represented by Eqs. (5a) and (5b), can be drawn as the kinked curve $X_{-i}(X_{-i})_0 ab$ in Fig. 13-1. A move from point b to a, along this reaction function, implies a fall in the profits earned by the firm i—from monopoly profits to a zero profit.

In an oligopolistic market composed of more than three firms, it is easier to determine the Cournot–Nash equilibrium by redefining an individual firm's reaction function $x_i = r(X_{-i})$ in terms of total industry output using the relation $x_i + X_{-i} = X$. If this redefined reaction function is expressed by $x_i = R(X)$, $R( )$ satisfies

$$R(X) = r[X - R(X)] \tag{7a}$$

which, in turn, can be defined as a function satisfying

$$P(X) + P'(X)R(X) - C'[R(X)] = 0 \tag{7b}$$

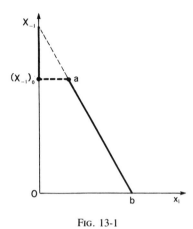

FIG. 13-1

especially when $R(X) > 0$. Note that for $R(X) > 0$, the slope of the reaction function, from Eq. (7a) satisfies

$$R'(X) = r'[X - R(X)]/\{1 + r'[X - R(X)]\} < 0 \qquad (8)$$

The negative sign on the right-hand side of this equation, from Eq. (6), is due to strategic substitutability of firm strategies. Moreover, the reaction function R shows the same properties as reaction function r (drawn in Fig. 13-1), and is kinked as depicted by the curve XX_0AB in Fig. 13-2. Note that, since $X_0 = (X_{-i})_0 + r[(X_{-i})_0]$, at point A the representative firm earns zero profit.

Having done the ground work, the Nash equilibrium for the Cournot competition at stage 2 of the game with n firms can be determined simply as follows. Since the individual firms are symmetric, the Cournot–Nash equilibrium that

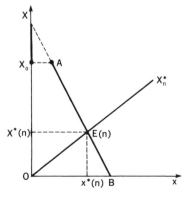

FIG. 13-2

emerges is also symmetric. Hence, the equilibrium can be defined, in relation to the total number of firms n and output of the representative firm $x^*(n)$ as $[n^*, x^*(n)]$. If total industry output in equilibrium is $X^*(n)$, the equilibrium $[n^*, x^*(n)]$ must satisfy the following conditions:

$$X^*(n) = nx^*(n) \tag{9a}$$
$$x^*(n) = R[X^*(n)] \tag{9b}$$

Figure 13-2 is the diagrammatic representation of the Cournot–Nash equilibrium thus obtained. Curve XX_0AB is the reaction function $R(\ )$ of the representative firm and the straight line OX_n^*, with slope given by the number of firms, depicts the relationship between output of the representative firm and total industry output corresponding to Eq. (8). The equilibrium with n firms in the industry is defined by $E(n)$, the point of intersection between the two curves. The profits earned by individual firms in equilibrium are determined solely by the number of firms in the industry. If $\pi^*(n)$ represents profits in equilibrium, $\pi^*(n)$ must, by definition, satisfy

$$\pi^*(n) = p^*(n)x^*(n) - C[x^*(n)] = \{p^*(n) - \mathrm{AC}[x^*(n)]\}x^*(n) \tag{10}$$

assuming $p(n) = P[X^*(n)]$.

13.2 FREE-ENTRY COURNOT EQUILIBRIUM

The previous section discussed Cournot oligopoly equilibrium with a fixed number of firms. In this section, we deal with the properties of equilibrium that emerges in stage 1 of the game, i.e., when a firm makes a decision on whether to enter the industry or not, aware in advance of the fact that the stage 2 subgame results in equilibrium.

Figure 13-3 is a reproduction of Fig. 13-2. If there are n firms in the industry to begin with, the equilibrium point is given by point $E(n)$. Since this point lies below point A, individual firms earn a positive excess profit. If every firm is fully aware of this situation, and there are only n firms existing in the industry, new entry is induced. Consequently, the number of firms in the industry expands, moving the straight line OX_n^* in an anticlockwise direction. This results in the following changes.

First, the equilibrium level of output produced by individual firms declines. Since the new entrants bring additional output to the market, the output of the existing firms declines. This results from strategic substitutability of the firm strategies.

Second, total industry output rises and market price falls. Although output of the existing firms declines with new entry, the decline falls short of the increased output by the newly entered firms. This result is explained by the forward-falling reaction function of the representative firm as depicted in Eq. (8). Since the nega-

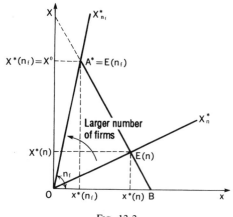

FIG. 13-3

tive sign on $R'(X)$ in Eq. (8) follows from Eq. (6), the above result, in the last analysis, can be attributed to the stability condition.

Third, since equilibrium in the stage 2 subgame shifts up to the left along XX_0AB, the reaction function of the representative firm, it can be easily seen that output and, hence, profits of the representative firm decline. That is, total industry output, following the second property above, rises, causing the market price to fall. This reduces the maximum profit that individual firms can obtain.

If the number of firms in the industry can be depicted by continuous real numbers,[3] entry of new firms and exit by the existing firms stops when the number of firms exactly equals the slope of the straight line $OX_{n_f}^*$. This is because A depicts the equilibrium point for stage 2 of the game and all the firms earn zero profits. If n_f is the number of firms in this situation, the equilibrium of the game encompassing decisions to enter or exit freely—the free-entry equilibrium below—can be defined, in relation to number of firms n_f and output of the representative firm in the new situation $x^*(n_f)$, as $[n_f, x^*(n_f)]$. By definition, such an equilibrium must satisfy the following conditions:

$$X^*(n_f) = n_f x^*(n_f) \tag{11a}$$
$$x^*(n_f) = R[X^*(n_f)] \tag{11b}$$
$$\pi^*(n_f) = \{P[X^*(n_f)] - AC[x^*(n_f)]\}x^*(n_f) = 0 \tag{11c}$$

Finally, since the average cost curve for individual firms is forward falling as shown by Eq. (1), note that the firms in the free-entry equilibrium do not exhaust the scale economies completely.

In the subsequent discussion, the number of firms in the free-entry equilibrium n_f is referred to as the equilibrium number of firms since this corresponds to the number of firms in the long-run equilibrium under the conditions of perfectly free entry and exit.

The next section uses the Cournot oligopoly framework to discuss the effect of competition-promotion policies on economic welfare.

13.3 ENTRY RESTRICTION AND ECONOMIC WELFARE

Granting, for the sake of discussion, the notion that increasing competition raises economic welfare, an increase in the number of firms, as compared to the number of firms in the oligopolistic equilibrium determined in the previous section, should further raise economic welfare. This follows from the above notion stating that restricting new entry to blunt intraindustry competition is undesirable on the grounds of economic welfare.

In the following, we assume that government has relatively weak regulatory power over the industry. That is, we assume that the government, having given a free hand to the firms in the oligopolistic industry to follow a profit-maximizing behavior, retains the power to regulate the entry of new firms and exit of the existing firms only on the basis of economic welfare considerations.

There are two reasons for placing such restrictions on the powers of the government. First, the very fact that the government can regulate firm behavior in an oligopolistic industry is fraught with the danger of generating serious distortions in resource allocation. For example, if new entry into the industry is restricted, the existing firms will no longer feel threatened by potential entry. These existing firms, therefore, can jack up the market price without any fear of inducing new entry. Moreover, since the existing members are fixed, cartelization becomes easier. Regulating output levels of and prices charged by the existing firms can give rise to still serious distortions in resource allocation. For example, if the government can intervene in the decisions regarding output level, individual firms will tend to invest resources in lobbying activity to get a production quota most favorable to themselves. This form of rent seeking is nothing but waste of resources from a social viewpoint.[4]

It is the possibility of the distorting effect of regulations that makes us limit government regulatory powers only to entry and exit decisions of a firm.

The policies adopted (even under ideal conditions) by a second best government, in the sense that its powers are limited, cannot be first best policies. It may be possible, for an ideal government (one that keeps the undesirable side effects discussed in the earlier paragraphs), to achieve economic results that a second best government cannot hope to attain by carefully distinguishing between regulation of entry–exit and price–output decisions. But, here, we have a theoretical pitfall.

For the sake of argument, assume that the performance of free oligopolistic competition, as compared to the performance under ideal government regulation, leaves something to be desired from the viewpoint of economic welfare. This fact, by itself, cannot serve as a justification for government policy intervention in the real world since the governments, in reality, are not ideal. In other words, government regulations that serve as a reference point for discussion over whether competition is excessive or too little in the context of industrial and competition policies are necessarily second best. This is the second reason for limiting the regulatory powers of the government in our model.

Following the conventions of standard partial equilibrium analysis, welfare judgments in our model are made with reference to total social surplus W, the sum of the consumer surplus CS, and the producer surplus PS. In an industry with n firms, and equilibrium output for the stage 2 subgame defined by $X^*(n)$, Eq. (12) gives the consumer surplus as

$$CS = CS(n) = \int^{X^*(n)} P(z)dz - P^*(n)X^*(n) \tag{12}$$

Furthermore, the producer surplus, since it is the sum of profits earned by all the firms operating in this industry, is given by

$$PS = PS(n) = n\pi^*(n) = P^*(n)X^*(n) - nC[x^*(n)] \tag{13}$$

Total surplus, therefore, is given by

$$CS(n) + PS(n) = \int^{X^*(n)} P(z)dz - nC[x^*(n)] \tag{14}$$

Can competition promotion, through policy-induced new entry in this oligopolistic industry by a second best government, raise economic welfare? The answer to this question is provided by an examination of the effect of a change in number of firms on total surplus.

As seen in the previous section, an increase in the number of firms in an industry changes the output level of each firm, total industry output, and prices. Representing the changes in these variables by Δn, Δx, ΔX, and Δp, respectively, we determine the changes in the consumer surplus, the producer surplus, and the total surplus (represented by ΔCS, ΔPS, and ΔW, respectively).

Let us, first, consider changes in consumer surplus ΔCS. As the number of firms in the industry increases as a result of new entry, the existing firms' control over price setting weakens and market price falls ($\Delta p < 0$). The increase in consumer surplus, in this case, is nearly proportional to the amount of consumption before the fall in price. Thus, change in consumer surplus can be represented as

$$\Delta CS = X(-\Delta p) \tag{15}$$

The change in producer surplus ΔPS, on the other hand, is composed of the change in the profits earned by the existing firms ($n\Delta\pi$) and profits earned by new entrants [$\pi^*(n)\Delta n$].

$$\Delta PS = n\Delta\pi + \pi^*(n)\Delta n$$

The first term on the right-hand side can be further broken up into two components. First, we have the change in profits resulting from a change in output of each firm. This change in profits is proportional to the difference between $P^*(n)$, the market price of a marginal unit increase in output, and the marginal cost $C'[x^*(n)]$. That is, the profits change by $\{P^*(n) - C'[x^*(n)]\}\Delta x$. The second component is composed of changes in profit as a result of a change in price induced by new entry. The change in profits as a result of a change in sales price is proportional to output being produced before the change occurred. For individual firms, this equals $x^*(n)\Delta p$. Thus, total change in profits of all the existing firms taken together is given by

$$n\Delta\pi = n\{P^*(n) - C'[x^*(n)]\}\Delta x + X^*(n)\Delta p$$

Thus, the change in producer surplus ΔPS can be depicted as follows:

$$\Delta\text{PS} = n\{P^*(n) - C'[x^*(n)]\}\Delta x + X^*(n)\Delta p + \pi^*(n)\Delta n \qquad (16)$$

From Eqs. (14), (15), and (16), change in total surplus can be determined as

$$\Delta W = \Delta\text{CS} + \Delta\text{PS}$$
$$= n\{P^*(n) - C'[x^*(n)]\}\Delta x + \pi^*(n)\Delta n \qquad (17)$$

The first term on the right-hand side of Eq. (17) gives the resource-allocation effect while the second term reflects the increase in total profits as a result of new entry or, in other words, the competition-promotion effect.

Let us now consider if new entry by an additional firm, in a free-entry equilibrium, raises welfare. From Eq. (17), it is clear that the competition-promotion effect represented by the second term is zero if the initial equilibrium is a free-entry equilibrium ($n = n_f$). This result follows from Eq. (11c), which states that all firms earn zero profits under a free-entry equilibrium. Therefore, competition promotion affects economic welfare only through the resource-allocation effect. It is amply clear from the discussion in the previous section that this resource-allocation effect is negative.[5] Thus, promotion of new entry causes a decline in economic welfare, a result at loggerheads with the prescription of the traditional theory of industrial organization.

In the case of strategic substitutes, under consideration, a rise in the number of new rivals concomitant on new entry results in a reduction of output produced by individual firms. The benefits arising from scale economies, which are already being underutilized by the individual firms operating in a free-entry equilibrium, are further reduced. This leads to an increase in social cost of producing the product in question. That is, overlapping investment in entry costs reduces social welfare.

Thus, in an oligopoly with homogeneous products characterized by scale economies, entry by new firms over and above the number viable for a free-entry equilibrium leads to a reduction, rather than an increase, in total surplus generated. Economic welfare, instead, can be raised by restricting the number of firms below the viable number for a free-entry equilibrium. Put differently, when a government, having no control over price–output decisions of the firms but which can regulate entry and exit, tries to maximize economic welfare, the optimal number of firms (second best number of firms) falls short of the equilibrium number of firms. Hence, the following theorem, known as the excess-entry theorem, is established.[6]

> When the products produced and supplied in an oligopolistic market are strategic substitutes, restricting the number of firms to less than that viable under free-entry equilibrium raises economic welfare.

13.4 EXCESS-ENTRY THEOREM AND ITS ECONOMIC INTERPRETATION

The analysis in the previous section indicated that in an oligopolistic industry characterized by scale economies there is a tendency for the number of firms to become too numerous from the point of view of economic welfare. How realistic is this excess-entry theorem?

Assuming linear variable cost and inverse demand functions and allowing the fixed cost to decline, the equilibrium and optimum number of firms were calculated.[7] As shown in Table 13-1, the equilibrium as well as the optimum number of firms rises as fixed costs decline. Furthermore, the difference between the two rises at a much faster pace, indicating that tendency for excessive entry gets stronger the lower the fixed cost.

As shown in the last column of Table 13-1, welfare loss due to excess entry is as high as 8%. As fixed costs decline, the corresponding welfare loss, as a percentage of total surplus, gradually declines from 7.8 to 5.2 to 3.8%. These calculations assume an extremely static form of firm competition. In the case of dynamic competition over time, the welfare loss may well be the unavoidable social cost needed to preserve dynamic efficiency such as technological innovation. Furthermore, following the analysis in this chapter, if the number of firms in an industry is found to be excessive at some point in time and new entry is regulated, degree of competition in the industry may decline as existing firms form tacit cartels or no longer feel threatened by new entry.

TABLE 13-1

Optimum number of firms	Equilibrium number of firms	Loss in welfare (%)
3	7	7.8
5	13	5.2
8	26	3.8

The argument that the government enforces its regulatory powers for any and every oligopolistic industry, taking the excess-entry theorem on its face value, begs a number of other questions, besides those mentioned above.

First, our analysis is couched in terms of Cournot oligopoly and deals with strategic substitutes only and the excess-entry theorem fails to hold for an oligopolistic industry with strategic complements. In this case, the first term in Eq. (17), giving the effect of new entry on economic welfare, i.e., the resource-allocation effect, is positive. This follows from the fact that in the case of strategic substitutes, increase in industry output as a result of new entry increases the output level for each firm. Economic welfare considerations, in this case, imply that the government should promote new entry even by granting subsidies.

Second, even in the case of strategic substitutes, the effect of new entry on economic welfare may be understated by Eq. (17) if the oligopolistic industry is characterized by quality differences. The reason is that qualitative differences in goods and services produced by individual firms give rise to an additional source of social benefits from new entry in the form of product diversity. In modern economies characterized by a fast pace of technological innovation, it is quite possible for new entrants, even in the industries which have traditionally produced homogeneous products, to market new products that differ from available products in that these embody new technology and knowledge. *Ex ante* entry restrictions, in this case, can stifle the emergence of socially beneficial new products and the society foregoes the benefits of an increased diversity in consumption.

Third, one may refer to the limited capacity of the government to gather information necessary to regulate entry. In the context of the problem of qualitative differences in goods and services as discussed above, effective regulation of new entry by the government requires accurate prior information on whether the existing industry is an oligopoly producing a homogeneous product or an oligopoly producing qualitatively different products. Even when the new entry is to be regulated, decisions regarding the number of firms to be allowed in an industry require substantial and detailed information.

As discussed above, the regulatory authorities cannot make a decision, just on the basis of the fact that the industry in question presently produces a homogeneous product. They must determine whether or not the industry will continue to produce such a homogeneous product in future. Effective entry regulation becomes possible, including this point, only if there is prior information on technological opportunities available to the firms, including the potential entrants, over time and also on the possible future changes in consumer preferences. We are quite skeptical about the ability of government to collect all the information accurately.

Fourth, entry restrictions emphasized in the excess-entry theorem raise important issues from the viewpoint of equitable distribution. This theorem states that a free-entry equilibrium number of firms exceeds the optimum, making it socially desirable to restrict the number of firms. If so, which of the existing firms should be made to exit? The process through which each firm passed before gaining entry into the industry may differ from firm to firm but it remains a fact that every one of the existing firms is a winner in the interfirm competition. It is impossible to determine which one of these firms is inferior and therefore to be eliminated. If, somehow, such a distinction is made, the basis of discrimination must be unfair to the firm called upon to exit.

The problem of distribution also emerges among the consumers and the producers. Welfare improvement by regulating entry was seen to result from greater exploitation of scale economies as the existing firms increased their output. However, from another perspective, this leads to a reduction in consumer surplus since it raises market price by reducing total industry output. The welfare increase concomitant upon entry regulation arises because the rise in producer surplus outweighs the decline in consumer surplus. It is difficult to say whether consumers will accept a policy protecting producers at the cost of consumers.

Taking everything into consideration, a defense of the excessive competition argument based on a one-sided interpretation of the excess-entry theorem and indiscriminate restriction of interfirm competition could be dangerous. The real significance of this theorem does not lie in justifying entry regulation but in the fact that it shows that the notions supported by traditional theory of industrial organization do not necessarily hold under all circumstances.

NOTES

1. In the subsequent discussion we assume that a firm produces a positive output when profits are zero. This is absolutely a simplifying assumption and has essentially no effect on the analysis.

2. This assumption automatically holds if the market demand function is linear and if the products supplied by each firm are substitutes in the normal sense. This, however, does not stand for a market demand function with constant price elasticity. For a detailed discussion of this point, see Bulow, Geanakoplos, and Klemperer (1985).

3. Using continuous numbers to represent the number of firms does not have any significant impact on the essence of the subsequent discussion. The minor adjustments necessitated if the number of firms is constrained to be a natural number are discussed in Suzumura and Kiyono (1987).

4. For a discussion of problems associated with government controls, see Chapter 16.

5. Denoting average cost function, when the output level is x, by AC (x), the resource-allocation effect can be rewritten, using the well-known relational function $C'(x) = AC(x) + xAC'(x)$, as

$$\{P^*(n) - C'[x^*(n)]\}\Delta x = \{P^*(n) - AC[x^*(n)]\}\Delta x - x^*(n)AC'[x^*(n)]\Delta x$$
$$= -x^*(n)AC'[x^*(n)]\Delta x$$

The last of these equations follows from the fact that in a free-entry equilibrium, the profit is zero and price equals average cost. This transformation shows that the negative sign on the resource-allocation effect derives from the fact that average costs decline ($\Delta x < 0$), that is, due to the existence of scale economies. The essence of the resource-allocation effect lies in the fact that scale economies in an oligopolistic industry are not exhausted even in a free-entry equilibrium.

6. The excess-entry theorem, in fact, is composed of the following two propositions: (1) If the government can fully control the price–output and entry–exit decisions of the firms, the first best number of firms for maximizing economic welfare falls short of the equilibrium number of firms in a free-entry equilibrium. (2) If the government can control only the entry–exit decisions of the firms, the second best number of firms for maximizing economic welfare is less than the equilibrium number of firms.

The excess-entry theorem discussed below corresponds to proposition (2) above. For a detailed discussion, the reader is referred to Suzumura and Kiyono (1987), Kiyono (1986), Mankiw and Whinston (1986), and Perry (1984).

7. Here we depend on Mankiw and Whinston (1986).

14

Investment Competition and Policy Intervention

14.1 INVESTMENT COMPETITION AS A FORM OF EXCESSIVE COMPETITION

The last chapter considered the possibility of excessive competition emerging in the form of an equilibrium number of firms in oligopolistic competition exceeding the number of firms needed to maximize economic welfare in an industry characterized by scale economies in production technology. It was shown that there is a distinct possibility for the number of firms to be too numerous in the limited sense that economic welfare is higher with free competition among a restricted number of firms, if the number of firms can be regulated through entry restriction policies, than under free competition with free entry. Besides the discussion, in the previous chapter, regarding the extent to which the existence of the concept of excessive competition, as described above, is related to the real economy, especially to the postwar Japanese debate over excessive competition, there are a number of other aspects which need further probing.

It is true that the term "excessive competition" has also been used to imply an excessive number of firms in an industry. More often than not, the concept is used to represent a phenomenon (or apprehension) whereby economic welfare for the society as a whole is lowered on account of overzealous production, investment or price strategies adopted by individual firms that lead to lower profits, not only for the other firms in the industry but also for the firms themselves.

With this in mind, a proper understanding of the concept of excessive competition in the real world needs an investigation into the possibility, or otherwise, that severe competition in, say, investment or research and development activities leads to excessive investment or research and development from the viewpoint of welfare of the economy as a whole. It is especially important to consider if the social excess in these activities is the result of strategic firm behavior taking the behavior of other firms explicitly into account. The present chapter tries to determine whether the investment activity, in an industry in which new entry is restricted due to some unspecified reason, tends to be excessive or too little and, if excessive, under what circumstances.

163

14.2 A Two-Stage Game Including Investment Competition

We assume each firm to produce a homogeneous product. In contrast to the previous chapter, there is no free entry or exit due to the existence of entry barriers and there are n firms operating in the industry. The industry is characterized by a two-stage competitive process. At the first stage, the firms compete for the level of investment. Competition at the second stage is for output levels based on cost conditions emerging as a result of investment competition at stage one. Further, we assume that the government has no policy control over the level of output and leaves it to be determined by competitive forces. It, however, has policy control over levels of investment, the precondition for production activity. Does the government need to increase, or decrease, investment levels to raise social welfare? Investment competition may be considered excessive if a reduction in investment raises social welfare, and insufficient if social welfare rises with an increase in investment.

Let us consider the following model. $P(X)$ is the inverse demand function for the industry in question, with X representing total industry output and $P(X)$ its price. All firms have similar second stage (related to production) cost functions $C(x, K) = c(K)x$, where x is the output level of the given firm and K is the amount of investment (in first stage). Given K, the investment level $c(K)$, the marginal cost of production, is a constant. The subsequent discussion assumes that marginal cost $c(K)$ satisfies $c'(K) < 0$ and, hence, declines as K rises. It follows that by increasing the level of investment in the first stage, the firm improves its competitive position in stage 2 as its marginal costs decline. It goes without saying that investment level in stage 1 is a commitment made by the firm before production is started and cannot be changed later (in stage 2).

The firms engage in stage 2 competition (subgame) using output strategies constrained by the combination of investment levels $\mathbf{K} = (K_1 \ldots K_n)$ selected in stage one, and the outcome of this competition is given by Cournot equilibrium. That is, an individual firm i tries to maximize its quasi-rents (or revenue less costs of production)

$$\pi_i(x_i, x_{-i}) = P(x_i + x_{-i})x_i - c(K_i)x_i \tag{1}$$

where $x_{-i} = \Sigma_{j \neq i} x_j$. The output combination, emerging as a result of each firm trying to maximize its own quasi profits, taking the output of its rivals as given, is the Nash equilibrium of the given subgame. Let us represent this combination as a function of the combination of investment levels as $\mathbf{x}^*(\mathbf{K}) = [x_1^*(\mathbf{K}), x_2^*(\mathbf{K}) \ldots x_n^*(\mathbf{K})]$.

Figure 14-1 represents stage 2 competition for a two-firm ($n = 2$) case. That is, given the level of investment (K_1, K_2) selected in stage 1, intersection of the reaction functions of the two firms, point N, gives the Cournot equilibrium. Now, Fig. 14-1 has been drawn for the case of linear demand functions and, in

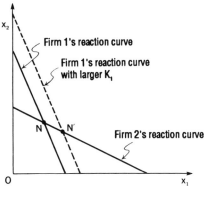

FIG. 14-1

the subsequent discussion, we assume the Nash equilibrium to satisfy the stability condition, namely, the absolute slope of the reaction functions of the two firms is less than unity.

Let us assume that firm 1 increases its investment level K_1 in stage 1. Its reaction function, reflecting an improvement in its competitive position, shifts to the right. As a result, firm 1 output level in the new (stage 2) equilibrium rises while firm 2 output falls. This is obvious since Fig. 14-1 depicts the case of forward-falling reaction functions for both the firms, i.e., the strategies (output) of the two firms are strategic substitutes. Increased investment, in this case, while making firm 1 more offensive, makes firm 2 more defensive.[1] In the process, quasiprofits for firm 1 rise and those for firm 2 fall. Moreover, total industry output, as long as the reaction functions satisfy stability conditions, unequivocally rises.[2]

Each firm tries to determine its investment level at stage 1 by guessing the Nash equilibrium expected to emerge as the result of the stage 2 subgame. Selecting the units properly we can use K_i to represent the costs incurred by firm i for an investment level K_i. Firm i, then, tries to maximize its total profits over the two stages,

$$\Pi_i[x_i^*(\mathbf{K}), K_i)] = P[X^*(\mathbf{K})]x_i^*(\mathbf{K}) - C[x_i^*(\mathbf{K}), K_i] - K_i \qquad (2)$$

where $X^*(\mathbf{K}) = \Sigma_{i=1}^{n} x_i^*(\mathbf{K})$. Let us represent the resulting (perfect Nash) equilibrium by $\mathbf{K}^* = (K_1^* \ldots K_n^*)$. Since all the firms have the same cost functions and are symmetric, we can expect the perfect Nash equilibrium also to be symmetric and $K_i^* = K_j^*(i, j = 1 \ldots n)$ to hold. Again, stage 2 equilibrium output is also assumed to be symmetric such that $x_i^*(\mathbf{K}) = x_j^*(\mathbf{K})$, $(i, j = 1 \ldots n)$, holds.

Let us briefly interpret strategic behavior in the context of the type of competition being discussed in this section. By strategic behavior, here, we imply that the firm, while taking a decision on its level of investment at stage 1, foresees the effect of such investment on the behavior of the other firms in stage 2. Thus, firm i, while opting for investment level K_i, knows that firm j will select its stage 2 output level in the form of $x_j^*(\mathbf{K})$, and maximizes its profits taking this factor into account.

If this firm does not engage in strategic behavior, it follows that the firm does not consider its investment decisions to have any effect on the output by other firms. In other words, investment decisions of a firm that does not engage in strategic behavior take the investment levels as well as the second stage output levels of other firms as given. Such a firm, thus, acts on the assumption that its own investment decisions do not affect the investment and output of other firms.

14.3 CHANGES IN INVESTMENT LEVELS AND SOCIAL WELFARE: RESOURCE-ALLOCATION EFFECT

Social welfare, in an oligopolistic equilibrium, can be determined as the sum of consumer and producer surpluses. Social welfare $W(\mathbf{K})$, when investment configuration $\mathbf{K} = (K_1 \ldots K_n)$, is given by

$$W(\mathbf{K}) = \int_0^{X^*(\mathbf{K})} P(X)dx - P[X^*(\mathbf{K})]X^*(\mathbf{K})$$
$$+ \sum_{i=1}^n \{P[X^*(\mathbf{K})]x_i^*(\mathbf{K}) - C[x_i^*(\mathbf{K}), K_i] - K_i\} \qquad (3)$$

The sum of the first two terms on the right gives the consumer surplus while the third term represents the total industry profits, i.e., producer surplus.

Let us now consider how social welfare changes if a single firm i, in the oligopolistic equilibrium configuration $\mathbf{K}^* = (K_1^* \ldots K_n^*)$, raises its investment level K_i. The changes occurring in this situation can be divided in two. First, social welfare is affected by a change in output concomitant upon a change in investment level. Second, there is a direct effect of a change in investment level on the firm concerned (both on the investment as well as production costs).[3] The former of these effects is referred to as the "resource allocation effect" and the latter as the "strategic effect" of investment. The reasons for using this terminology are self-evident from the analysis that follows.

First, as for the resource allocation effect, the analysis of the previous chapter can be directly applied. That is, if we represent prices, output, and marginal costs, before the change in investment is affected, by P, X, and MC, change in prices by ΔP, changes in quantity demanded = change in total output by ΔX, the change in consumer surplus ΔCS can be approximated by the difference between the change in total benefits $\int P(Y)dY$, equivalent to $P\Delta X$, received by the consumer, and the change in total expenditure given by $P\Delta X + X\Delta P$. Thus, we can write

$$\Delta \text{CS} = P\Delta X - (P\Delta X + X\Delta P) \qquad (4)$$

The change in producers' surplus (quasirent, or receipts less production costs) in stage 2, on the other hand, is given by the difference between the change in receipts $P\Delta X + X\Delta P$ and the change in production costs $MC\Delta X$:

$$\Delta PS = (P\Delta X + X\Delta P) - MC\Delta X \qquad (5)$$

Adding Eqs. (4) and (5), we get

$$\text{Resource allocation effect} = (P - MC)\Delta X \qquad (6)$$

As discussed in the previous chapter, marginal revenue of an oligopolistic firm, on account of its monopoly power, is lower than the price. Since in such an industry marginal revenue = marginal cost, prices in an oligopolistic equilibrium are above the marginal costs. That is, marginal benefits derived by the consumer from additional output of the product exceed the marginal costs of producing such output. The behavior of an oligopolistic firm—maximizing private profits by restricting output and raising prices—generates distorted (inefficient) resource allocation and socially desirable additional output does not come forth.

Thus, the resource-allocation effect ultimately depends on the sign of ΔX, or $\partial X^*/\partial K_i$. As was seen in Fig. 14-1, an increase in investment by a single firm led to a rise in output of the industry as a whole. Thus, the resource-allocation effect (as long as the equilibrium satisfies the stability condition) is always positive. That is, increased investment by a firm raises social welfare if the resource-allocation effect is the only consideration.

Thus, we find that the resource-allocation effect results in a less than socially optimum investment. This fact is also amply clear from the behavior of oligopolistic (or monopolistic) firms as we know them. That is, output in the competitive equilibrium in an oligopolistic industry is invariably below the socially optimal levels since each firm tries to raise prices using its monopoly powers. Low output leads to weaker incentives for cost reduction and, hence, investment is also low. A policy to raise investment levels, in this case, improves social welfare.

14.4 CHANGES IN INVESTMENT LEVELS AND SOCIAL WELFARE: STRATEGIC EFFECT

The strategic effect, on the other hand, refers to the changes in the behavior of other firms in stage 2 in response to the change in investment level by a given firm at stage 1. Conversely, the strategic effect is nothing but the difference between the direct effect of a unit increase in investment, i.e., reduction in production costs concomitant upon increased investment $-\Delta C$ and an increase in investment costs resulting from the increase in investment. Thus,

$$\text{Strategic effect} = -\Delta C - 1$$

If each firm believes that the behavior of its rivals will not change whatever it does to its own investment level (i.e., ignores strategic considerations) the strategic effect is bound to be zero. This follows from the fact that each firm, ignoring strategic considerations, will choose an investment level where reduction in its (own) production costs as a result of additional investment $-\Delta C$ is equated with the costs of such an investment.

But in the model of strategic competition being considered here, the investment decisions of a firm are guided not only by cost considerations but also by strategic considerations. An increased investment by a firm in stage 1 raises its output in stage 2 equilibrium at the cost of output produced by other firms that stand in a strategic substitutability relationship. The stage 2 profits for the firm in question are also higher. Thus, the firms try to increase their investment levels with a view to raise their profits by strategically reducing the output of their rivals. As a result, the strategic motivation leads to socially excessive investment. Therefore, the strategic effect (as private marginal benefits of investment to a firm exceed $-\Delta C$ if outputs of the competing firms are strategic substitutes) is always negative and results in competitive equilibrium levels of investment far in excess of the socially optimum levels.

Given that the resource-allocation effect leads to underinvestment and the strategic effect to overinvestment, whether the level of investment in a competitive equilibrium is excessive or too low depends on the relative size of the two effects. There is nothing to guarantee that one of the two effects always overwhelms the other. In general, (1) the greater the number of firms in an industry, and (2) the stronger the substitutability between the outputs if the output of the industry is not homogeneous, the more the strategic effect tends to exceed the resource-allocation effect and it is possible to show that there is a greater probability that investment levels exceed the social optimum level.

Leaving the technical details to the Appendix (Section 14.5), let us consider the intuitive reasoning behind this argument. If the number of firms in the industry is large, the strategic effect of increased investment is spread over a larger number of competing firms. That is, an increase in investment leads to a reduction in output of a large number of firms. As a result, there is a greater increase in the profits of the firm, increasing investment, and the strategic effect becomes relatively stronger than the resource-allocation effect. If, on the other hand, outputs of the firms are weak substitutes, the interfirm competition in production is weakened and the strategic effect of increased investment on the competing firms is smaller. Conversely, when the outputs of different firms are close substitutes, as in the case of homogeneous products considered above, the strategic effect can be considerable as improved competitiveness of one firm can have serious repercussions on the competing firms.

Thus, the larger the number of firms and the greater the substitutability among the outputs of the firms, the greater is the possibility that the strategic effect dominates the resource-allocation effect and excessive investment is more likely. We close the discussion in this chapter by putting some reservations on the conclusions derived above.

First, it is quite possible for the strategic effect to dominate the resource-allocation effect and investment to be socially excessive even when the number of firms is small. Especially in the case of Cournot competition with homogeneous output and a linear demand function, as considered in this chapter, it can be shown that investment will always be excessive. Therefore, socially excessive investment competition considered in this chapter is quite pervasive.[4]

Second, we concluded that the larger the number of firms, the greater is the possibility of excessive investment. However, it is possible to argue that if there is a sufficiently large number of firms, a change in the behavior of one firm may not have a significant effect on the industry as a whole. In this sense, strategic behavior loses importance when the number of firms is large and the economic significance of the concept of excessive investment, dealt with in this chapter, is also reduced. That is, even though the strategic effect may dominate the resource-allocation effect, the absolute value of both the effects may decline and it may not be very productive to consider these effects. Therefore, excessive investment becomes an issue in the industries where the degree of monopoly and inefficiency in resource allocation is not very high but the outputs produced by the firms are close substitutes and interfirm strategic behavior is important.

14.5 APPENDIX[5]

The stage 2 (subgame) equilibrium can be represented by the state in which each firm maximizes Eq. (1), that is, satisfies the first order condition,

$$\partial \Pi_i / \partial x_i = P'(x_i + X_{-i})x_i + P(x_i + X_{-i}) - C_x(x_i, K_i) = 0 \qquad (7)$$

where C_x is the derivative of C with respect to x_i, i.e., marginal cost, and P' is the slope of the inverse demand function.

The (perfect) equilibrium over the two stages is given by the state in which each firm maximizes Eq. (2) and satisfies the first order condition,

$$\partial \Pi_i / \partial K_i = (P - C_x)(\partial x_i^* / \partial K_i) + x_i^* P'(\partial X^* / \partial K_i) - C_K - 1 = 0 \qquad (8)$$

where C_K is the derivative of C with respect to K_i. Using Eq. (7), Eq. (8) can be rewritten as

$$(P - C_x) \sum_{j \neq i} \partial x_j^* / \partial K_i = -C_K - 1 \qquad (9)$$

Now, let us assume that a firm i in the perfect equilibrium configuration $\mathbf{K}^* = (K_1^* \ldots K_n^*)$ increases its investment by a small amount. A partial differentiation of Eq. (3) with respect to K_i and canceling out the overlapping terms gives the change in social welfare as

$$\partial W / \partial K_i = (P - C_x)(\partial X^* / \partial K_i) - C_K - 1 \tag{10}$$

The first term on the right-hand side of this equation is the resource-allocation effect and the second is the strategic effect.

The resource-allocation effect is the same as discussed in the text but the strategic effect, using Eq. (9), can be written as

$$(P - C_x) \sum_{j \neq i} \partial x_j^* / \partial K_i \tag{11}$$

the sum of the two effects, thus, is given by

$$\partial W / \partial K_i = (P - C_x)[(\partial X^* / \partial K_i) + \Sigma_{j \neq i} (\partial x_j^* / \partial K_i)]$$
$$= (P - C_x)[2(\partial X^* / \partial K_i) + (\partial x_i^* / \partial K_i)] \tag{12}$$

Since price in perfect equilibrium is above the marginal costs, the sign on Eq. (12) depends on whether the term within the brackets is positive or negative. A positive sign on this term implies an excessive investment while a negative sign indicates that investment is socially too low.

Figure 14-2 looks at this term for the general case of n firms. All the firms have exactly similar reaction functions as investment configuration under perfect equilibrium, $\mathbf{K}^* = (K_1^* \ldots K_n^*)$ is the same for all the firms. The left-hand side of Fig. 14-2 presents the reaction function of a specific firm i, given the total output of all the other firms $\Sigma_{j \neq i} x_j$. Based on this, the reaction function of the firm i, given the total output (including firm i's own output) $X = \Sigma_{j=1}^n x_j$, is drawn as rr in the first quadrant of Fig. 14-2. Vertical addition of these individual reaction functions for n firms gives the curve RR. In this case, the total industry output in the Nash equilibrium for the subgame $X^*(\mathbf{K})$, is given by N, the point of intersection between curve RR and the 45° line. Moreover, each firm produces

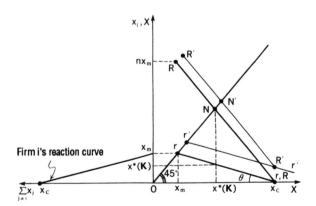

Fig. 14-2

the same amount of output, the value of which $x^*(\mathbf{K})$ is given by the ordinate of the individual reaction function given the total industry output.

Curve $r'r'$ is the (individual) reaction function when the investment level is slightly higher as compared to that represented by rr. Since investment is higher, the marginal cost of production is lower now than with rr and the firm in question becomes aggressive. The optimum output for this firm, even though the total industry output stays the same, rises. The curve depicted as $R'R'$ in Fig. 14-2 is the vertical integration of the reaction functions of individual firms when only firm i raises its investment level by a small amount, moving to a reaction function $r'r'$ while all other firms maintain their original investment levels and their reaction functions stay at rr. The new stage 2 Nash equilibrium in this instance is given by N', the point of intersection between $R'R'$ and the 45° line. It is obvious that total industry output, as well as the output level of the firm increasing its investment, rise while the output of the other firms falls. Increased investment makes the firm in question more aggressive, raising its output, while making other firms producing strategic substitutes relatively more defensive, thereby reducing their output.

Figure 14-3 reproduces Fig. 14-2 for differing number of firms, n and n' ($n > n'$). If only a single firm raises its investment by one unit, the vertical sum of individual reaction functions RR (RR'), with n (n') number of firms, shifts vertically upward by a given amount irrespective of the number of firms. It can be easily read from Fig. 14-3 that the change in total industry output as a result becomes smaller as the number of firms becomes larger. That is, the resource-allocation effect becomes smaller as the number of firms becomes larger.

The size of the strategic effect, on the other hand, is determined by the decline in output of the other firms when one of the firms raises its investment level. The higher the value of this effect, the greater is the increase in profits resulting from the strategic investment by this firm. If ΔX is the increase in total industry output as one of the firms raises its investment level, the decline in output of the firms

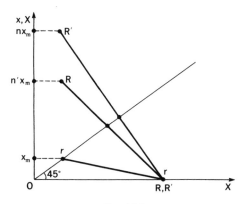

Fig. 14-3

that do not increase their own investment, as is evident from Fig. 14-3, is given by $\Delta X\theta$, the slope of rr. In other words, the output of the firms that do not increase their own investment levels always declines by a fixed proportion of the increase in total output irrespective of the number of firms. Therefore, as the number of firms becomes greater, an increase in investment by one firm generates relatively greater decline in output of other firms as compared to the increase in its own output, thereby increasing the size of the strategic effect (relative to the resource-allocation effect). This is what was referred to as characteristic [1] in the main text.

Notes

1. In Cournot competition with homogeneous products, the outputs of individual firms are necessarily strategic substitutes if the demand function is linear and marginal costs are constant. Moreover, the reaction function for each firm in this case is forward falling. The subsequent analysis deals with this case unless stated otherwise.

2. For details, see Chapter 8.

3. Refer to Eq. (10) in the Appendix to this chapter.

4. For details, refer to Okuno-Fujiwara and Suzumura (1987).

5. This Appendix is a mathematical treatment of the arguments presented in the text. The readers, except for those interested in mathematical exposition, can skip this Appendix and proceed to the next chapter without any loss in continuity. On the other hand, readers interested in pursuing the topic in greater detail are referred to Okuno-Fujiwara and Suzumura (1987).

15

Competition and Economic Welfare: A Reconsideration of the Concept of Excessive Competition

15.1 SOME REMAINING PROBLEMS

The last two chapters reconsidered the accepted notion that increasing competition raises economic welfare. The analysis in Chapter 13 revealed that in an oligopolistic industry with homogeneous products, where the outputs produced by different firms are strategic substitutes, the number of equilibrium firms invariably exceeds the social welfare-maximizing optimum number of firms. In such cases, therefore, restricting new entry to prevent the number of firms from exceeding the optimum, rather than simply allowing the intensity of competition to rise as a result of profit-motivated entry of new firms, can increase economic welfare. Further, in Chapter 14, it was seen that strategic investment for cost reduction could become socially excessive in oligopolistic industries with homogeneous products where outputs are strategic substitutes. Moreover, the tendency for investment to be excessive was seen to be greater the larger the number of firms in the industry. In this light, the assertion of the traditional economic theory—that excessive competition is a nonexistent phenomenon and competition leads to maximization of social welfare—may not be appropriate.

In this chapter, we discuss the relationship between competition and economic welfare in a more general perspective and also present a tentative evaluation of the concept of excessive competition. Using this generalized framework, we also try to clarify the problems associated with administrative intervention based on an industrial policy with excessiveness of competition as its core argument.

The first of these points relates to the interpretation, in the Japanese context, of excessive competition as a phenomenon that results in socially undesirable consequences as firms, in a bid to outlast the severe dynamic competition in the struggle for survival, indulge in competitive behavior incomprehensible in terms of static profit maximization. Given this interpretation, the (primarily static) framework of equilibrium theory, as discussed in Chapters 13 and 14, cannot properly treat the phenomenon of excessive competition in the Japanese context. The next section provides an economic analysis underlying this line of reasoning.

173

The second point relates to "cooperation" or "collusion." Rejection of the accepted notion that increasing competition raises economic welfare does not, *ipso facto*, imply acceptance of the alternative notion that competition is bad, cooperation is good. The analysis of Chapters 13 and 14 (including that of the next section) simply shows that government intervention in the organization of industry and investment decisions can raise social welfare provided interfirm competition (using output or pricing strategies) is maintained. Alternatively, the policies intended to control competition in some form or another can be effective only if competition among the private sector firms, within the limits set by these controls, is ensured.

The third point is the appropriateness of administrative intervention based on the notion of excessive competition. Administrative intervention is not always justified just because there is a market failure in the sense that competition among private sector firms leads to excessive competition. This is because the possibility of policy failures can be as high as the possibility of market failures. It is possible that the so-called excessive competition in the Japanese context may have been, ironically, induced and aggravated by the very policies intended to do away with excessive competition.

Finally, administrative intervention may not only result in policy failures and intensification of excessive competition but, at the same time, is highly likely to impede competition in the original sense of the word, hurting long-term economic activity. In the ultimate analysis, it is the free and fair access to all economic opportunities by all economic agents that underlies the functioning of the politico-economic processes in a free society.

15.2 DYNAMIC PROCESSES AND EXCESSIVE COMPETITION

Until now, our discussion of competition, including the two-stage competition treated in the previous chapter, has basically been within the framework of static equilibrium theory. This is simply because all the firms know, at stage 1, the exact nature of profit opportunities available at stage 2 as well as the means to exploit them. In such an analytical framework, time does not play any substantive role except for demarcating stage 2 from stage 1. Competition, in such analyses, emerges only as a result of efforts to obtain profits by bringing down prices and capturing bigger markets.

Time, however, invariably plays a more substantive role in the competitive process in the real world economy. Once a profit opportunity is grasped, it generates profits over a longer period, due to the irreversibility of time; if lost, it is not easy to recoup it once again.

For example, if a firm is able to corner the semiconductor market, acquisition of greater skills in production technology through experience can bring down average production costs as the outage rate of faulty products declines. In contrast to this, a firm that loses its market is unable to continue production and falls behind in technology. Besides, development of new products for the future or even production technology for such a purpose also become difficult. Even in the case of industries where scale economies do not operate, once a firm is able to establish its image and product credibility among the consumers and is able to set up a network of retail outlets, it is possible for the firm to sell its products at a higher price, or even an inferior product, in large quantities. A newly entering firm, lacking these advantages, cannot hope to compete with the existing firms except either by undertaking to run a large-scale advertising campaign at a substantial cost or by taking time to convince the consumers and build its own retail network.

Thus, given this irreversibility of time, competition for markets and products is centered more on how quickly a firm can enter and capture a market than on how cheap and good quality a product it can offer. This is what is meant by "competition over time." Since all the firms are fully aware of this aspect of competition, they are also aware that every competing firm in the same line of business is speeding up development in order to capture the market. Therefore, a firm, in order to capture the profit opportunities by suppressing other firms, needs to devote much greater developmental efforts than its rivals, who are quickening the pace of their own development. Such competition involving time unleashes exceptional competitive pressures on the private sector firms trying to generate and capture profitable opportunities at their earliest.

Development of excessive competition under such competitive pressures is quite likely, in the form of firms trying to introduce large-scale integrated circuits much earlier than would have been the case if competition was absent, and pricing below costs in order to capture markets. Can this form of competition lead to socially desirable results?

Competition over time (or development rush), as discussed in Chapter 18 in detail, can easily lead to socially excessive competition. There must be a socially optimum time for profit opportunities to materialize, that is, a time when social welfare attainable from such a profit opportunity is maximized. However, competition for an early acquisition of such an opportunity is inevitable as long as this profitable opportunity generates positive profits for the firm that acquires it first. Profits (producer surplus) earned from the materialization of such a profitable opportunity, at least, are higher if it is possible to delay the realization of such an opportunity. As long as there is no matching decline in consumer surplus, social welfare is higher with delayed materialization of the profit opportunity.

Thus, emergence of excessive competition, in the sense that competition exceeds the socially optimal level, is more likely if dynamic competition, with characteristics differing fundamentally from those of static competition, is taken into account. In this case, too, the understanding of the traditional economic theory that competition is always good and that competition ensures socially optimal state does not sound right.

At the cost of repetition it must be noted that pointing out the problems caused by competition does not amount to saying that competition is always bad. The main point to be noted here is, rather, that it is highly probable that the very efforts to rectify the problems of competition generate social "evils." In the remaining sections we discuss the problems associated with policies to regulate competition and the suitable form of the policies to deal with excessive competition.

15.3 COMPETITION AND COOPERATION

As mentioned earlier, advocacy of competition-regulatory policies, just because the sufficient condition for competition to be excessive is satisfied, is premature. Intervention into the competitive process does not guarantee improved social welfare just because the conditions discussed in Chapters 13, 14, or the previous section (details in Chapter 18) are satisfied. The industries where efficiency or strategic considerations are important are inevitably oligopolistic and are composed of a small number of firms. There are sufficient incentives, in such industries, for the firms to cooperate and collude in raising prices and earn monopoly profits. Moreover, repeated cooperation over time can lead to the formation of cartels, explicit or implicit, with internal rules that force the member firms to set monopoly prices.

If a firm tries to sell at less than the agreed price and usurp the share of the other firms, other members, by (implicit) understanding, take retaliatory action and the members fearing such retaliation must abide by the agreed prices. There is a distinct possibility that excess capacity, usually cited as an indicator for the existence of excessive competition, may be artificially created to make the internal rules of the cartel or the threat of retaliation more credible (see, for example, Benoit and Krishna, 1984).

Such cooperative behavior, through monopoly price setting that maximizes collective profits of the firms participating in the cartel, tramples on consumers' economic welfare and generates inefficiencies in resource allocation. Inefficiencies generated in this way differ substantially from those discussed in Chapters 14 and 15. The group of firms entering into a cartel can control the industry and there is nothing to control this monopoly power. In contrast to this, if there are a number of competing firms, the monopoly power of each firm is severely curtailed by competitive pressure from its rivals.

Moreover, destruction of the competitive environment due to cartelization and the inactivity of the existing firms due to cooperation benumbs the process of "constructive destruction" and denies fair access to profitable opportunities by the nonmember firms. In this sense, cooperation, by destroying free competition and negating the incentives for development of new products and for technological innovation, imposes severe (in some cases, crucial) long-run social costs on the economy.

15.4 EXCESSIVE COMPETITION AND ADMINISTRATIVE INTERVENTION

The administrative authorities, as a part of the bureaucratic system, are characterized by pursuit of power to serve vested interests. Therefore, the administrative authorities have an incentive to intervene administratively not only when it is desirable from the viewpoint of social welfare but also in cases which do not require any intervention. Even if one grants, for the sake of argument, that the administrative authorities are able to put aside such incentives and are guided purely by social welfare considerations, there is no guarantee that the decisions made, as a result, will always be proper. In contrast to the market system, where competitive pressures guarantee a minimum level of efficiency, no system of automatic checks is available for policy decisions made by the administrative system, based primarily on the capabilities and good intentions of individual bureaucrats alone.

Moreover, regulation competition through administrative intervention invariably generates benefits (rents) for some economic agents. These agents, in their pursuit of rents arising from regulation of competition, try to intervene in the political decision-making process. As far as administrative machinery is subordinated to the political set-up, the political maneuvers in quest for rents build up political pressures for regulating competition strong enough to overwhelm the administrative set-up trying to formulate socially fair policies.

The politico-administrative system designed to counter excessive competition resulting from market failures is too weak in the face of incentives for internal power within the bureaucracy, the pressures applied in the pursuit of rents generated by a competition-regulation policy. It is clear, in this light, that policy failure can be as or even more prevalent than market failures. A careful consideration of the competition-regulation policies that deprive the economy of the competitive environment, the minimum condition for sustaining an economic system, is indispensable not only for its economic implications but also its political and administrative ramifications.

Furthermore, it is quite possible that the market system is transformed as a result of administrative intervention and fails to perform its original functions. The well-known example of such a phenomenon is the emergence of excessive competition as a result of administrative intervention intended to counter it. As "motorcars are traveling faster than they otherwise would because they are provided with brakes," (Schumpeter, 1941, pp. 88),[1] excessive competition develops precisely because there is some form of governmental rationing.[2] Let us explain this mechanism briefly in the remainder of this section.

It is a well-known fact that "rationing and licensing systems, like foreign exchange rationing, cartels for curtailing operations, production quotas, funds allocations and licensing for introducing foreign capital and other purposes adopted by the trade and industry ministry authorities and in various other forms within the industry circles were quite prevalent in postwar Japan."[3] However, the rations and licenses tend to be granted on the basis of the relative position of a firm in the industry in terms of existing production capacity and market share, etc. In such cases, "the firms do not concentrate on competing on the basis of socially beneficial product improvement, cost reductions and sales services and engage in socially wasteful competition in order to obtain maximum alloca- tions."[4] For example, if import allocations for crude oil are to be decided on the basis of the existing petroleum-refining capacity, the petroleum companies, to secure market share and profits, will be induced to invest far in excess of what is rational under the present market conditions. It is ironic that the rationing and licensing systems, meant to avoid excessive competition within the industry and to set the stage for orderly expansion of production facilities, end up triggering excessive competition.

The allotments for construction of ethylene plants in the petrochemical indus- try are often given as an example where such a case actually occurred. The sekiyu . . . kai (petrochemical industry association), under the *kanminhoshiki* (an association where both the government and private firms participate) started in 1964, tried to circumvent the problem of excessive competition and exces- sive entry into the petrochemical industry by preventing new entry by setting up minimum standards for plant constructions and, in the process, avoiding rapid expansion of capacity and the resulting excessive competition. In more concrete terms, by disallowing construction of plants below a capacity of 100,000 T (later 200,000 T), it tried to curtail entry by new firms that lagged behind in terms of financial resources and market development. However, controls introduced under this scheme, instead, gave rise to a scramble by a large number of firms to enter the petrochemical industry at an early date to reap profits by participating in the cooperative. This resulted in a huge excess capacity when the oil crisis struck.[5]

The problem lies in having relative shares of the existing firms as the basis of allocations and licensing. These standards are based on the implicit understand- ing that it is equitable to make the allotments based on the past performance of the firms. But the considerations of equity based on past performance invariably result in excessive competition. That is, there is a trade-off between equity and efficiency.

Let us consider two firms engaged in Cournot competition with a homoge- neous product. Further, let (x_1, x_2) be the output produced by the two firms and $\pi_i(x_1, x_2)$ be the profits resulting from the productive activity of firm i ($i = 1, 2$) in the current period. The normal Cournot–Nash equilibrium in this case is ob- tained when each firm is maximizing its profits, that is, satisfying

$$\partial \pi_i(x_1^*, x_2^*)/\partial x_i = 0 \qquad (i = 1, 2) \qquad (1)$$

Again, this Cournot–Nash equilibrium can be represented as point N in Fig. 15-1.

Now, let us assume that the government decides to allot quotas in the next period on the basis of production shares in the current period. If the profits of a firm are higher the greater the allocation, the next period profits (discounted present value) of firm i can be depicted as an increasing function of the current production share $\Pi_i[x_i/(x_1 + x_2)]$. As a result, firm i tries to maximize

$$\pi_i(x_1, x_2) + \Pi_i[x_i/(x_1 + x_2)]$$

The firms maximize the sum of the (discounted present value of) profits over time $\pi_i + \Pi_i$ and not the current profits π_i.

Each firm, in this case, becomes more aggressive in its production behavior than it would in an effort to maximize current profits alone. The rationale is easy to follow. Higher output, assuming the rival output to be given, not only raises current profits but future profits as well, since an increase in current share raises next period allocation out of the government quota.

As a result the reaction function of firm 1 shifts to the right and that of firm 2 shifts upward, moving the equilibrium to the right, to a point like N' in Fig. 15-1. Thus, competition among the firms is stiffer with quotas than without them. In other words, government quotas, imposed with an intention to control excessive competition, in fact, give rise unnecessary excessive competition.

Thus, we find that there is a trade-off between equity and efficiency. Basically, most of the policy measures adopted by a government intervening in a decentralized economy or society are indirect measures guiding the private economic activity into socially desirable directions by affecting the incentive structure of individual firms. Besides, in the formulation and implementation of such policies, it is socially necessary to ensure that these measures are applied to all the interest groups involved in an equitable manner, taking the past performance of the private firms into account. But as the adoption of policy measures becomes a known fact, private firms try to maximize their own profits by taking the implementation of these measures as a datum. As a result, the policy measures considered to be socially desirable and equitable may, at times, end up producing results

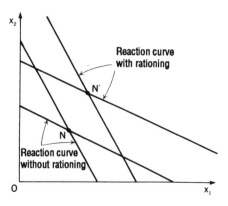

Fig. 15-1

quite opposite to the intentions of policy authorities. The trade-off discussed above indicates that such a result, in fact, is likely to be quite pervasive. It is also clear that policy implementation in a decentralized society is subject to constraints.

15.5 FREE COMPETITION AND GOVERNMENT INTERVENTION

Even when competition is excessive in some sense and there is a need for policy intervention, a number of alternative policy measures could be devised to meet the situation. It is possible to check the degree of competition in an industry with excess entry or investment by imposing additional corporate taxes or investment taxes. There is no necessity to limit the government intervention for excessive competition to measures like approval of cartelization or regulation by the government.

As against this, most of the competition-regulation policies based on the concept of excessive competition in postwar Japan have been, as compared to the other economic policies undertaken by the government, quite peculiar. That is, these competition-regulation policies, in a bid to avoid excessive competition, limit the free decision-making process in the private sector by requiring, explicitly or implicitly, government licensing or administrative guidance in almost all aspects of firm activity like investment, plant construction, output, prices, introduction of new products, and so on. Such licensing and administrative guidance inevitably result in rendering entry of new firms into an industry almost impossible without government approval. These competition-regulation policies cast the regulatory net of controls over almost all aspects of firm activity and, besides, these regulations tend to discriminate in favor of the large or the existing firms within the industry.

Thus, a discriminate protection only of the existing firms and the very fact that the environment of free competition among the firms is destroyed is the aspect feared by the more wary proponents of modern democracy, who believe that the society can function properly only under free competition. This is because in a society where the interests of the constituents do not necessarily converge, coordinated decision making that encompasses contradictions and still is able to develop in an overall desirable form requires an adherence to the principle of free and fair access to all economic and political opportunities by all the constituents of the society. The failure of the early socialist countries' experiment with guaranteeing "equity as an end" unrelated to the amount of effort and labor involved lies precisely in its denial of free competition, which ensures greater rewards to an individual who works harder than other members of the society. The individuals make efforts and the firms adopt revolutionary management techniques only because they can earn their living and reap profits. That is, there are incentives for labor and creativity. If the efforts undertaken do not product matching rewards, the very basis of drawing on individual efforts and creative ideas necessary for the society as a whole crumbles.

It goes without saying that free competition is not omnipotent. Competition weans the strong from the weak. In this sense, if the weak that have lost in competition due to some misfortune are not aided or the strong that have won with unscrupulous means are not punished, the society will lose its basis of existence. But such aid to the weak and punishment to the unscrupulous become meaningful only if all the members of the society have a free and fair access to economic and political opportunities and the principle that these opportunities can be obtained through free competition is ensured. If the workers (or new firms contemplating entry) are the weak and the aristocracy (or existing firms) are the strong, would the former be satisfied with a meager amount of aid?

In this sense, it is important to make a clear distinction between the arguments over whether excessive competition exists and those over whether competition should be curtailed. As shown here, it is quite possible for excessive competition, in the sense that competition is socially excessive, to exist. But direct government intervention in the competitive process in the form of regulation of competition for this purpose may destroy the basic precondition for the political and economic functioning of the society as a whole. In the presence of excessive competition, therefore, it is necessary to devise policy measures that do away with the incentives for excessive competition while maintaining the principles of the competitive process, namely, free competition and equitable opportunity. We leave the discussion of the desirable policy measures needed for this purpose to the future and refrain from offering a hasty analysis.[6]

NOTES

1. See Schumpeter (1941). Also see Nakamura [1969, 1974, and 1978 (Chapter 6)], the latter referring to "the 'mountain hut' functions of industrial policy."
2. See Komiya (1975), Chapter 10.
3. See Imai *et al.* (1972), Vol. 3, p. 253.
4. See Imai *et al.* (1972), Vol. 3, p. 254.
5. See, for example, Tsuruta (1982), pp. 174–180 on this point.
6. Economic welfare can be improved by curbing excessive competition through a universal tax on all the firms in an industry. See, for example, Okuno and Suzumura (1985).

V

Research and Development Investment

16

Characteristics of Technical Knowledge and Incentives for Research and Development

16.1 CHARACTERISTICS OF TECHNICAL KNOWLEDGE
AND ITS PUBLIC GOOD NATURE

Research and development (R & D) of and learning about new technologies and products plays an important role in determining the performance of an economy. It is necessary for Japan, now that the era when advanced technology could be imported from the foreign countries and improved upon is over, to develop its own unique technologies and accumulate basic knowledge not only for its own further development but also to meet the increased international responsibilities concomitant with its increased share of the world economy. Moreover, the undulations of the new information society, based on computer and related technologies, have increased the pace of technological change and have made research and development all the more important at the level of a firm, an industry, a country, or even the world.

However, R & D activity is quite distinct from any other economic activity. Due to a number of reasons, optimum resource allocation for R & D activities fails to materialize on the basis of market forces guided by private incentives alone. Hence, to complement the market mechanism to attain socially optimal R & D and learning activities is an important policy problem not only for the country concerned but for the world economy as well. As discussed in detail below, some of the characteristics relevant in this context are difficulties of the monopolizing of technology and new products or in other words the possibility of externalities and spillovers, competition and externalities in the use of technical knowledge, the intertemporal competition among the firms for R & D and the concomitant rush to invent, risk and uncertainty involved in R & D, and the irreversible impact of technological accumulation on the cost structure of the firms and the resulting tendency for oligopolization of the markets.

These characteristics, while generating market failures by impeding the functioning of the market system in a desirable manner, also uniquely distinguish the process of developing new technology and products and the process of technical

185

learning from other economic activities. It is these very features of technology that account for the divergence of free R & D activity and the process of technical learning based on private incentives from socially optimum levels. Moreover, some of these features cause the R & D to be suboptimal while others make it excessive. In the light of the diverse and complex nature of factors affecting R & D and the process of technical learning, an evaluation of and a decision on what policies a government should or should not adopt need very careful analysis.

Before we begin our discussion of industrial policy in the context of R & D, there is one point that the reader must note. In a discussion of the process of development and accumulation of technology, in addition to development of technology and R & D by the private sector, the role played by R & D activity undertaken by public institutions cannot be neglected. Our purpose, however, is to discover the impact of industrial policies, designed as a measure to complement the functioning of the market economy, on technological development and R & D activity of the private sector and the resulting effect on economic welfare of the society as a whole. In this sense, the analysis undertaken below, compared to the usual economic analyses of R & D or technology, emphasizes R & D activities undertaken by the private sector rather than by the public sector. Moreover, the policy measures discussed here are mostly those that intervene in the private sector R & D.

This circumscribing of the topic in no way implies that public R & D activities are useless. It is rather due to the fact that fundamental R & D activities, undertaken at the public level by government-related institutes like the industrial technology institutes and National Research Institutes or by public and private universities, are not easily brought within the area of our interest. Besides, it is a well-known fact that Japan lags behind many other countries in terms of public assistance to the so-called fundamental R & D and accumulation of knowledge. There is no doubt that an increase in public assistance to fundamental R & D is the most important issue facing the future science and technology policy in Japan.

The policies related to introduction of foreign technology by way of technological assistance, joint ventures, and licensing are also important from the viewpoint of technological progress and accumulation in a country. Limitations of space, however, prevent us from discussing such policies for introduction and transfer of technology.

16.2 CONSTRUCTIVE DESTRUCTION AND CAPITALISM

Part IV dealt with the impact of market competition on the economic welfare of the society as a whole. But the model used there was a static model capturing "competition within a rigid pattern of invariant conditions, methods of production, and forms of industrial organization in particular."[1] Dynamic competition based on the development of new products and new technologies, discovery of new sources of supply, development of new forms of organization—breakthroughs that "incessantly revolutionize the economic structure from within"[2]— could not, however, be treated. Competition for technological innovation through R & D refers to this dynamic competition characterized by a Schumpeterian process of constructive destruction.

The process of constructive destruction emerging as the result of the coming together of a sudden transformation of an industry based on the fruits of R & D activity and superior entrepreneurial skills results in "an element of genuine monopoly gain in those entrepreneurial profits which are the prizes offered by capitalist society to the successful innovator."[3] If so, entrepreneurial profits that a superior entrepreneur can earn, by pushing ahead with the process of constructive destruction, serve as the engine of growth of capitalism. In the subsequent analysis, we try to look into the factors determining the size of incentives for R & D activity, i.e., entrepreneurial profits.

These entrepreneurial profits (innovator's profits or incentives for R & D), however, are threatened by imitators from the instant that the process of constructive destruction results in success. In this sense, difficulty of imitation governs the effectivity of the "engine of capitalism" and the size of incentives for R & D activity.

But, again, imitation is also important from the viewpoint of the society as a whole. The full potential of the results of R & D and the sudden transformation of industry that revolutionizes industrial structure from within are realized only when these reach the farthest corners of economic activity and society. As long as the fruits of development are restricted within one firm, R & D activity, although contributing toward higher monopoly profits for the firm concerned, do not raise consumer or social welfare as these contribute neither to a fall in product prices nor to an improvement in overall product quality in the industry. The merits of newly acquired knowledge and new forms of organization percolate down to society as a whole only through diffusion of the fruits of development.

Diffusion of the fruits of development can result in new applications or development of new products that may have been overlooked by the original inventor; thus, development of new production technology and forms of organization may be of help not only to the inventor or his or her organization but also to the efficient functioning of various other aspects of economic activity and organizations. Imitation, or "copying," the simplest and most universal form of diffusion, has a great hidden potential for substantially increasing social welfare. In the absence of imitation, since the inventor is a monopolist, there is a strong possibility that the fruits of development are absorbed fully in monopoly profits and the consumer gets nothing. Imitation corrodes the position of the inventor as a monopolist and thereby leads to a dispersion of the fruits of development in the form of lower prices for the consumer and thus to increased economic welfare.

In this sense, the subsequent analysis is concerned mainly with the factors determining the size of incentives for R & D activity, primarily profits for the inventor, and for imitation that leads to diffusion of the fruits of development.

16.3 ECONOMIC ASPECTS OF RESEARCH AND DEVELOPMENT

Research and development activity is the process of generating new knowledge through investment of productive factors. This new knowledge, by being embodied in new products (product innovation) or by reducing production costs through an improvement in the existing production techniques (process innovation), or, again, through technology sales in the form of licensing, gives rise to economic profits. The knowledge gained through R & D activity, like nuclear physics, cannot be directly applied to economic activity. While a part of this knowledge has only a very bleak possibility for profit making, there are other developments, such as superconductivity at room temperature or new drugs, which ensure huge rewards to the inventor if successful. How can one classify such economically different forms of R & D activity?

Traditionally, the R & D activities have been classified into fundamental, applied, and development categories. Fundamental R & D refers to discovery and invention of absolutely new branches of knowledge on the basis of creative research. Applied research, on the other hand, investigates the possibility of applying the knowledge, discovered or invented on the basis of fundamental research, to specific uses. The last category, developmental research, involves the development of new products and replacement of existing technology with low-cost production technology, using the results of applied research. Even after new products have been developed and new technology has been introduced, R & D for product and production technology improvement continues. Besides, technological improvement also takes place during production activity, not explicitly directed toward R & D, through the accumulation of and learning about production technology and know-how.

The results of fundamental research are usually of universal importance and it is considered good to have the benefits of such research spilled over to economic agents other than the inventor. As detailed in the next chapter, the fruits of research with a low degree of competition in consumption can raise economic welfare if widely publicized and used in various aspects of social life. In contrast to this, the results of developmental research, when imitated, have been considered to lower the profits of the inventing agent. The reason is that, compared to fundamental R & D, the fruits of developmental research have a high degree of competition in consumption. However, recent research has clearly shown that this categorization of R & D activities on the basis of stage of research is not necessarily fruitful for economic analysis. The fundamental and applied R & D activities are not carried out for their own sake alone but are closely related to final product development.

For our purposes, the spectrum of various R & D activities and processes of technical learning should be classified into two categories, not on the basis of stages of research, which may not be necessarily appropriate, but on the basis of requirements of economic analysis.[4] These are "inventions" and "innovation." Invention refers to the discovery of new knowledge that cannot be predicted *ex ante* and usually corresponds to the stage of fundamental research. Invention, by itself, is both the objective and substance of research by a scientist. However, it is basically independent of the entrepreneurial activity guided by profit motive since the results cannot be predicted *ex ante*. Thus, inventions are an exogenous factor for industrial policy and cannot be brought under policy controls.

Innovations, on the other hand, involve commercialization of the fruits of inventions—"seeds"— in the form of new products or production technology aimed at recovering the costs and posting profits. Thus, the possibility of commercialization is predictable to some extent in the case of innovation activity and success is guaranteed to produce substantial economic profits. The private sector R & D activity is guided by the profit motive and hence innovation R & D forms the basic object of our analysis.

The subsequent analysis looks at the R & D activity undertaken with a view to quick, cheap, and certain commercialization of the already existing seeds (inventions) with such a possibility. Even the results of R & D activity for innovation are uncertain. It is possible that commercialization fails even when seeds are there. Alternatively, even if a firm succeeds in commercializing the invention, profits may turn out to be zero because some other firm has already commercialized the product. Thus, uncertainty is one of the important features of R & D activity.

It is also important to distinguish between two types of innovation. One of these is the "creative development activity" which involves developing heretofore nonexistent new products and technology. Such R & D and the resultant profits to the inventor are the Schumpeterian engine of capitalism, as mentioned above. In contrast to this, a new development competition develops as soon as the fruits of creative R & D become known. This involves R & D activity for imitation and improvement in the search for profits based on corrosion of inventor's profits through imitation of and improvement over new products or technology.

The R & D activity for imitation and improvement differs economically from the creative R & D activity on the following counts. The possibility that the commercialization effort, even though seeds exist, will successfully generate economic profits is unknown in the case of creative R & D and there is a high degree of uncertainty. In the case of activities directed at imitation and improvement, on the other hand, the degree of uncertainty is quite low since the product or the technology is already established.

Further, the size of rewards for creative R & D is independent of the existing technological levels and product quality. If the results of such activity are successfully commercialized, the traditional product or technology becomes obsolete and loses its competitive edge. In contrast to this, the R & D for imitation and improvement, even when successful, does not weed out the existing product or technology completely. The existing technology can continue to hold some competitive power. Thus, the size of the profits based on the fruits of R & D for imitation and improvement depends on the traditional technological level and product quality, and also on the type of firms holding such technology and products.

Before embarking on the actual analysis, let us emphasize one particular perspective within which an economic analysis of R & D activities can be conducted. The incentives for R & D are given by the difference between opportunity profits (profits over and above what could be earned if R & D was not undertaken) and the cost of R & D. Thus, opportunity profits resulting from R & D, in most cases, emerge in the market where new products or products using new technology are sold. Research and development competition, therefore, is not restricted only to competition for R & D activity alone but also depends heavily on product market competition for recovering the costs. Subsequent analysis concentrates on how strategic behavior among the firms, based on the structure of the product markets and the differences in the positions of firms engaged in development, affects development incentives.

16.4 ORGANIZATION OF PART V

In the light of the above discussion, Section V deals with an analysis of economic factors determining R & D activity and also tries to provide an economic evaluation of direct or indirect industrial policy intervention into R & D activity.

Chapter 17 discusses the traditional view that R & D activity tends to be too little from the viewpoint of social welfare. Research and development is an activity that produces knowledge, a public good. That is, imitation results in a flow of economic rewards, which would otherwise have been earned by the inventor, to the imitator. As a result, it is difficult to recover the costs of undertaking R & D through the functioning of the market mechanism. Thus, private incentives for R & D fall short of social incentives and private sector R & D tends to contract. Moreover, a part of the benefits from R & D activity flow down to the consumers in the form of lower prices. This effect also results in lowering private incentives for R & D compared to social incentives. That is why the traditional discussion of R & D emphasizes the tendency for R & D to be socially small.

There are, on the other hand, factors that tend to make R & D activity socially excessive. These characteristic competitive factors of R & D and their economic significance are treated in Chapter 18. Research and development activity differs from other economic activities and is strongly characterized by intertemporal competition. A firm can reap the benefits of R & D only if it beats its rivals in the development process. There are no rewards for coming in second or third, or the rewards are at least substantially lower as compared to the winning firm. Thus,

R & D competition provides incentives to the firms to invest more than their rivals in a bid to win the race for development and reap the first mover advantages. Again, R & D produces a public good in the form of knowledge. Therefore, investment in R & D that is socially sufficient if undertaken by a single economic agent is duplicated when a number of economic agents invest in similar R & D activities. Whether R & D levels are socially excessive or low depends on the relative size of the factors tending toward lower R & D, as discussed in Chapter 17, and the factors tending to make it excessive, as discussed in Chapter 18. No unequivocal solution can be found.

Chapter 19 deals with the impact of industrial organization forms on incentives for R & D. The level of R & D is determined by taking strategic considerations into account since R & D activity plays an important role in determining the future course of a firm. As a result, the size of development incentives depends on whether the industry in question is a monopoly or competitive and whether the said firm has already made a place for itself in the industry or is a new entrant. These problems are discussed in Chapter 19 separately for the creative R & D case and the case of R & D for imitation and improvement.

Chapter 20 uses the analyses in the previous chapters to discuss the significance of policy intervention in R & D activity. Besides the traditional policies for R & D activities, an economic analysis of R & D associations, which have attracted considerable attention in recent years, is also carried out in this chapter.

NOTES

1. See Schumpeter (1950), p. 84.
2. See Schumpeter (1950), p. 93.
3. See Schumpeter (1950), p. 103.
4. Scherer (1986) emphasizes this distinction.

17

Traditional Theory of Research and Development and Underinvestment

Research and development (R & D) has been a widely discussed topic. The main point of controversy revolves around whether private incentives result in excessive or too little R & D activity as compared to the socially optimum level. On this point, the traditional explanations concentrate on the public goods nature of technology and knowledge, as discussed later, and conclude that, given private incentives alone, R & D activity tends to be socially too little and some form of government assistance to R & D is necessary. The present chapter presents a critical overview of such a traditional theory of R & D.

17.1 Technology as a Public Good and Research and Development Incentives

Knowledge or technology, defined as a disembodied economic good, is usually referred to as a public good. All technology and knowledge is characterized, to a greater or lesser degree, by "impossibility of exclusion from use" and "noncompetitiveness (collective nature) in use" as defined below.

The agents developing new technology are always threatened with the possibility of imitation by other economic agents. The entities that do not engage in technology development can get to know about the newly developed technology, without incurring as high a cost as the developer of that technology, by deducing the technological content from the marketed product, or by drawing away technologists from the parent firm, or by using industrial spies. On the other hand, the developer of technology can try to preclude imitation by taking special measures to prevent others from determining the technological content from the marketed product, by paying high remuneration to prevent its technologists from leaving and by introducing sophisticated anticrime systems and using security companies to prevent industrial spies. That is to say, precluding access by other economic agents to a given technology through imitation involves considerable exclusion costs.

192

This problem is also sometimes referred to as the problem of appropriability. It is impossible for a developer of technology and knowledge to monopolize it without preventing imitation by other firms at a cost. Whether or not a developer monopolizes the technology developed or, in other words, whether or not it undertakes efforts to prevent imitation by other firms, depends on the relative size of costs of preventing imitation and profits generated by such prevention measures. Obviously, preventive measures are unfruitful as long as the former outweighs the latter. Although monopolization is desirable from the viewpoint of the developer, imitation occurs since the rewards for undertaking preventive measures are often insufficient.

The unappropriated technology or knowledge usually tends to spill over to other firms, raising their benefits (profits), a result that follows from the "noncompetitiveness in use" feature of technology and knowledge allowing a number of economic agents to use it simultaneously. This raises benefits (higher profits or an increase in profits).

It is clear, therefore, that technology or knowledge is characterized simultaneously by a possibility of imitation (or impossibility of exclusion) and noncompetitiveness in use. The private benefits of development of technology or knowledge can be measured by the increase in profits that results from its actual use. Net profits, calculated by deducting private development costs from the above, define the size of private incentives. In general, private benefits from such technology or knowledge are much smaller than benefits to the society as a whole, including the spillover benefits showered on other firms, since technology or knowledge has a public good character as discussed above. As a result, development activity, like any other public good, tends to fall below the socially optimum levels if left at the mercy of market forces alone, which are guided exclusively by private incentives. Even when social benefits exceed (private) development costs, the private benefits of R & D to the developer fall short of such costs and production and development of socially desirable technology fail to materialize.

Considered in the above perspective, government assistance to R & D becomes necessary and there is a need to raise the level of R & D activity to the socially optimum level. This is the most traditional argument advocating policy intervention in the R & D activities. Taking this argument on face value, however, is beset with problems. This is because the developer, as well as society and the economy, have devised various measures to make the imitation of development results, by economic entities other than the developer, difficult without proper compensation. Leaving aside the patent system as discussed in Chapter 21, the measures used for precluding imitation by other firms can be categorized in the following three broad groups.

First, a firm, by erecting some form of market barriers, at the same time as technology is embodied into a product and before any other has a chance to imitate, can obliterate the opportunity of making profits through imitation. That is to say, it can blot out the incentives to imitate. To achieve this end, it must be possible to raise entry barriers in the product market. One well-known example in this context is erection of entry barriers in the form of product image established on the basis of extensive advertising campaigns at the time of introducing the new product, embodying newly developed technology, into the market.[1] Such a strategy is successful only when the product market is characterized by product differentiation and it is possible to raise product image through advertising. One way of introducing entry barriers in product markets is to use sunk costs of large-scale investment as an irreversible strategy.[2] However, entry barriers based on investment are flawed in the sense that they reduce incentives for introducing new technology or renovating the old technology as and when a new technological innovation occurs.[3] In any case, firm image is important for effectiveness of entry barriers based on psychological factors like product image while entry barriers through investment involve substantial costs. Hence, the existing firms that have already established an image for themselves or for their products have a greater incentive for conducting R & D activities than do medium- and small-scale firms or the new entrants.

A second way of preventing imitation by other firms is to specialize in the development of high technology by using superior technological levels as compared to other firms, thereby making it difficult for others to understand and learn about new technology even if they want to. To attain technological levels superior to those of the other firms, a firm is required to organize a large number of researchers and maintain a high level of R & D activity. Moreover, technological level, being a stock, is the accumulation of the flow of R & D activities over an extended period of time. In this sense, again, the existing large firms have an advantage over the medium- and small-scale firms or the new entrants. These firms use accumulation of R & D efforts as an irreversible strategy to raise entry barriers in the R & D market. While speaking about superior technological levels, it must be kept in mind that technology is accumulated in an organization basically in the form of technicians and researchers as individuals or in the form of know-how. The case of computer industry in the United States and software industry in Japan are typical examples indicating that the extent to which such technology is appropriable depends on the interfirm mobility of human resources.[4]

A third method of preventing imitation by other firms is to quarantine new technology by designating it as a company secret, thereby preventing disclosure to other firms. The effectiveness of such a strategy is particularly dependent on the nature of the technology involved. For example, in the case of technology closely related to the marketed product, other firms can easily discern the technology from the product and imitate it. In contrast to this, if the technological innovation concerns a production process and is not embodied, imitation is difficult without drawing away the technologists conversant with the technology or stealing related information.

Besides the fact that imitation is preventable to a certain extent, there are other factors indicating that the stress placed on public good characteristics of technology and knowledge is inappropriate. Technology or knowledge, unlike the public goods (pure public goods), is a quasipublic good with a higher degree of competition in use. For example, development of new computer software by a firm can be imitated in a relatively short time by other firms, leading to a loss of market for the firm that first develops it. Such spillover or imitation of technology, through market encroachment by rival firms, restricts the benefits to the firm that has developed the technology at a lower level than would be the case in the absence of such imitation. As a result, recovery of development costs of technology that is not easily appropriable becomes particularly difficult since, even when developed, an imitator can easily usurp the earnings. In this sense, private incentives for development are particularly low for technologies where preclusion from imitation is difficult and the degree of competition in use is high.

Given similar technological innovations, the proportion of developer's profits corroded by other firms through imitation is smaller and the degree of competition in use lower the closer the innovation is to development of basic technology rather than to development of new materials, with wider applicability, or to technological innovations related to universalized production technology. On the contrary, technological development, specific to individual products with a narrow range of applications, such as development of new products or product improvement, tends to have a higher degree of competition in use. This provides the basis of the argument, as stressed by the traditional theory, that fundamental research, rather than applied or development research, and creative research, as against research for imitation and improvement, should receive greater public assistance.

17.2 SPILLOVER TO CONSUMER AND DEVELOPMENT INCENTIVES

As shown above, in the discussion on the public goods character of technology or knowledge, private incentives for development decline the lower the degree of appropriability. That is, even if a firm tries to gain a competitive edge over its rivals in the product market by making use of the fruits of development of new technology, the existence of externalities among the firms in the form of imitation and spillover makes private benefits emanating from the development process as such lower than its social benefits. That is why the private benefits tend to be socially low. This, however, is not the only route by which the fruits of development spill over. Benefits also flow down to the consumer through lower prices and increased diversity in consumption. The developer cannot reap the full social benefits of development due to the increase in consumer surplus or spillover to consumers. Thus, the private valuation of the rewards of development for the firm that undertakes such development falls short of the social value and the scale of development activity becomes socially small.[5]

To make this point clear, let us take the example of a process innovation that reduces production costs for an already existing product. The argument, as developed here, is also applicable to product innovation. This is because the latter exhibits process innovation characteristics in the sense that the product that could not be produced at a cost acceptable to all the consumers with the existing technology can now be produced and supplied at a lower cost. It must, however, be stressed that product innovation involves other peculiar problems. The emergence of an entirely new product in the latter case implies a more diversified menu of consumption possibilities that raises social benefits.[6]

Using Fig. 17-1, let us look at the private and social benefits arising from the development of a new technology that has a marginal cost advantage over the existing technology. Curve BD in the figure represents the total market demand. Let us assume that, initially, the product was being competitively supplied with AS_1 representing the supply curve. Thus, AS_1 is the social marginal cost curve and C_1 is the marginal cost of producing this product. Now, assume that costs of production fall to C_2 as a result of development of new production process. FS_2 represents the social marginal cost curve under this new technology (fixed costs of production are assumed away for the sake of analytical simplicity). How can we measure the social benefits generated by the new technology?

Assuming that use of the new technology does not involve any costs, making the technology and the knowledge available to all the economic agents at no cost is socially desirable. In this case, since the product can be produced at a lower cost C_2 with new technology, by selling the product at this price, the increase in total consumer surplus for society as a whole is given by the area $AEGF$ in Fig. 17-1. This is the social benefit or change in social benefit generated by the new technology. The firm engaged in R & D activity, however, cannot secure the full amount of the change in social benefits for itself. Let us elaborate on this point further.

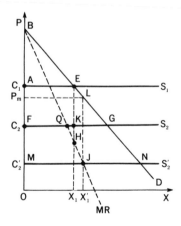

FIG. 17-1

Let us consider the case when the firm that develops the new technology uses it exclusively to supply the product. The marginal cost curve, in this case, is clearly FS_2. If the firm is able to monopolize the market, its marginal revenue curve is given by the straight line B–MR. The developer, therefore, wants to produce FQ output. But this is impossible in the case of the marginal improvement in technology as assumed above. The price, in this case exceeds C_1 and other firms enter (or do not exit) the market to meet the demand since they can reasonably expect to earn positive profits using available technology.

The actual demand curve facing this firm is AED since it is not in a position to charge a price above C_1. The marginal revenue curve corresponding to this average revenue function (demand curve) is given by the kinked line AEH–MR and the firm maximizes its profits by charging a price slightly below C_1. The firm, therefore, sets its price at C_1 and produces X_1 output for total private benefits given by the area $AEKF$. The social benefits of new technology, on the other hand, are given by the area of trapezoid $AEGF$ and benefits corresponding to the area of triangle EKG flow out in the form of consumer surplus. Thus, private benefits of R & D fall short of its social benefits.

The case of new technology that reduces costs by a margin large enough to make the old technology obsolete can also be treated in a similar fashion. This case is represented in Fig. 17-1 by a sufficiently large shift in costs from C_1 to C_2' such that the postdevelopment marginal cost curve MS_2' intersects the marginal revenue curve B–MR to the right of X_1. As in the case of technological change resulting in small cost reductions, the developer maximizes its profits by equating marginal revenue, given by curve AEH–MR, to its marginal cost, given by curve MS_2'. This gives an output level of X_1' and the price charged P_m. Since P_m is less than C_1, the average cost of other firms, the old technology is rendered obsolete with a zero economic value. As a result, the monopoly profits earned with output at X_1' and price at P_m are given by the area P_mLJM. The social benefits from the new technology bringing about such a large reduction in costs are given by the area of trapezoid $AENM$. It can be seen that in this case, too, the private benefits fall short of social benefits as a part of R & D profits flow out to the consumer.[7,8]

All R & D activity, for which social benefits exceed the R & D costs, is desirable on economic welfare grounds. In contrast to this, private incentives dictate that no development activity, for which private benefits of R & D fall short of R & D costs, be undertaken. What we have shown above is that there is a tendency for the private benefits of R & D to fall short of social benefits due to spillover of social benefits to the competing firms or the consumers. Therefore, this may lead to the relation that

Private benefit of R & D activity $<$ R & D costs $<$ social benefit of R & D

Research and development activity in this case, although socially desirable, fails to be carried out due to lack of private incentives.

The divergence between the private and social benefits following R & D activity, in this sense, is the result of the failure of the firm undertaking such activity to recover all the benefits of development in the product market. Such a phenomenon is inevitable, even when imitation is completely prevented, as long as the benefits from development flow away from the developer in the form of consumer surplus. Now, let us consider the circumstances under which the private and social benefits do not diverge. The following three cases can be pointed out.

First, in the case when the demand for the product is perfectly price inelastic such that the demand curve is vertical, it is easy to verify that private and social benefits do not diverge.

Second, we have the case when the product lends itself to, for example, perfect price discrimination and the firm is in a position to siphon off all of the consumer surplus. Such cases, although highly specific, stress the dependence of private incentives for R & D activity on the nature of the product.

The third case, a special case, is highly interesting as it pinpoints the most fundamental cause of divergence. This is the case of marginal improvement in technology. In terms of Fig. 17-1, this is the case when the developed technology results in a marginal reduction in costs (therefore, the case discussed at the very beginning) and the divergence between the private and social benefits from technological development (area of triangle EKG) can be neglected. In this case, the developer can corner almost all of the social benefits generated by the development of new technology. Thus, the divergence between private profits and social benefits, considered here, results from the fact that R & D normally produces noticeably large improvements in technology, rather than marginal improvements, and hence a decline in price cannot be ignored.

17.3 STRUCTURE OF PRODUCT MARKET AND PRIVATE BENEFITS OF RESEARCH AND DEVELOPMENT: THE ARROW EFFECT

Whatever the case, the private incentives for R & D activity, except for highly specific cases, fall short of social benefits and provide a basis for some form of government assistance or intervention. The only problem is that private incentives for R & D are not socially low just because technology and knowledge are indivisible. It is a fact that the market structure in which a firm operates are also important.[9] That is, structure of the product market in which market intervention is to be operative, if undertaken, must be taken into account.

Figure 17-2 compares the extent to which incentives for R & D activity differ when the said industry is a monopoly or perfectly competitive. The curves basically correspond to those of Fig. 17-1. As discussed earlier, in the context of Fig. 17-1, private benefits from R & D activity, if the industry is characterized by perfect competition before technological development occurs, are given by the area $FIHE$.

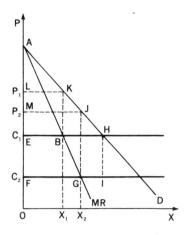

FIG. 17-2

As compared to this, if the firm undertaking R & D monopolizes the market to begin with, it must be supplying X_1 output at price P_1 since its marginal cost before the new technology is developed is C_1. Research and development reduces this cost to C_2 and the firm now supplies X_2 amount of output at price P_2. If the fixed costs of production after R & D activity is undertaken stay the same as before, profits rise from *EBKL* (equals *ABE,* the difference between total revenue *ABX_1O* and total costs *EBX_1O*) to *FGJM* (equals *AGF*). The profits of the monopolist, due to the success of the development effort, have risen by area *EBGF* in Fig. 17-2. Therefore, private benefits of the monopolists from a successful development effort, i.e., the private incentives for R & D, are further reduced as compared to those of the perfectly competitive firm.

This results from the fact that the monopolist earns a huge amount of profits before the introduction of new technology and the increase in production after the new technology is introduced is not very high. This phenomenon, whereby R & D incentives decline due to the fact that the increase in profits is small on account of large predevelopment profits, is termed, hereafter, the "Arrow effect," after Kenneth J. Arrow, who first pointed it out. This Arrow effect has been emphasized in the traditional theory to argue that R & D incentives under monopoly are even smaller than when the product market is competitive.

17.4 A RECONSIDERATION OF UNDERINVESTMENT IN THE RESEARCH AND DEVELOPMENT ARGUMENT

Up to here, we have discussed the effects of (1) the public goods nature of technology and knowledge, (2) the indivisibility of technology developed, and

(3) the structure of competition in the product market where the fruits of development are infused, on the development and acquisition of technology. The main findings can be summarized as follows:

1. The private benefits from development efforts generally fall short of the social benefits, causing R & D investment to fall below the socially optimum level.

2. The private incentives for a development effort differ with the structure of the product market in which the results of development are utilized. In general, private incentives for R & D are higher the greater the degree of product market competition.

Thus, the traditional argument finds making the product markets competitive along with some form of assistance to private sector R & D investment activity desirable.

These arguments, however, cannot be taken at face value, as the results derived from the above analysis are dependent on some important presumptions. The following points require especially close attention in discussing the economic significance of the traditional analysis.

First, *post facto*, R & D costs that are sunk as fixed costs tend to make the product market oligopolistic by generating scale economies. As a result it is practically impossible to meet the traditional theory presumption that policies adopted should lead to competitive, preferably perfectly competitive, markets. What the government should aim at is a second best policy in which an oligopolistic market is taken as a precondition.

Second, the traditional theory presumes that government intervention into private sector economic activity invariably leads to attainment of the best possible state. But this presumption is difficult to accept, as discussed in Chapter 1. This, again, calls for considering a second best policy.[10]

Finally, the traditional argument presumes that development activities are undertaken by only one entity and competition and rivalry for such activity itself does not have any effect on social performance of R & D. In practice, however, a large number of developers engage in and fiercely compete for R & D activities using R & D investments or investments for technology acquisition. We pointed out in Section 16.5 of Chapter 16 that first mover advantages and the monopoly profits concomitant on succeeding in development before any of the rivals provide incentives for R & D activities. Future R & D competition is expected to take the form of moves to get ahead of other firms in the search for monopoly rents and the process of intertemporal competition itself.

The behavior of individual firms, in the process of such competition, can seriously affect the profitability of their own R & D activities as well as those of their rivals. Therefore, the R & D activity of individual firms becomes highly strategic in such circumstances since, by undertaking advance investment far in excess of the other firms, it is possible to subdue the urge of rivals to engage in R & D and gain first mover advantages.

Reconsidering R & D activity in the above perspective, it is possible for private development incentives, unlike in the case of the traditional argument, to be socially excessive. This point is discussed in the next chapter.

Notes

1. For example, cf. Schmalensee (1982). In recent years, network externalities in information and communications industries have received a great deal of attention. These refer to externalities in consumption in the sense that the higher the number of consumers of these goods and services, the greater are the benefits derived even when these goods and services are of the same quality. A firm, in the case of industries characterized by such externalities, that initially introduces a product into the market can also raise effective entry barriers just as in the advertising case. See Katz and Shapiro (1985) and Farrel and Saloner (1985) on this point.

2. See Chapter 7 for details.

3. In this sense, large firms, with huge production facilities and a large market share at present, may not be as keen on new technology as the small-scale firms. See Chapter 19 on this point.

4. For example, the firms like Amdhal, formed as an independent company by erstwhile IBM technologists, are the examples of such technological spillover.

5. While discussing the infant industry protection argument in Chapter 4, it was pointed out that the presence of pecuniary external economies, due to the indivisibility of certain factors, results in set-up costs. The present case is substantively similar.

6. See Chapter 18 for problems related to this point.

7. Here we have considered the case where the firm developing the new technology engages in production activity by itself. The same amount of profits can be earned by selling the new technology to another firm. For example, in the case of new technology that leads to only small cost reductions, the buyer of technology (possibly a number of firms) can be charged AF (or marginally lower)/unit of production carried out with the new technology as technology fees. In the case of technology resulting in substantial cost reductions, the firm that gains a monopoly position in the industry as a result of purchase of the new technology can be made to pay the whole amount of expected monopoly profits (or a slightly lower amount) as technology charges, independent of the level of output.

8. Charging technological fees in proportion to output produced results in unnecessary inefficiencies. This is because such a fee structure gives rise to problems similar to those of a successive monopoly that have been often discussed in the context of the problem of vertical integration. For example, see Vernon and Graham (1971).

9. The analysis, hereunder, follows Arrow (1962). Also see Demsetz (1969).

10. Although a patenting system is in effect to deal with the impossibility of appropriating technology and knowledge, this system also has severe drawbacks from the viewpoint of efficiency of resource allocation. See Chapter 20 on this point.

18

Research and Development Competition and Excess Investment

18.1 INTRODUCTION

As seen in the last chapter, the underinvestment argument of the traditional theory presumes the attainment of the best state by rectifying the divergence between the private and social benefits of R & D through policy intervention by the government. But a number of studies since then have shown that theoretical difficulties involved in attainment of the best state in practice are insurmountable and the traditional theory has come under a review. It is clear from these studies that there is a distinct possibility for private incentives for R & D activity to become socially excessive rather than being too low. This argument can be, broadly, approached in two ways.

The first of these approaches deals with nonconflicting R & D competition assuming that there are a large number of development seeds in existence and that a number of inventors, operating in their own product market, are engaged in the generation of economic value independent of each other. In the traditional theory, there is only one development objective and no firm, except the one that succeeds first in attaining this objective, can reap the first mover advantage. In reality, however, in a number of cases, R & D competition takes the form of substitution or complementarity relations in demand or the form of indirect competition in factor markets but there is no direct competition for the development objectives.

For example, development of super alloy in the steel industry does not hinder development of new materials in the petrochemical industry. The two new materials, in this case, may either compete with or complement one another. Even when the products are in a competitive relationship, early development of one of the products does not kill all incentives for developing the other product. Thus, the first approach uses this perspective to review the results of traditional theory, based on the operation of the Arrow effect, that development incentives under monopoly are weaker as compared to those in a competitive market.

The second approach considers the case where a number of inventing firms are

202

fiercely competing for the same development objective. The traditional theory assumed that there is only one inventor but, in reality, a number of inventors compete for the monopoly rents expected from a particular development. Concentrating on this aspect, the later discussion reveals that the scale of R & D activity in the society tends to be socially excessive due to incentives for the firms to move ahead of its rivals, overlapping of investment due to multiplicity of inventors, and externalities resulting from movement of "common pool" among the inventing firms.

The subsequent discussion uses the first of these approaches to reconsider the traditional arguments as developed in the previous chapter.

18.2 Nonconflicting Research and Development Competition and Industrial Linkages

The assumption of the traditional theory that no firm other than that of the inventor can reap the rewards of development is, in most cases, unrealistic. In a substantial number of cases, there is no direct competition for the invention as such although indirect competition based on relationships of demand substitutability and complementarity or via the factor markets may prevail.

Research and development in different industries, referred to earlier, is a clear example of such relationships. However, manufacturing methods or processes, even when firms within the same industry engage in development of similarly performing new products, tend to differ in a large number of cases. The differences between VHS and Beta formats in the VCR industry and the differences in production methods for optical fibers between Japan and the United States are some typical examples. In this case, even if a firm is the first to invent VCRs or optical fibers, the latecomers can use a different production methodology to develop a close substitute to the first mover product. In this sense, the profits of the latecomer from R & D cannot be brought down to zero.

Let us now reconsider the traditional underinvestment in the R & D argument, especially the significance of the Arrow effect, which posits that development incentives fall as the degree of monopoly in the industry increases, in this perspective. Let us consider a simple, monopolistically competitive market in which the firms, engaged in development activity, are interdependent in terms of demand and factor inputs but do not directly compete for results of development efforts.

The economy is composed of n types of goods and services. Each firm produces a single good or service and requires a given level of fixed costs to start production. Hereunder, for the sake of simplicity, we assume that cost conditions for each good or service are symmetric (i.e., except for differences in goods or services produced, cost conditions are the same). Fixed costs are denoted by f and the unit cost of production, assumed to be fixed, is represented by c. Further, if we assume the demand function for each good or service to be perfectly symmetric, the equilibrium, given the number of firms, i.e., the number of goods and services, at n, is also expected to be perfectly symmetric. Moreover, the final long-run profits of the representative firm must be zero since potential entrants keep introducing new products into the market by investing in fixed costs as long as individual firms earn a positive profit.

This model of monopolistic competition can be interpreted as a model of investment competition for product development. The fixed cost f represents investment cost for product development, and quasirents earned in the product market x (= total revenue − total variable cost) reflect the private profits from R&D. Let us first consider whether investment for product development is socially low in this case. This is done by investigating whether a government, incapable of intervening in the firm behavior in the product market but which can control private sector investment for product development, can raise economic welfare by increasing the number of products as compared to the state of equilibrium noted above.[1]

The change in welfare Δw, when the government increases the number of products by one, is effectively equivalent to the change in welfare concomitant upon new entry. Equation (17) of Chapter 13, describing the change in welfare as a result of new entry, therefore, is theoretically applicable to this case as well. The only major point of departure is that we now need to consider the benefits to the consumer of a diversification in consumption of goods. Thus, we get

$$\Delta w = n(p - c)\Delta x + [(p - c)x - f]$$
$$+ \text{ benefits of increased diversity in consumption}$$

where n is the number of products in equilibrium, Δx is the change in output of the existing firms as a result of new entry, p is the equilibrium price of individual goods, and x is the equilibrium output of each good. As discussed in Chapter 13, the first term on the right-hand side represents the resource-allocation effect and the second term reflects the competition-promotion effect. If the number of products in equilibrium is sufficiently large, the competition-promotion effect can be approximated by the profits of the representative firm and is zero. Therefore, it is sufficient to concentrate only on the first term, the resource-allocation effect (the first term), and the third term, the effect of increased diversity.

It is a widely known fact in the literature of monopolistic competition that new entry, in a monopolistically competitive market, has two opposing effects. Each firm, in the long-run equilibrium that emerges as a result of monopolistic competition, operates at a point where average costs are still falling and economies of scale are not fully exploited. A newly entering firm, in its bid to encroach upon the demand for the existing firms' products, ends up reducing the profits arising from scale economies. This corresponds to the negative sign on the resource-allocation effect, the first term in the expression. As far as this is concerned, additional entry in market equilibrium results in reducing economic welfare. At the same time, it also calls forth socially excessive entry or excessive investment in product development since the social welfare–reducing new entry gives rise to private profits. On the other hand, introduction of new products into the market is beneficial to the extent that the consumption menu is widened, as reflected in the third term. There is no unequivocal way to determine which of the two effects dominates.[2]

The resource-allocation effect, as discussed above, tends to dominate the effect of increased diversity if product innovation takes the form of improved design of an already existing product or does not make a significant difference in the eyes of the consumer even when production technology differs. The technology development competition between VHS and Beta formats in the case of VCRs and the American and Japanese methods of producing optical fibers fall in this category. In the case of process innovation, which does not entail any benefits from increased diversity, the tendency for excessive investment in technology development is expected to be stronger, as discussed in Chapter 14.

18.3 External Diseconomies of Common Pool and Research and Development

Thus, the traditional theory, stressing underinvestment in R & D, leaves a substantial scope for reconsideration if nonconflicting technology development competition is taken into account as discussed above. What happens in the case of rivalry in technology development competition?

When a number of firms compete for the same development objective, the benefits from successful invention go only to the firm which is first to succeed. A firm that lags behind cannot reap any profits. In these circumstances, development investment by a rival gives rise to external diseconomies in the sense that the probability that an individual firm will succeed before any of its rivals falls as compared to a situation when such investment is not undertaken. But since profits in the case of delayed development are zero, individual firms try to retrieve the situation by incurring greater development expenditures than before. The traditional theory does not take the effect of such competition or rivalry for development activities itself into account.

For society as a whole, on the other hand, success in any one of the R & D efforts is enough and the rivalry among the firms strongly tends to resource waste. In any case, simultaneous investment by a number of firms in R & D for a technology that is highly collective or noncompetitive in consumption is socially unnecessary duplication, and the possibility of loss in efficiency of resource allocation is high.

This tendency to overinvest results from the commitment by a number of firms to development since it is impossible for any one to prevent a firm, potentially capable of such development activity, from undertaking it. Moreover, such a commitment does not take the effect on other firms into consideration. In this sense, overinvestment originates in the unclear specification of ownership rights to potential fruits of development. Such external diseconomies are referred to as diseconomies of "common pool" or congestion diseconomies arising usually when individuals use facilities like forest areas, fishing areas, and roads, which can be used collectively by a number of economic entities with disregard for the effects on other entities. However, it is usually the uncertainty characterizing technology development activities, as discussed below, that lies at the back of socially excessive R & D investment, when a number of inventors engage in R & D competition by undertaking development activities simultaneously.[3]

Our discussion to this point, inclusive of the discussion of the traditional theory, implicitly assumed that each inventing firm knew, with certainty, how fast it could succeed in creating an invention given an amount of investment. But R & D activity, in fact, is a highly uncertain economic activity and requires the inventing firms to bear substantial risks. Regardless of the amount of development expenditure incurred by a firm, the time when the desired innovation actually materializes is uncertain. Moreover, such obscurity gives rise to uncertainty as to which firm is first to succeed in invention. But a firm that undertakes R & D risks and succeeds in inventing the coveted technology, before any of its more successful rivals, is assured of enormous first mover advantages. It is precisely due to this that a large number of small-scale firms or joint ventures invest in technology development side by side with the large-scale firms that have extensive development funds.

Below, we look at the process by which external diseconomies of common pool in technology development competition give rise to overinvestment in R & D, using a simple model incorporating above-mentioned uncertainties accompanying R & D activity.[4]

Let us assume that a number of firms possess seeds for the same potential innovation. Each firm undertakes R & D investment aimed at commercializing the innovation in the form of a product and introducing it into the market before any of its rivals. If successful in this attempt, the firm earns a monopoly profit Π (>0) by supplying a new product.[5] Further, the number of firms engaged in development activity is assumed to be constant at n.

To begin with, R & D activity requires a firm i ($i = 1 \ldots n$) to pay a fixed cost f and later to bear additional variable costs x_i. The former represents costs like those incurred for the setting up of an R & D proposal, or provision of research facilities and, for simplicity of exposition, are assumed to be the same for all the firms. The latter refers to costs incurred after the R & D plan is put into operation and is determined by the number of research personnel and the desired pace of research. The size of these latter-type costs incurred by a firm determines the speed of its development effort, the success of which requires completion before any of its rivals' efforts. In other words, these costs determine the degree of R & D uncertainty faced by the firm.

In what follows, we take the uncertainties associated with R & D activity into account and represent the probability P_i with which a firm i succeeds in its development efforts in front of its rivals as a function of its own development expenditure x_i and the total development expenditure of the industry as a whole, $X = \Sigma\, x_j$, as

$$P_i = P(x_i, X) \qquad (i = 1 \ldots n) \qquad (1a)$$

This function is assumed to satisfy the following conditions for $x_i > 0$ and $X > 0$:

$$0 < P(x_i, X) < 1 \qquad (1b)$$
$$P_x: \partial P(x_i, X)/\partial x_i > 0; \qquad P_{xx}: \partial^2 P(x_i, X)/\partial x_i^2 < 0 \qquad (1c)$$
$$P_X: \partial P(x_i, X)/\partial X < 0 \qquad (1d)$$

That is, if all firms invest in R & D, no firm can be fully certain of successful invention over the heads of its other rivals [Eq. (1b)]. Given the amount invested by the other firms, increased investment by an individual firm raises the probability of its success before the rivals but the rate of improvement in the probability of success declines [Eq. (1c)] as investment increases. On the other hand, the probability of success for an individual firm declines if the rivals increase their development expenditures [Eq. (1d)].

We assume here that total investment in the industry stays constant even if investment by an individual firm rises. This implies a sufficiently large number of firms so that the effect of an increase in investment by an individual firm on total industry investment can be neglected.[6] Further, for simplifying the analysis, it is assumed that the relation determining the probability of success in Eq. (1a) is the same for all the firms so that the probability of a multiple number of firms succeeding in the invention activity simultaneously is zero.[7]

Under these circumstances, the expected net benefits of R & D activity v_i that a firm i can look for can be represented as

$$v_i(x_i, X) = P(x_i, X)\Pi - x_i - f \qquad (2)$$

An individual firm maximizes its net benefits with respect to its own investment, taking total industry investment as given. If we assume the resulting equilibrium to be symmetric, this depends on the number of firms. Representing the investment of an individual firm in equilibrium by $x^*(n)$, the following equation must be satisfied.

$$B_P[x^*(n), X^*(n)] - 1 = 0 \qquad (i = 1 \ldots n) \qquad (3)$$

where $X^*(n) = nx^*(n)$ and

$$B_P(x, X) = P_x(x, X)\Pi \qquad (4)$$

represents private marginal benefits of development expenditure undertaken by individual firms.

Is the level of R & D activities for the industry as a whole, in this case, the socially desirable le$\overset{\backslash}{\text{v}}$el? Representing the value of R & D to the whole society V as the sum of expected benefits from invention to all the firms, we can write

$$V = \sum_{i=1}^{n} P(x_i, \Sigma x_j)\Pi - \sum_{i=1}^{n} x_i - nF \qquad (5)$$

The socially desirable investment level for each firm is also symmetric in this case. If this is represented by $x_S(n)$, in view of its dependence on the number of firms, it must satisfy, following Eq. (5),

$$B_S[x_S(n), n] - 1 = 0 \qquad (6)$$

where

$$B_S(x, n) = [P_x(x, nx) + nP_X(x, nx)]\Pi \qquad (7)$$

and is the social marginal benefit from development expenditure.

Provided the second order condition for maximization of social net benefits is satisfied, we invariably get $x^*(n) > x_S(n)$. This is represented in Fig. 18-1. The horizontal axis shows the development expenditure undertaken by individual firms. Curve MC with a unit height is the marginal cost curve of development expenditures while curve B_S (or B_P) reflects social marginal benefits (or private marginal benefits) from R & D investment. The socially desirable investment level satisfying Eq. (6) is given by the intersection of B_S and MC as $x_S(n)$ and the investment level in competitive equilibrium satisfying Eq. (3) is given by the intersection of B_P and MC as $x^*(n)$.

Comparing Eqs. (4) and (7), it is clear from Eq. (1d) that social marginal benefits B_S are lower than private marginal benefits B_P. This follows from the fact that increased investment by an individual firm generates external diseconomies in the form of reduced probability of success by the other firms, as depicted

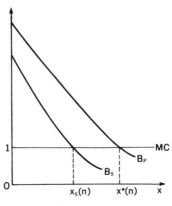

FIG. 18-1

by the second term within parentheses on the right-hand side of Eq. (7). Consequently, the social marginal benefit curve B_S lies below the private marginal benefit curve B_P, indicating that development expenditure by individual firms is socially excessive. This is referred to as external diseconomies of common pool coming into operation when technology development competition is beset with rivalries.

Again, the phenomenon of overinvestment arising on account of external diseconomies of common pool also implies duplication of investment. The socially desirable investment level is below that attained under competitive equilibrium. That is, the excess investment is socially unnecessary and results from duplication of investment by individual firms. Finally, it must be noted that inefficiencies resulting from duplication of investment are compounded by the inefficiencies due to excessive entry that occur under conditions of free entry and exit as discussed in Chapter 15.

18.4 RANK-ORDER TOURNAMENT IN TECHNOLOGY DEVELOPMENT AND RUSH TO INVENT

The previous section focused on uncertainties associated with R & D to analyze the relation between external diseconomies of common pool resulting from technology development competition involving conflict and overinvestment in R & D. As has been stressed over and over, it is the monopoly rents entailing the fruits of research activity that provide an economic motive for R & D. In the context of dynamic competition, involving competition among the firms for their continued existence, as opposed to static perfect competition, each firm vies for these monopoly rents by risking its very existence. The analysis in the last section does not fully capture the competition-through-time aspect of the technology development.

It is difficult for a firm that begins development at a later date, as compared to another that has already started its development activities, to earn monopoly rents unless it invests far more than the already existing firm. Conversely, if a latecomer does undertake such investment, it becomes difficult for the existing firm to earn those monopoly profits without undertaking still higher investment. Since the probability of success at an early date rises for the firm investing the most, the resulting emulation effect operates among the firms to increase their eagerness for larger and larger R & D investment.

This emulation effect can also be interpreted as an external diseconomy of common pool, discussed earlier. But this effect comes into operation only because R & D competition resembles strongly a rank-order tournament involving time or competition through time. In this sense, R & D competition differs from price competition in one fundamental respect. This gives rise to what has been termed as the rush to invent since private incentives for development tend to be socially excessive. We take recourse to Barzel's (1968) model to explain this phenomenon as well as the significance of the concept of competition through time.[8]

Let us assume that there exists one R & D opportunity. This R & D opportunity generates V as monopoly rent (discounted present value terms) for the firm that succeeds first, irrespective of the timing.[9] Now, if the invention materializes at time t, the discounted present value of monopoly rent thus generated is $b(t)V$ ($= e^{-rt}V$, where r is the rate of discount). It is obvious that a lengthening of time required for invention raises t and lowers $b(t)$. This R & D does not involve uncertainty but compressing the invention process involves costs. More concretely, if t is the time allowed for achieving success, $c(t)$ is the development cost (discounted present value terms) needed to succeed after period t. The function $c(t)$, representing the cost of R & D investment, is assumed to be decreasing in $t [c'(t) < 0]$. The longer the time taken for successful invention, the lower are the development costs since the economy as a whole shows technological progress in the meanwhile and, moreover, the development activity gets a breathing space.

Let us assume the net profits earned by a firm as a result of succeeding in this R & D effort at time t, before the others, to be

$$a(t) = b(t)V - c(t)$$

tracing a humped curve as depicted in Fig. 18-2. The cost of compressing the invention process within a short period of time are tremendous, resulting in negative net profits. By increasing the time required for the inventive activity, R & D costs decrease, increasing net profits. But if time taken is exceptionally long, invention comes about far in the future and reduces the present value of net profits earned.

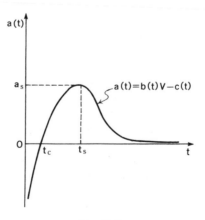

Fig. 18-2

To simplify the matter, let us assume that the rewards of this R & D do not flow out to consumers, despite the indivisibility involved, so that the private benefits to the firm engaged in the inventive activity equal its social benefits. The socially optimum time needed for R & D, in this instance, is t_S, where net benefits from R & D activity (= social net benefits) are maximized. It is clear that if a private sector firm A undertakes socially optimum R & D, it earns a_S [$= a(t_S) > 0$] as net private profits. But this induces the firms, competing for private profits, to conduct the same development activity in a shorter time.

The reason can be easily elaborated by considering firm B, which is able to succeed in the invention in a slightly shorter period of time than t_S. As a result, firm B is able to preempt the monopoly rents being earned by firm A. But firm A, or some third firm C, can preempt firm B's monopoly rents by undertaking a higher R & D investment and hastening the process still further. This rush to invent by the firms trying to preempt the monopoly rents of their rivals by hastening the pace of development continues relentlessly as long as the net profits arising from successful invention ahead of others $a(t)$ are positive. This is nothing but rank-order tournament involving time.

The rank-order tournament through time (as in the case of Bertrand competition, which is a rank-order tournament involving prices) continues until total profits are competed down to zero, i.e., the invention comes about at time t_C. In the case of R & D competition for technologies that are appropriable, the firms do not look for marginal profits $a'(t)$ but compete for the total profits $a(t)$ concomitant on an early success in invention. The competition for preemption of monopoly rents leads to completion of an R & D activity, which should have socially been undertaken in time t_S, by period t_C, and the level of R & D investment becomes socially excessive.

18.5 PRIVATE INCENTIVES FOR RESEARCH AND DEVELOPMENT: A REVIEW

In this chapter, we considered the possibility that private incentives for R & D (in a second best sense), granting that the first best state assumed by the traditional theory cannot be attained, could become socially excessive. However, a proper understanding of the excessive investment outcome as presented in this chapter requires a careful look at the following points.

In our analysis of rank-order tournament (rush to invent), the social value placed on technology development was assumed to equal its private value. In practice, however, as discussed in the previous chapter, the social value exceeds private value by the spillover effect that benefits other firms and the consumers. To this extent, the private R & D incentives tend to fall short of social benefits, as dictated by the traditional theory. The main focus of the excessive investment argument, as developed in this chapter, is to show that, when a number of firms are involved in development activity, the private R & D incentives are stronger than suggested by the traditional theory due to the competitive interdependence of the firms in terms of demand and factor input structure or the external diseconomies of common pool and so on. In this sense, when the degree of excessive investment is not too high, there is a distinct possibility for R & D activity, on the basis of private incentives alone, to come close to the optimum level as posited by the traditional theory.

An evaluation of the excessive investment argument in this perspective does not shed any new light on the controversy over whether private incentives for R & D are socially excessive or too little. As discussed toward the end of the last chapter, R & D competition is a process of strategic behavior in which each firm vies to succeed in its development efforts ahead of its rivals. The Barzel model lucidly presents such a strategic competitive process. But the Barzel model has the following shortcomings.

In the Barzel model, although a number of firms compete, if any one of the firms aims to complete the invention by period t_C, no other firm has an incentive to engage in the same R & D activity. In this sense, while the number of potential developers is large, only a single developer undertakes the R & D activity. Excessive investment arises only when there is a threat of potential new entry in the sense that the firm actually engaged in R & D loses its development profits to the other firms by reducing its own R & D investment. But how is such a leading firm determined? The Barzel explanation lacks a mechanism to determine a developer firm.

It is also plausible to think that a firm gaining access to the development seeds before the others monopolizes R & D activity. The most important point, however, is the position held by the existing firms in the product market. For example, a large firm with an extensive share of the product market, if overtaken by a small firm, stands to lose a substantial proportion of the market if the invention in question is a cost-reducing new technology. In contrast to this, a small firm has very little to lose if the large firm overtakes it. In this sense a large firm has a relatively greater incentive for R & D activity and is a good candidate for becoming the leading firm in the Barzel model. Thus, the firm holding the highest R & D incentives is intricately related to the structure of the product market or, alternatively, to the position that an individual firm holds in the product market. The next chapter discusses the relationship between the structure of the product market and R & D incentives under oligopolistic strategic interdependence of the firms.

NOTES

1. The analysis below depends heavily on Dixit and Stiglitz (1977) and Stiglitz (1984). Also, cf. Okuno-Fujiwara and Suzumura (1987).

2. Dixit and Stiglitz (1977) show that under certain conditions the strategic effect of the benefits from increased diversity exactly balance out and diversity in goods supplied under competitive equi-

librium coincides with the socially optimum level in the second best sense. This result, however, is dependent on a number of assumptions in their model and cannot be easily generalized.

3. For a discussion of uncertainty in the context of R & D, see Kamien and Schwartz (1982).

4. The analysis here is based mainly on Loury (1979), Lee and Wilde (1980), Stewart (1983), and Dixit (1985).

5. Here, Π represents the discounted present value of the flow of profits beginning from the time the firm succeeds in R & D. In a strict sense, the discounted present value of profits from development activity depends on the timing of development. For the sake of simplicity, the present analysis assumes the discounted present value of profits to be independent of the timing of development.

6. The subsequent analysis is applicable to the case when a change in investment by a single firm affects the total investment in the industry. For details, see the literature cited in Note 4 above.

7. In continuous time, the probability of simultaneous success in development by multiple number of firms is zero if, for example, the technological uncertainty associated with R & D is assumed to follow a Powerson process.

8. Dasgupta and Stiglitz (1980a) present another study that sees R & D competition as a rank-order tournament involving time.

9. Strictly, V depends on the timing of development also. See Note 5 above.

19

Market Structure and Research and Development: Innovation, Improvement, and Imitation

This chapter addresses the relationship between strategic R & D incentives and market structure using the framework developed in the previous chapter. The Schumpeterian creative destruction, as discussed in Chapter 16, forms the basis of dynamism shown by a capitalist economy. Even though a firm is in a position to earn substantial pioneer profits for some time by introducing a new technology drastically different from the existing one, based on creative invention or discovery, the technology spreads out to other firms through the process of imitation and improvement. The inappropriability of technology and knowledge, pointed out in Chapter 17 as a factor causing development incentives to become too little, also makes the diffusion of new technology and knowledge through marginal improvements and imitation by the other firms that makes it possible to avoid a monopolization of market by the firm pioneering new technology and gives rise to widespread incentives for the development of new technology.

In this perspective, the received theory of R & D has the following two drawbacks.

First, the received theory deals primarily with "drastic technological innovations"—innovations that oust all the other firms from the market and change the market structure drastically—while the "marginal technological innovations" receive a light treatment. However, in reality, in most cases all or some of the existing firms may be able to stay in the market even after a technological innovation has occurred. Technological innovation, in this case, does not raise the competitive power of the adopting firm enough to drive out other firms but improves the competitive position of the innovating firm relative to its rivals. Technological innovations that do not result in radical changes in the market structure are referred to as marginal technological innovations. The R & D activities related to diffusion-like improvement and imitation fall in the category of marginal technological innovations. In this sense, improvement- and imitation-related R & D activities have been neglected in the traditional theory.

Second, the traditional theory also pays little attention to strategic behavior adopted by firms in the context of R & D competition. Technological innovation, by giving the innovating firm a competitive edge, makes it possible to capture rival markets. This aspect has been more or less ignored in the traditional theory. Such neglect, in an oligopolistic industry, can lead to an underestimation of private benefits from R & D as discussed below.

The private benefit from R & D is the difference between (1) the profits concomitant on appropriation of the fruits of development and (2) the profits that can be earned if the firm fails to appropriate these fruits. The profits under (1) are composed of direct profits generated by cost reduction, assuming the output of the innovating firm to be constant and the profits emerging as a result of wresting the market share of other firms. The latter type of profits do not materialize in monopolistic markets of the traditional theory. Profits under (2), on the other hand, are smaller as compared to profits earned if innovation fails to materialize. This follows as the relative competitiveness of a firm overtaken by a rival declines, causing a loss in market share. This strategic effect also fails to emerge in the monopolistic and perfectly competitive markets analyzed by the traditional theory. Thus, private benefits from R & D in an oligopolistic industry, taking these strategic effects into consideration, are higher than predicted by the traditional theory.[1]

These private benefits from R & D differ, depending on whether the technological innovation in question is a radical innovation or a marginal improvement, or on the position that the innovating firm holds in the product market. The subsequent analysis considers the relationships involving radical technological innovations or marginal improvements and the relative position of an individual firm in the industry.

19.2 THE POSITION OF A FIRM IN THE INDUSTRY AND RESEARCH AND DEVELOPMENT INCENTIVES

Competition for preemption of monopoly rents is, in fact, a struggle for rents arising out of successful R & D. If the size of these rents varies over the firms, the firms with the highest rents will also have the greatest incentives for R & D, and also for hastening the pace of R & D. As the size of rents emanating from successful R & D depends on the position of a firm in the industry, competition preemption of rents, or the rank-order tournament for R & D, determines whether the position of the firm in the industry changes over time or not.[2] In this sense, an analysis of the endogenous determination of market structure—how and which characteristics of the market itself determine the structure of the market—requires an explicit consideration of preemptive competition for rent when the size or the position of the firms within an industry differs.

Let us use a simple Barzel-type model of duopoly (1968) to analyze the effect of the position of a firm in an industry on preemptive competition for rent and how the latter, in turn, affects the relative position of the firm over time.[3]

We consider an industry with only two firms and also assume that only these two firms engage in the R & D under consideration. Further, assume that there is no technical uncertainty involved in this R & D and the profits of a firm from the R & D activity depend on which firm is first to succeed in development of this technology (or a superior technology) or, in other words, the firm that wins in the R & D competition. The table below depicts the manner in which the profits of the two firms are determined depending on which firm wins the competition. $W(i)$ and $L(i)$ in the table are the profits of firm i ($i = 1$, 2) when it wins and when it loses. Here, $W(i) > L(i) \geq 0$ ($i = 1$, 2).

	Firm 1 profits	Firm 2 profits
Firm 1 wins	$W(1)$	$L(2)$
Firm 2 wins	$L(1)$	$W(2)$

The firm that succeeds in developing and implementing the technology before its rival (or develops a superior technology) wins the competition for preemption of rents. Furthermore, let the timing of innovation and its implementation, following the Barzel model as discussed in the previous chapter, depend on the size of R & D investment by a firm. If the firms do not differ in terms of their stock of technology and knowledge needed for R & D, a firm that invests more than its rival, however small, will be the first to obtain the fruits of R & D. To simplify the matter let us assume, in the subsequent discussion, that a firm that invests more than its rival wins the R & D competition with a probability of 1. The problem facing us now is, how does R & D investment by individual firms vary and which of the two firms improves its position within the industry as a result when profits, as depicted in the table above, differ among the firms and there are interfirm differentials in technological levels needed for technological development itself?

Let us calculate firm i's ($i = 1$, 2) private incentives for R & D, i.e., the maximum amount of R & D investment $X(i)$ that a firm is ready to undertake for the given R & D activity. Let us take firm i and assume that in the initial situation the rival is sure to win the R & D competition. But if it is possible to reverse the results of competition by increasing R & D investment, firm i has an incentive to undertake R & D expenditure to the tune of

$$X(i) = W(i) - L(i) \qquad (i = 1, 2) \qquad (1)$$

As long as the costs of R & D competition to firm i fall short of this incentive, $X(i)$, the firm tries to annex the monopoly rents by hastening the pace of development relative to the rival and winning the R & D competition.

Let us, first, consider the relationship between position of a firm in the industry and R & D incentives assuming that the cost of R & D investment $c(t)$ is the same for both the firms. It is obvious, here, that firm i, with a relatively greater private incentives for R & D as measured by $X(i)$, can certainly win the R & D competition by investing slightly more in R & D than the maximum amount of investment $X(j)$ that its rival is ready to undertake.   •

Thus, the sufficient condition for firm 1 to win in R & D competition, when the cost of R & D investment is the same for both the firms, is given by

$$W(1) - L(1) > W(2) - L(2) \qquad (2a)$$

or, by rewriting Eq. (2a),

$$W(1) + L(2) > W(2) + L(1) \qquad (2b)$$

Let us consider the conditions under which Eq. (2a) or (2b) is satisfied and R & D incentives for firm 1 exceed those of firm 2. Gilbert and Newbery (1982) clarify this point.[4]

For analytical simplicity, assume that firm 1 monopolizes the market (monopoly owner of a technology slightly inferior to the one aimed at by the present R & D activity) before the R & D succeeds. Now firm 2, a potential competitor in this monopolized market, tries to enter the market by developing a new technology.

If firm 1 is able to develop the coveted technology before firm 2, the latter fails to enter the market. Firm 1 not only maintains its monopoly of the market but the profits earned on the basis of the developed technology $W(1)$ are also higher than before. Since firm 2 has failed to enter the market, it earns zero profits in this market. But if firm 2 succeeds in development, instead, the market must be divided among the two firms. The profits of the two firms, in such a duopolistic market, are $W(2)$ and $L(1)$, respectively.

The new technology under consideration here is a marginal new technology in the sense that it represents only a small improvement over the old technology. Therefore, aside from the division of profits between the two firms, the total industry profits can be higher if the existing firm utilizes the new technology in a monopolistic market without a competitor than if the new firm possessing the new technology competes with the existing firm using old technology. This is because the profits earned by the former are the maximum attainable using the new technology. That is, Eq. (2b) is satisfied.

This point can be intuitively explained using Eq. (2a). If firm 1, having a monopoly in the market, is able to introduce the new technology earlier, it earns monopoly profits. But if it fails to do so, it loses its market share to the new entrant, firm 2. In contrast to this, if firm 2 is the first to introduce the new technology, it can capture a part of the existing firm's market but it has nothing to lose if firm 1 overtakes. Since firm 1, with a monopoly in the market, suffers a reduction in its profits if overtaken by the rival, it tries to introduce the new technology earlier to avoid this situation.

This result stands even if the product market is competitive to begin with and stays competitive even after the new technology is introduced as long as the new technology is marginal. Let us now visualize the case when firm 1 holds a larger market share on account of superior cost conditions, as compared to firm 2, and effectiveness of its advertisement campaign. By failing to introduce the marginal new technology, it loses market to its rival and incurs losses. Generally, the loss is greater the bigger the market share and the greater the profit margin due to superior cost conditions before the new technology is introduced. As a result, the larger the share of the market held by a firm to begin with, the greater are the incentives for introducing the marginal new technology.

19.3 THE STRENGTHS AND WEAKNESSES OF THE GILBERT–NEWBERY MODEL

As discussed in the previous section, successful innovation by a firm holding substantial monopoly power, based on technology in use or the image of the firm, leads to a further monopolization of the market after the innovation is introduced and total industry profits rise. In contrast, the market becomes more competitive if an existing, relatively lower ranked, small firm or a new entrant to the industry succeeds in creating the said innovation. Therefore, under the assumption of no interfirm differentials in technological levels needed for R & D activity itself, the firm with an already established monopolistic position is always the first to undertake technological innovations, thereby preempting the monopoly rents associated with R & D. A relatively low-placed firm loses in R & D competition and makes an exit from the industry and a firm contemplating new entry into the industry also fails to beat the monopolistic firm.

How far can one generalize this result derived from the Gilbert–Newbery model? The conclusion, based on their analysis, that market concentration increases over time and only the large firms end up conducting R & D activities, is at variance with the experience of R & D competition in the high-technology industries that we usually hear about. Moreover, this conclusion diverges significantly from the concept of dynamic interfirm competition based on the Schumpeterian creative destruction.

What are the drawbacks of the above model? In the remainder of this section we concentrate on two main drawbacks of the Gilbert–Newbery model that also provide a basis for the discussion carried out in the next section.[5]

First, the new technology in the Gilbert–Newbery model is a marginal rather than a path-breaking technological innovation. A path-breaking technology replaces the existing technology by a totally new product. A path-breaking technological innovation gives the innovating firm, irrespective of whether the firm is an existing monopoly or a newly entering venture business, the same monopolistic position in the industry. The loser in this competition, on the other hand, loses all profit opportunities in the said market without any regard to its position in the industry before the innovation materializes. That is, $W(1) = W(2) > 0$ and

$L(1) = L(2) = 0$. The conclusions of the Gilbert–Newbery model, as derived above, therefore break down under these conditions and all the firms hold exactly the same R & D incentives. In this sense, the Gilbert–Newbery model treats only the marginal R & D, i.e., R & D for technological improvement producing a marginal increase in profits, rather than R & D through which the firms struggle for their very existence.

Second, the model is flawed because it ignores the fact that R & D activity is fundamentally full of uncertainties and risky. The real-world firms cannot capture the monopoly rents with absolute certainty simply by increasing their R & D investment, as posited by the Gilbert–Newbery model. There is an intrinsic risk of being overtaken by the rival no matter how large the R & D expenditures are. Therefore, R & D-related decisions are not as straightforward as a decision on whether or not to undertake a particular R & D project. What is important for the firm, instead, is the extent to which it is advisable to change the probability of success ahead of the rivals through an increase in its own R & D investment, i.e., marginal adjustments in and choice of investment levels.

The next section takes explicit note of the uncertain nature of R & D activities and sets up a more generalized model, allowing for development of a path-breaking technology, in order to analyze the significance and limitations of R & D activities of private sector firms involved in dynamic competition. However, there is still another important point left unexplained by the Gilbert–Newbery model, i.e., the role of accumulation of R & D technology as a barrier to prevent new entry into R & D activities. The remainder of this section discusses this point.

The Gilbert–Newbery model assumes that firms are similar in terms of technology needed to undertake R & D, i.e., they have exactly similar development cost functions $c(t)$. But R & D costs depend on the accumulated knowledge and know-how regarding R & D as well as the quality and number of technicians and researchers employed by a firm. A firm, with a sufficiently large stock of accumulated research in the concerned area and already sunk costs needed for such research, is likely to be in a better position to develop the technology at a lower cost as compared to a firm that does not have these advantages. In this sense, even if the returns on R & D investment, i.e., R & D incentives, are the same for all the firms, a firm with an insufficient accumulation of research will not be inclined to make as large an investment in R & D as its rival and hence cannot win the development race.

On the contrary, the firm holding a sufficiently large stock of accumulated research, by reducing the R & D incentives for the competing firms and by subduing new entry, can very well ensure a monopolistic position for itself in the product market over the long run. It goes without saying that, as a result, the industry is divested of competitive forces and monopoly pricing becomes possible, giving rise to inefficiencies in resource allocation. Such barriers to entry in the field of R & D itself are especially important from the viewpoint of industrial policy, as discussed later.

19.4 STRATEGIC RESEARCH AND DEVELOPMENT COMPETITION: INNOVATION, IMPROVEMENT, AND IMITATION

When the R & D results are uncertain, an entity engaged in R & D is not faced with a clear-cut win or lose situation. It must consider the possibility of successful development by both itself and its rival at the same time, or of both failing in this effort. Let the profits earned by the two firms, given all the possible states that R & D results can take inclusive of the above two cases, be as depicted in the table below.[6]

	s_2	f_2
s_1	(D_1, D_2)	(W_1, L_2)
f_1	(L_1, W_2)	(F_1, F_2)

The term s_i (f_i) depicts the state of success (failure) in R & D by firm i and the two terms enclosed within the parentheses represent the profits earned by the two firms in each of these states, with the left term standing for firm 1 and the right for firm 2. For example, success in R & D for firm 1 and a failure for firm 2 implies the emergence of the state depicted by row 1 column 2 of the table such that the profits of firms 1 and 2 are W_1 and L_2, respectively.

Now, let p_i represent the probability of successful R & D by the ith firm and assume that this probability is a function of the size of R & D investment, x_i. That is, firm i's R & D-related technology can be represented by

$$p_i = p_i(x_i) \tag{3}$$

where $p_i(0) = 0$ and $p_i(\infty) = 1$. Further, for all $x_i > 0$, $p_i'(x_i) > 0$. That is, no firm can succeed in R & D without making an investment and no firm can be certain of success no matter how many resources it invests in R & D. But a firm can increase the probability of success by increasing its R & D investment.

Under these conditions, if the two firms invest (x_1, x_2) in R & D, expected profits of the ith firm V_i can be represented as a function of this investment as follows:

$$\begin{aligned} V_i &= V_i(x_1, x_2) \\ &= p_i[(1 - p_j)W_i + p_jD_i] + (1 - p_i)[(1 - p_j)F_i + p_jL_i] - x_i \end{aligned} \tag{4}$$

where $i, j = 1, 2$ $(i \neq j)$, and $p_k = p_k(x_k)$ $(k = 1, 2)$.

The (Nash) equilibrium of such a game is the combination of strategies (x_1^*, x_2^*) that equalizes marginal benefits (marginal incentives for R & D) from R & D investment for each firm $p_i'[(1 - p_j)(W_i - F_i) + p_j(D_i - L_i)]$ to the marginal cost $(=1)$ necessary for such investment. Thus, the Nash equilibrium, given by (x_1^*, x_2^*), satisfies

$$\partial V_i(x_1^*, x_2^*)/\partial x_i = p_i'[(1 - p_j)(W_i - F_i) + p_j(D_i - L_i)] - 1 = 0 \tag{5}$$

where $p_k = p_k(x_k)$, $p_k' = p_k'(x_k)$ $(k = 1, 2)$ and $i, j = 1, 2$ $(i \neq j)$.

Equation (5) leads to the following results. The greater the increase in profits $W_i - F_i$ of firm i when it succeeds in R & D while the rival fails, and the higher the profits $D_i - L_i$ recoverable by succeeding when the rival firm has also succeeded, the higher are the (marginal) incentives for R & D. Therefore, R & D incentives are larger (1) the higher the W_i due to development of a technology superior to its rival, and (2) the lower the profits attainable due to a failure in R & D on account of inferiority of production technology as compared to the rival or due to inferior firm image F_i or when R & D fails to produce results L_i. These results, especially point (2), stand in contrast to those of the Gilbert–Newbery model.

For example, consider a radical technological development that renders the existing technology obsolete (valueless). In this case, as already discussed, since $W_1 = W_2 > 0$, $L_1 = L_2 = 0$, and $D_1 = D_2$, the marginal R & D incentives are higher for the firms with a low F_i. That is, if a firm already earning high profits in the market develops the new radical technology, it loses a part of its existing profits. As a result, a firm holding a large share of the market can expect only a small increase in profits and, hence, has smaller R & D incentives as compared to the firms with a smaller share of the market. This is nothing but the Arrow effect considered in Chapter 17. It is, rather, the smaller firms with inferior cost conditions and low profits that hold higher incentive for development of radically new technologies.

NOTES

1. In this sense, strategic interdependence or rivalries among oligopolistic firms probably tend to make private benefits from R & D socially excessive. It is, therefore, clear that cost-reducing investment competition among the oligopolistic firms, as discussed in Chapter 14, causes private benefits from marginal technological innovations to become socially excessive.

2. The endogenous determination of market structure was also discussed in Chapter 14 in the context of cost-reducing investment competition.

3. Also see Gilbert and Newbery (1982), Fudenberg, Gilbert, Stiglitz, and Tirole (1983), and Fudenberg and Tirole (1986).

4. See Gilbert and Newbery (1982) for details.

5. Reinganum (1983, 1984) provides the basis of the subsequent discussion inclusive of that in the next section.

6. In general, the probability of success associated with each firm is not independent as assumed here but correlated. In this case, a firm can allow its rival to proceed with the R & D activity and gain information from the results of such activity that helps it determine the feasibility of its own R & D activities. Therefore, the time at which a firm gets involved with the R & D activity is also an important factor in such cases. The discussion below ignores this problem in order to keep the analysis simple. Those interested in the details of the alternative set-up may refer to Kiyono and Okuno-Fujiwara (1987).

20

Research and Development and Industrial Policy: With Special Reference to Research and Development Associations

As seen in Chapter 19, our knowledge regarding economics of R & D activity is still far from sufficient. It was, however, pointed out at the beginning of Part V that the Japanese economy, at the present juncture, is faced with an environment that calls for a careful consideration of industrial policies appropriate for R & D activities. This chapter, therefore, is devoted to a search for desirable economic policies in the light of the economic analysis of R & D activities as developed in and up to Chapter 19.

Policy intervention in R & D activities can be categorized into four major types: (1) Setting up of a legal framework such as a licensing system and copyrights to protect intellectual property, (2) government-sponsored R & D activities through the network of national universities, national research institutes, and other institutions, (3) policies to foster and assist private sector R & D based on various types of subsidies to R & D activity, interest subsidies, tax reductions and exemptions, and so on, and (4) assisting in the organization of R & D associations by rallying private sector firms and policies to foster and assist such organizations. In what follows, we discuss the relative merits and demerits of these policies, with special reference to the research associations mentioned under point (4).

20.1 LICENSING SYSTEM AND INTELLECTUAL PROPERTY

As is well known, protection of intellectual property rights by way of legal systems such as patents, copyrights, and design registration is intended to legally ensure monopoly rights for ownership and use of the fruits of intellectual activities, based on R & D, to the inventor. Therefore, in an ideally working system the problem of inappropriability of the R & D results vanishes and *ex ante* R & D incentives increase. However, since a patenting system is an attempt to ensure appropriability to fundamentally inappropriable knowledge in an artificial manner, it invariably leads to some unavoidable contradictions.[1]

The first, and perhaps the most fundamental, problem with a system of ensuring intellectual property rights, as represented by a patenting system, is that in attempting to increase R & D incentives by solving the problems related to inappropriability of inventions it gives rise to inefficiency from the viewpoint of competition in use. The cost of R & D activity, in the postsuccess stages, is sunk both privately and socially. In post-development stages, therefore, the fruits of R & D activity should be exploited in a way, independent of development costs, that maximizes social benefits from such development.

The fall in inventor's profits as a result of diffusion of the development results is small, especially if competition in use for the results of development is weak. The technology developed, in such cases, should be widely publicized. This is because, by widely publicizing the fruits of R & D, the technology concerned may find further uses in diverse areas of social activity and the economic welfare derived from such R & D activity may be maximized in an *ex post* sense. But if the technology is protected by a patenting system, the patent holder monopolizes the technology and tries to increase its profits from the development results by charging high licensing fees. It is, therefore, quite possible for the private costs—the costs that a nonpatent holder must incur for the use of technology protected by a patent—to be excessive as compared to social costs. In such cases, the fruits of R & D are socially underutilized.

Thus, we find that the patenting system involves an inherent contradiction in that while it raises *ex ante* R & D incentives by extending property rights, it also renders the diffusion of the developmental fruits, socially desirable in an *ex post* sense, difficult. It is, therefore, necessary to determine the content of the patent and the period for which protection is provided carefully by taking into consideration the trade-off resulting from this contradiction.

A second problem with the patenting system is related to the monopoly power that it entails. A patenting system, by allowing monopolization of development results, gives rise to transactions in licensing rights—an artificially created "product"—thereby internalizing the externalities, and tries to attain an efficient resource allocation. But the licensing rights for the use of each patent are monopolistically supplied and the licensing fees are determined by negotiations rather than in the market. As a result, there is no guarantee for the licensing fee to be determined at an efficient level and for development results to be used in an efficient manner.

Third, a patenting system is not designed to cover knowledge in its totality but to protect only those parts which involve originality. Therefore, taking computer software as an example, the extent of originality of programs usually becomes a bone of contention among rivals. Thus, a patenting system is beset with uncertainty over the coverage of protection and the content. In this sense, it cannot guarantee perfect appropriability. Again, in an international perspective, since each country formulates its own patenting system, it is undeniable that the firms of countries signatory to the international patenting system, as set down by the Paris convention, are put at a disadvantage against the firms from countries that have not joined this convention.

The widely discussed issue of intellectual property rights in recent years is nothing but an attempt to address the problems of the existing patenting system by setting up comprehensive international guidelines to govern exclusive property rights to intellectual property like designs, trademarks, and copyrights. It is clear, from the earlier discussion, that appropriability of the economic good—knowledge—by an inventor is technically infeasible in the absence of a well-equipped legal system covering the rights to such goods and internationally implemented to exclude the possibility of imitation. It is therefore important, for ensuring R & D incentives as well as providing free and fair access to economic opportunity for all (the very basis of a competitive society), to formulate a system of intellectual property rights that guarantees internationally recognized rights to knowledge and ideas.

Punitive trade restrictions have received attention, in the recent discussions on a system of intellectual property rights, as an effective measure to guarantee such rights. Such measures are aimed at empowering the home government to impose punitive tariffs on specified imports or imports in general, from those countries lacking a well-equipped patenting system or failing to give proper consideration to protection of intellectual property rights, to enable the home firms to stay competitive. There is no questioning the fact that imposition of punitive trade controls on other countries will raise R & D incentives for the home firms. However, since the issue of intellectual property rights is totally unrelated to the trade problem as it stands, punitive measures should be restricted only to areas that have a direct bearing on intellectual property rights. Besides, once imposition of discriminatory trade controls on foreign firms is possible, and as long as there is no guarantee that such measures will not be politically and arbitrarily implemented, the emergence of rent-seeking political lobbying, as discussed in Chapter 15 (Section 15.4), becomes highly likely. Finally, comprehensive protection of intellectual property rights through trade restrictions can easily lead to protection of knowledge that should not be protected on economic welfare grounds. This can nip the future radical innovations in the bud. In this sense, a system of intellectual property rights needs to be approached with extra caution at the formative stages.

20.2 PUBLIC RESEARCH INSTITUTES

Research and development activity undertaken directly by the government through public research institutes, the second major type of government policy intervention mentioned at the beginning of this chapter, implies that the property rights to the fruits of development (assuming the existence of a patenting system) are vested with the government and hence lend themselves easily to socially optimum utilization. In this sense, this system is superior to the patenting system discussed above. However, the efficiency of the R & D activity itself may be impeded since the institutions involved in R & D are not profit motivated and there is nothing to ensure that the R & D activity is carried out at the socially minimum cost. A lack of profit motive or private incentives, in conjunction with the moral hazard problem as discussed below, can give rise to a particularly high degree of inefficiency in the case of R & D activities involving uncertainty.

The moral hazard problem is common in public R & D activity, as well as in the third major type of government policy intervention, which includes pecuniary incentives like subsidies and tax reduction or exemption measures. Even when pecuniary assistance to a fundamentally uncertain economic activity like R & D ends in failure, it is not clear whether the failure was the result of negligence on the part of technicians, researchers, or the development firms that undertook the development activity and the subsidies, or sheer bad luck despite all-out efforts by the persons involved. It is rather possible that those undertaking such development activity, knowing well that the fiscal authorities or the supervisor cannot determine the cause of the failure, may try to use uncertainty as a scapegoat for failure resulting from insufficient effort on their part. In this sense, public R & D and development assistance in the form of pecuniary incentives leads to excessively small R & D investment, as compared to the situation when R & D is left to private incentives alone, and there is an inherent possibility for resource allocation to become inefficient.[2]

20.3 POLICIES TO PROMOTE AND ASSIST PRIVATE FIRMS

Policies to provide direct pecuniary inducement and assistance to R & D by private sector firms or government procurement of equipment embodying such R & D can raise private incentives for R & D. Such policies, since they do not hamper dispersal of the fruits of development while raising R & D incentives, are more desirable than a legal system as represented by the patenting system.

The private sector assistance policies, however, are easily susceptible to problems associated with information asymmetry, including that of moral hazard. For example, pecuniary subsidies and assistance for R & D do not provide sufficient R & D incentives since those performing the R & D can obtain such subsidies without conducting the R & D activity except when the government is able to detect a breach of agreement. Similarly, one of the objectives of procuring defense- and space development-related machinery and equipment from the private sector in the United States is intended to be promotion of private sector R & D. However, cases of private sector procurement where development has ended in failure despite substantial investments or where final costs have far exceeded the initial estimates have been pointed out time and again.[3] One of the influential factors here is the fact that the firms are in a position to shift the responsibility for failure or for excessive costs onto chance, as discussed earlier. Again, while the firms involved in development are fully aware of the content—for example, production costs required for commercializing the product—of the development activity, the procurer, i.e., the government, is not. The private sector firms use this information asymmetry to bid for large-scale contracts at low bid prices and later to inflate these prices, taking recourse to reasons like inflationary pressures.

As discussed in the Appendix to this chapter, a solution to the problems associated with moral hazard requires ingenuity.[4] First, subsidies for R & D should not be fixed amount subsidies to be granted irrespective of the results but should follow a percentage system such that success, as judged on the basis of some set standards, is rewarded by larger amount of subsidy than a failure. Besides, by refusing to grant subsidies for a failure in a project with a low degree of uncertainty, and where success is quite certain, a penalty can be quite effective in removing the moral hazard.

Second, in the case of procurement of equipment embodying R & D from the private sector, procurement costs should be minimized by making the content of the contract explicit to the maximum extent possible and inviting tenders from a multiplicity of firms. But sticking strictly to the bid prices for payment purposes implies a unilateral shifting of the risks of fluctuations in R & D and raw material costs onto the bidding firms. It is desirable however, that the government should bear all such risks to lessen the burden of the private firms that have a weak capacity to bear these risks. It is possible, for the sake of removing moral hazard while appropriately distributing the risk burden at the same time, to formulate the procurement contracts as follows: The contract goes to the firm with the lowest bid price (x) but the procurement price, considering the *post facto* development and production costs (y), can be fixed such that the total amount satisfies $ax + by$ ($0 < a, b < 1$). This is termed as an incentive contract.

Summarizing the above discussion, the following conclusions can be drawn. First, in the case of creative inventions or unanticipated intellectual developments, production tends to be excessively low if left to private incentives alone due to difficulties in preventing imitation and the problem of inappropriability. On the other hand, since creative inventions normally have universal applicability and can also greatly benefit entities besides the developer, leaving such R & D to the public sector is desirable. One distinctive feature of creative inventions, thus, is the production of universal knowledge. This feature provides a successful developer with an incentive, distinct from material profits, in the form of social status as a pioneer developer of knowledge and, hence, excessive worry about the lack of private incentives is unwarranted in this case. The fruits of creative inventions, instead, are more likely to have a noncompetitive character and hence the developed technology should be made publicly available without cost such that all the segments of the society can make full use of such development. In this sense, too, it is desirable to leave such development to public research institutions.

In the case of R & D directed at improvement and imitation R & D within the context of innovations in the commercialization process, the problem of incentives and conflicts is relatively small. It is rather the market structure that poses problems. As seen in Chapter 19, the market for a given product tends to retain its monopolistic character over an extended period if it is already monopolized by a single firm. The improvement and imitation activity in this case tends to be subdued and can retard the increase in economic welfare concomitant on lower product prices and improved product quality. In this sense, increased mobility of researchers and maintaining competitive firms in the industry may be important for raising economic welfare.

In contrast to this, formulation of policies for original R & D is not at all easy. A theoretically desirable policy should increase R & D incentives while diffusing the development results as widely as possible at the same time. But, as seen above, policies intended to raise private incentives through pecuniary inducement and assistance are beset with information-related problems like moral hazard. Ensuring private incentives through legal systems like the patenting system, on the other hand, results in impeding the diffusion of development results. The remainder of this chapter, focusing mainly on original R & D activity, is addressed to the R & D association format of conducting R & D that has gained wide acceptance in recent years.

20.4 RESEARCH AND DEVELOPMENT ASSOCIATIONS AND INTERNALIZATION OF EXTERNALITIES

As discussed in Chapter 2, assistance to R & D activities has been one of the focal points of the Japanese industrial policy in recent years and assistance measures for development assistance have been centered around rallying the private sector firms to form research associations. This has been termed as the "R & D association system." Some of these research associations have succeeded beyond expectations. There is no doubting the fact that the importance of R & D activities is bound to increase in the future and the association system will continue to be an important policy measure in the tool kit of the policy authorities, charged with industrial policy, in the process of shifting from direct controls to indirect incentivist measures.

However, there is no serious analysis available, barring a few management-oriented studies, regarding the need for adopting an R & D association system or the most effective way of forming such associations from the viewpoint of the development objectives. The main reason for such a state of affairs, as is true for any other policy measure as well, is that an association system has been introduced as one of the "ideas" rather than on the basis of some clearly defined analytical framework. As a result, the outsiders had to perform a circuitous and tedious task of compiling case studies and analyzing individual research associations to be able to discuss the association system as a whole.

Fortunately for us, the stock of available case studies has been building up in recent years and the internal conditions of development associations are also coming to light.[5] In what follows, we base ourselves on available research in attempting an economic analysis of R & D associations.[6]

It may be useful, here, to summarize the discussion of Chapters 16–19 regarding the problems associated with R & D investments. We discussed the following four problems involving the effect of R & D investments on resource allocation:

1. Externalities or the problem of inappropriability
2. Duplication of investment or the rush to invent
3. Oligopolistic strategic behavior among the firms involved in development activity
4. Information asymmetry as reflected in moral hazard

Problems (1) and (2) are unrelated to the market structure in the industry and can emerge even when the industry is perfectly competitive. Let us first analyze these two aspects assuming that the industry is perfectly competitive.

Case (1) leads to an excessive lowering of private R & D incentives by giving rise to externalities through (a) an outflow of the fruits of development to competing firms by way of imitation, and (b) an outflow of benefits from development to the consumers. In contrast to this, case (2) leads to excessive development incentives by inducing a rush to invent as a result of investment competition among the firms for a development objective, whereas the society as whole would be equally well served with a single success. The common characteristics of cases (1) and (2) lie in the presence of externalities—external economies in case (1) and diseconomies in case (2).

Research and development associations, by allowing cooperative behavior among a number of firms in pursuit of a single R & D activity, in fact legalize cartelization. Such a system leads to appropriate development incentives by internalizing the inappropriability (externality) discussed under case (1), point (a). One way of internalizing the externalities, therefore, is to merge the generators and the recipients of externalities, or make them cooperate in the pursuit of collective maximization of profits and hence adopt socially optimum behavior. In the case of an association system, the development benefits are appropriable by the cartel as long as the outflow of such development benefits is to the firms within the cartel. Setting up of an appropriate system of distributing the benefits can solve the problem of appropriability. Similarly, cartelization tends to avoid unnecessary duplicate investment and competition through time by the firms. Therefore, as long as all the firms, having potential incentives to conduct the development activity, participate in the cartel, the R & D association monopolizing the said R & D activity will have socially desirable development incentives.

The outflow of benefits to the consumer, however, cannot be internalized even under an association system and externalities listed under case (2), point (b) above cause development incentives to be socially small.

20.5 RESEARCH AND DEVELOPMENT ASSOCIATIONS AND STRATEGIC BEHAVIOR

The R & D cost, once the development activity succeeds, is sunk. Therefore, development costs are treated as fixed costs in the product market that uses the fruits of such development and give rise to scale economies. That is why the industries, where R & D activity plays an important role, normally tend to be oligopolistic. Oligopolistic strategic behavior, mentioned under case (3) above, therefore, assumes an important role. The oligopolistic strategic behavior can have two effects. First, (a) it may result in inefficient resource allocation due to oligopolistic product market and thereby lower development incentives as compared to the socially optimum levels. Second, (b) development activity, by itself, serves as a strategic variable in the interfirm competition. As a result, R & D incentives are higher or lower compared to incentives in the absence of strategic interaction depending on whether the product market strategies of the firms are substitutes or complements. These aspects have already been discussed in detail in Chapters 8 and 15 and we simply summarize the main points here.

To begin with, an oligopolistic product market implies that each firm has at least some amount of monopoly power. This results in socially too little productive activity in the product market and underinvestment in development activities which are but one factor of production.[7] This is the essence of point (a) above and the development incentives are too little.

Next, let us discuss the strategic effects, concentrating on the case when the firm strategies in the product market are strategic substitutes. This represents the case when the reaction functions of individual firms are positively sloped. The firms, without considering the strategic aspects of R & D, will increase their R & D activities to a point where marginal profit from an additional unit of investment is zero. That is, the investment level is determined by the equality of marginal cost of development (assuming that the rival firm does not change its behavior in the market for inventions) and the marginal increase in profits earned in the product market. Let us now assume that one of the firms takes strategic behavior into consideration. That is, the firm undertakes development expenditure fully aware of the fact that a change in such expenditure brings about a change in the development results and changes the nature of competition in the product market.

Additional development expenditures make a firm more aggressive in the product market. If firm strategies in the product market are strategic substitutes, aggressive behavior by a given firm puts its rivals into a defensive (receptive) position. Since receptive behavior by the rivals raises the profits of the aggressive firms, development incentives taking strategic behavior into account are higher than would be otherwise. In contrast to this, if firm strategies in the product market are strategic complements, an increase in development expenditures by a firm calls forth more aggressive behavior by its rivals and leads to a decline in its profits. Strategic behavior in this case leads to a decline in development incentives.

Thus, development incentives are invariably too low if firm strategies in the product market are strategic complements. But no generalizations regarding whether adoption of oligopolistic strategic behavior results in excessive or too little development incentives is possible in the case of strategic substitutes.

How can one evaluate an association system from the viewpoint of strategic behavior in an oligopolistic setting? Adoption of an association system, like the establishment of the VLSI Technology Research Association, by rallying domestic firms to counter giant overseas firms with an established position in an environment of stiff international competition is deemed to make an impact in at least three respects: (1) development costs, (2) strategic behavior, and (3) monopoly power in the product market.

First, in case (1), development costs, formation of an association is believed to lower the development costs for the participant firms by excluding the possibility of duplicated investments and by making effective use of relative strengths of individual firms in development activities. That is, development activity can be undertaken with greater efficiency by bringing together the firms excelling in their respective fields. This results in higher development incentives for individual firms and hence to a rise in R & D activity.

Next, in case (2), the effect on strategic behavior, the formation of research association may lead to an overblown strategic response by foreign firms since the inventions, as a result of successful development, become available to all the participating firms simultaneously. If the firm strategies in the product market are strategic substitutes, increased development expenditures by domestic firms, as a result of formation into an association, may make the foreign firms more receptive, leading to a further rise in development expenditure by the domestic firms. It goes without saying here that even if R & D expenditures rise due to these factors, whether social welfare, especially of the world as a whole, increased or not is unclear.[8]

Finally, in case (3), monopoly power in the product market, implications differ according to whether an R & D association system gives rise to concerted behavior by participant firms in the product market or not. Let us assume that cooperation in the development activities does not extend into the product market and the product market stays competitive despite the formation of an association. In this case, adoption of the association system to assist R & D activity implies that competition in the product market rises, since the development results are collectively owned by the participant firms, and product prices fall. Thus, it is possible for an association system to increase competition in the domestic market while at the same time strengthening the domestic firms against the foreign firms.

Thus, it can be seen that the association system does have various merits. However, at the same time, it has a number of shortcomings, too. First, there is nothing to ensure a continued competitive environment once the association system is adopted. As discussed earlier, an R & D association allows cooperative behavior by a number of firms in the field of R & D. Ignoring the cooperative behavior in the R & D activities, if cooperation is extended to collusion in the product market, the product prices may rise, giving rise to inefficiency in resource allocation. In adopting the association system, therefore, it is necessary to set up a mechanism that ensures continued competition in the product market.[9]

Second, the participant firms in an association get a substantial amount of subsidies and also benefit from exchanges of research and knowledge. Despite this, selection of participant firms in the research associations is often arbitrary and the associations tend to be closed institutions with exclusive club characteristics. As a result, equality of opportunity between the participant and nonparticipant firms is lost and participant firms are placed at an advantageous position relative to the nonparticipant firms. Adoption of such regulated and discriminatory policy measures can also lead to continuation of firms that would not have been able to stay in the industry otherwise, at the cost of firms that may have been potentially strong. These points are all the more important for industries where research associations are repeatedly formed.

20.6 INTERNAL ORGANIZATION OF DEVELOPMENT ASSOCIATIONS

One of the points, invariably stressed, in the context of the internal organization of development associations is as follows. The success of the VLSI research association, a widely used example of successful association, is believed to be the result of the fact that it set up an independent research institute where the researchers deputed by the participating firms worked shoulder to shoulder for the development project. In contrast to this, most of the unsuccessful stories of development projects are found to be in cases where the overall project was divided up into small parts and participant firms were allowed to conduct their part of the research in their own facilities. It is not easy to explain these facts at a theoretical level and derive policy implications. But it is possible to consider the problem within the framework of agency theory as follows.[10]

As is explained in the Appendix to this chapter, it is easy for the government to generate development incentives, even in the presence of moral hazard, by formulating an appropriate contract if there is only a single firm (agent in the context of agency relationships) engaged in development. That is, the government can adopt a percentage system to share the development costs between the government and the developer by making the total amount of subsidies dependent on the results of development activity. In the real-world R & D association, the fact that the patent for invention is owned collectively by the participating firms that bear a part of the development costs in the form of a levy implies the existence of such a percentage system. The firms endeavor, through this percentage system, to succeed in the development project to earn the subsidy.

However, development associations are composed of a multiple number of firms. In this case, unless the percentage is set at an exceptionally high level, adoption of a percentage system does not generate development incentives since the increase in profits of individual firms upon successful completion of the project is small. This calls for a contract and an organizational structure other than a percentage system, as it is practically infeasible to set the percentage at several hundred percentage points. In what follows, we consider two such alternatives.

The first of these alternatives tries to look for incentives generated through self-discipline within the organization. That is, in the formation of an association by a multiple number of firms, the effort level chosen by individual firms tends to fall short of the desired level from the viewpoint of the association as a whole. This is because individual firms try to take a free ride on the efforts made by other participating firms and enjoy the fruits (subsidies) without the work. This provides each firm enough incentive to monitor whether the development efforts of other firms are up to the desired level or not. If the participating firms can settle on a system of mutual monitoring, appropriate development incentives can be generated. This is because monitoring leads to self-discipline in the association as an institution.[11]

Establishment of an independent research institute where the researchers from individual firms get together for the success of the project implies that the association gives rise to an independent organization with its own independent regulations. The research institute, thus, serves as a mechanism to keep a check on the efforts put in by individual firms since research workers from different firms monitor each other's activities.

The second type of mechanism is represented by rank-order tournaments.[12] If it is possible to observe the extent of development efforts put in by individual firms (which may be imperfect), the government can vary the amount of subsidy granted to individual firms on the basis of an evaluation of the level of development efforts put in by each firm. Since a firm putting in greater efforts gets larger subsidies than the others, each firm will compete to do its best in the development project. This is what is termed as a rank-order tournament.

In the case of a development association, it is possible to think of a rank-order tournament in reverse. That is, if the development efforts of a firm are deemed to be small, it is penalized by exclusion from the next research association formed. This forces each firm to put out its maximum effort for the project. Such a mechanism presumes the following characteristics in a development association.

First, the association should not be a once-and-for-all affair but must be repeatedly constituted with the selection of a firm in a subsequent association made dependent on its performance in the previous one. Second, and perhaps more important, is that the association should be formed of firms in relatively similar industries rather than in widely differing industries due to greater technological complementarity among the former group. This is because, in this case, benefits from being a member in the subsequent association are higher than being an outsider.

In any case, R & D associations leave much to be explained. Further accumulation of theoretical analyses, hearings, inquiries, and empirical studies is imperative for a proper understanding of the association system.

20.7 APPENDIX: MORAL HAZARD AND AGENCY RELATIONSHIPS

Information asymmetry leads to substantial lowering of development incentives as it induces firms to lay the blame of a failure in R & D on a chance factor. This problem of information asymmetry, especially moral hazard, assumes great importance in the context of deciding on the internal organization of a development association. The form of contracts for procurement from the private sector can also be analyzed within an almost similar framework. The problem of devising an internal organization or formulation of procurement contracts in the presence of information asymmetry is usually termed as the "principal–agent" or agency theory. It is, however, impossible here to discuss these theories fully and the theory of multiple agents, the main issue of interest here, is still in its formative stages. In the following, therefore, we restrict ourselves to explaining only the points that have a direct bearing on R & D associations and private sector procurement and discuss their policy implications.[13]

The agency theory deals with the analysis of the nature of contractual relationships or the internal organization desirable when an economic entity is unable, due to some reasons, to carry out the required economic activity by itself and delegates it to an agent. In terms of the immediate objective at hand, the government, aiming at maximization of economic welfare from R & D activity, delegates it to the private sector. In such cases, the behavior of the agent can diverge from the expectations of the client unless the interests of the two concur or the client provides sufficient incentives to the agent for the task. The interests of private firms who attempt to maximize their own profits, in the case of development associations, do not coincide with those of the government, which aims at maximizing total national economic welfare, inclusive of consumer surplus.

The agency relationship, in its simplest form, is depicted in Fig. 20-1. There is only one private sector firm acting as the agent and x is the level of R & D investment by this firm. The development activity does not involve any uncertainty and the level of R & D results y is uniquely determined by the production function

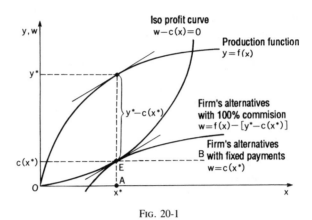

FIG. 20-1

$y = f(x)$, as represented in Fig. 20-1. While the firm, since it actually undertakes the investment, knows the level of investment x the client, i.e., the government, does not. But the government can, while delegating the task to the private sector firm, make the amount of subsidy granted, or the level of procurement x, depend on the function y since it knows the level of achievement as the result of the R & D activity.

The government, using the agency relationship, tries to maximize the total surplus $y - w$, the difference between the total benefits derived from development results and total expenditure. The private sector firm, on the other hand, earns the difference between development subsidy from the government w and the costs necessary for R & D investment $c(x)$ as profit. Thus, the locus of all combinations of (w, x) for which $w - c(x)$ is constant depicts the isoprofit curve and Fig. 20-1 depicts the isoprofit curve for zero profit. It is clear that the points lying above and to the left of this curve represent positive profits and those lying below and to the right are associated with negative profits. The private sector does not agree to undertaking government-sponsored R & D unless the profits are nonnegative, since the firm is better off by not undertaking the research activity. Point E in Fig. 20-1 represents the socially optimum state since it corresponds to zero profits to the firm while maximizing total surplus. That is, an investment level of x^* by the firm to attain y^* results with $y^* - c(x^*)$ as the amount of subsidies (procurement) is optimum.

Let us consider four alternative ways of disbursing the subsidy (or procurement payments). Let us first take the case of piece-rate payments where, irrespective of the outcome of the development activity, the government contracts to grant a fixed amount $y^* - c(x^*)$ to the firm. In this case, since the firm is ensured of $y^* - c(x^*)$ irrespective of the level of x, it can choose any point on the horizontal line passing through E. It is obvious that $x = 0$ is the optimum level of choice for this firm and the government must pay the subsidy without getting any results. This is precisely the problem of moral hazard.

This problem, however, can be solved by taking recourse to any of the following three type of contracts. The first of these is the time rate system. Let us assume that the firm can obtain the rights to the outcome of R & D if it agrees to pay $y^* - c(x^*)$ to the government. Thus, the firm receives a total of $w(x) = f(x) - [y^* - c(x^*)]$. As is clear from Fig. 20-1, the firm optimizes by choosing the investment level x^*. Thus, the firm, by its own free will, selects the socially optimum level of investment. That is, the time rate system offers enough incentives to the agent to make it come up to the expectations of the client.

A second contract form involves fixed payment of $y^* - c(x^*)$ by the government to the development firm as a subsidy, but if the result falls short of y^* the subsidy (or procurement) is zero. In this case, the choice frontier facing the firm is given by the curve $OAEB$ in Fig. 20-1 and the firm, by itself, decides on x^* as the investment level. Thus, the agent can be induced to come up to the client's expectations by imposing penalties on the agent for unsatisfactory performance.

The third type of contract to avoid moral hazard is the application of the first type mentioned above. Here, we assume the existence of a multiple number of firms, with similar cost conditions, ready to undertake the said development activity as long as profits are nonnegative. Further, assume that this contract is granted through tenders on the condition that the subsidy received by the successful bidder is proportional to its performance. A successful firm with bid price of b yen, receives $g(b) \equiv \max[f(x) - c(x) - b]$. If b^* is the expected successful bid by the rival firm, and as long as $g(b^*)$ is positive, the firm will be ready to raise its bid price to earn positive profit. The equilibrium bid price, as a result, is attained when $g(b^*)$ is zero and the successful firm invests x^*.

In the simple case discussed above, the client can attain a Pareto efficient resource allocation, just as in the case of perfect information where information asymmetry does not exist, by offering desired incentives to the agent by adopting an appropriate rate system, penalties, or tender systems. But is it normally possible to formulate such optimum contracts? The answer is a clear no. The main difficulty in formulating such optimum contracts is posed by uncertainties that are usually associated with the production function $f(x)$ and the cost function $c(x)$. In this case, it is necessary to share the risks emanating from an agency relationship which conflicts with the incentives. In the following, we discuss the case of uncertainties in the production function such that an investment level x does not result in a unique outcome.

Let us first consider the case of a time rate system. A 100% time rate system forces the development firm to bear the whole risk. If the firm is risk neutral, and hence indifferent to the risk involved, the time rate system solves the problem. But if the firm is risk averse, as is usually the case, the government, being relatively more risk neutral, should bear a large part of the risk arising from the agency relationship. Thus, taking risk sharing into account, the rate for the time rate system should be set at less than 100%. In general, incentives rise as the rate rises but forces the relatively risk-averse firms to bear greater risks. Therefore, this trade-off should determine the optimum rate (the second best to be precise).

If the uncertainty involved is not very high and the outcome is certain provided a large enough investment is undertaken, a contract with a built-in penalty is all the more desirable. This follows from the fact that if a subsidy is dependent on a certain minimum level of results, the firm will undertake sufficient investment to attain that minimum level. As long as the firm makes sufficient investment, it can certainly achieve results above those required by the government and does not have to bear exceptional risk. Thus, an appropriate mix of rate system and penalties can result in the formulation of socially efficient contracts even when information asymmetry and uncertainty coexist.[14]

A similar argument can be applied to procurement contracts with uncertainty in the cost function. In this case, a fixed price contract, equating the bid price x to the amount of payments $w(w = x)$ forces the firm to bear all the risk. A cost-plus contract where the government undertakes to pay the whole amount of ex post increase in costs $(w = y)$, on the other hand, undermines the firm's incentives to cut down costs. In this case, an optimum contract is the incentive contract, where the government meets a part of the increase in costs while, in principle, sticking to bid-price contract $(w = ax + by)$.[15]

The agency theory discussed to this point assumed a single agent. A development association, however, is composed of a multiple number of firms or agents. This is the subject matter of the theory of principal–multiagent relationships or the theory of rank-order tournaments.[16]

The difference between the multiagent and sole agent cases lies in the fact that the agents in the multiagent case adopt strategic behavior amongst themselves to vie for the subsidy. From the viewpoint of the government, the principal here, it is necessary to set the rules of the game in such a manner that the strategic behavior among the agents leads to the most desirable state of development activity.

To simplify the analysis, let us assume only two agents, 1 and 2, with respective investment levels x_1 and x_2. The outcome of the development activity y is assumed to be $x_1 + x_2$. Further, while the government knows the outcome y correctly it has only imperfect information on the effort (x_1, x_2) by individual firms. In more concrete terms, let us consider the following situation: The government investigates into the development efforts (x_1, x_2) by individual firms but due to observation errors, it can observe only $(z_1, z_2) \equiv [x_1 - (\varepsilon/2), x_2 + (\varepsilon/2)]$. Here, ε is a random variable with zero expectation and a density function defined by the humped curve $f(\varepsilon)$ in Fig. 20-2.

Let us assume that the government grants W_i $(i = 1, 2)$ as subsidy to the firms on the basis of its observation of (z_1, z_2).

$$W_i = \begin{cases} \overline{W} + W & (z_i \geq z_j) \\ \overline{W} - L & (z_i < z_j) \end{cases} \tag{1}$$

where W and L are positive constants. The firm with a higher level of observed effort receives an additional payment of W and the firm with a lower observed level of effort is penalized to the extent of L. Firms 1 and 2 play the game within the framework of subsidies represented by Eq. (1). Let us now analyze this game. If the firms are aware of each other's effort levels (x_1, x_2), firm 1 anticipates the subsidy grant as follows. Firm 1 receives $\overline{W} + W$ if $\varepsilon \leq x_1 - x_2$ but only $\overline{W} - L$ if $\varepsilon > x_1 - x_2$. That is, the expected profit of firm 1, when (x_1, x_2) is chosen, is given by

$$\Pi_1(x_1, x_2) = \overline{W} + W \int_{-\infty}^{x_1-x_2} f(\varepsilon)d\varepsilon - L\int_{x_1-x_2}^{\infty} f(\varepsilon)d\varepsilon - c(x_1)$$

Given x_2, a small increase in x_1 raises the probability of getting W by $f(x_1 - x_2)$ and reduces the probability of losing L by $f(x_1 - x_2)$. That is, the expected value of subsidies rises by $(W + L)f(x_1 - x_2)$. Since the cost of additional investment is $c'(x_1)$, firm 1 chooses its investment level x_1, given x_2, to satisfy

$$(W + L)f(x_1 - x_2) = c'(x_1)$$

and, thereby, maximizes its expected profits. This optimizing behavior is easier to understand by interpreting the above optimizing condition as follows.

Following the optimum factor demand condition in the standard theory of the firm, let probability density $f(x_1 - x_2)$ represent the marginal productivity of investment (factor of production) by firm 1, $(W + L)$ the marginal revenue product, and $c'(x_1)$ the marginal cost. It is easy to see, now, that the above optimizing condition simply equates marginal value productivity of the said factor (investment) to its marginal cost. Thus, the optimizing condition can be rewritten in terms of the equality condition for marginal profit (marginal productivity), measured in terms of the output of the firm and costs as follows:

$$f(x_1 - x_2) = c'(x_1)/(W + L)$$

Interpreted in this sense, the profit maximization by firm 1 can be depicted in terms of Fig. 20-2.

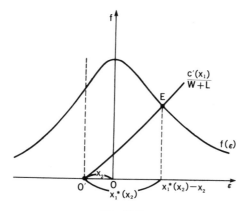

Fig. 20-2

The horizontal axis to the right of origin O measures ε and the vertical axis measures the probability density $f(\varepsilon)$. If x_2 is the investment level chosen by firm 2, firm 1's investment can be measured toward the right with O' as the origin. The curve $c'(x_1)/(W + L)$, starting at the new origin O', represents the real marginal cost curve of investment and the portion of the probability density curve $f(\varepsilon) = f(x_1 - x_2)$, lying to the right of O', gives the real marginal profit curve. With the investment level of firm 2 given at x_2, the optimum investment level for firm 1 is given by $x_1^*(x_2)$ corresponding to E, the point of intersection of the two curves. Moreover, $x_1^*(x_2)$ also defines the reaction function of firm 1. It is, however, not clear whether $x_1^*(x_2)$ increases or not as x_2 rises.[17]

Figure 20-3 is drawn for the case when $x_1^*(x_2)$ is an increasing function of x_2. The Nash equilibrium in this case is given by point N and each firm undertakes (x_1^*, x_2^*) amount of development effort.

Let us assume that the government raises W and L. Both the reward for a win and the penalty for a loss against the rival rise for the firm. If $f(\varepsilon)$ and x_2 in Fig. 20-2 are assumed to be given, the optimum level of effort by firm 1 rises since the curve $c'(x_1)/(W + L)$ rotates clockwise. In terms of Fig. 20-3, this implies that the reaction function of firm 1 shifts to the right. This new reaction function is represented by $x_1^{**}(x_2)$ in Fig. 20-3. Similarly, the reaction function of firm 2 also shifts upwards to $x_2^{**}(x_1)$ and the development effort in the new equilibrium, N', rises.

Thus, in a multiagent case where individual efforts can be observed to some extent, the client can increase development incentives by enlarging the gap between rewards for a win and a loss in the competition among the agents. This is the essence of the theory of rank-order tournaments.

As discussed in Chapter 16 (Section 16.3) in slightly different terms, one way of increasing development incentives is to provide greater subsidies or earnings in proportion with the increase in investment by an individual firm. Development

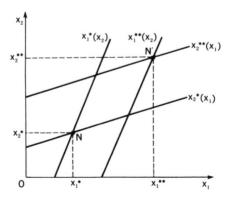

FIG. 20-3

incentives can be increased substantially by rank ordering the firms according to their investment levels and providing larger subsidies to firms with large investments and lower subsidies or even penalties to the firms with small incentives.

In the presence of information asymmetries, however, the client—government—cannot fully observe the investment level of individual firms. Moreover, in contrast to the single-agent case, while it may be possible to observe the achievements of the development association as a whole to a certain extent, the level of investment by each individual member of the association cannot be inferred. This is the main point of divergence between the multiagent and sole-agent models.

It may, however, be possible for the client to assess the level of investment undertaken by individual agents (firms), even though imperfectly (for example, excluding assessment errors). If so, the client can condition the amount of payment (subsidies) on the assessed levels and thereby generate sufficiently large development incentives for the agents. Especially as discussed earlier, incentives can be generated by ordering the agents by assessed levels and offering large rewards to the winners and imposing large penalties on the losers. The reason is that such a system ensures the agent a winning berth if it increases its investment level and raises its assessed level.

Thus, in a multiagent case where individual efforts can be observed to some extent, the client can increase development incentives by enlarging the gap between rewards for a win and a loss in the competition among the agents. This is the most important conclusion of the theory of rank-order tournaments.

NOTES

1. For a detailed discussion of the role of the patenting system in R & D, see Chapter 16 of Scherer (1980) and the literature cited therein.

2. A discussion of moral hazard and development incentives is carried out in the Appendix to this chapter.

3. See, for example, Fox (1974).

4. For the details of the subsequent arguments, see the Appendix to this chapter.

5. For example, see Ohtaki (1983), Wakasugi (1986), and Wakasugi and Gotoh (1985).

6. The analysis developed below is a piece-meal approach to the association system and the implications derived for the conduct of the association system are no more than one possible approach to the problem. We intend to use this analysis as a stepping stone for developing a systematic analysis of the research association system in the future.

7. This result is based on the implicit assumption that new entry is prevented in some way and the number of firms in the industry stays constant. If the industry is characterized by free entry, it is possible for the level of input–output activities to become socially excessive. See Chapter 14 for details.

8. The reason is that it is unclear whether development incentives in the absence of an R & D association were too small or not in the first place. Moreover, the rent being earned by the foreign firms must have declined.

9. Ordover and Willig (1985) and Katz (1986) contain an economic analysis of R & D associations and R & D cooperation.

10. In the following analysis, we consider subsidies as the only means to raise development incentives. In practice, various other measures, like granting patents for invention to the participating firms, deputation of researchers to the associations, bearing the costs of R & D facilities by the national treasury, can also have similar effects. Subsidies, a direct policy measure, have been chosen at the risk of neglecting all other measures only for expositional clarity.

11. Okuno (1984b) tries to explain worker loyalty to a firm in these terms.

12. See the Appendix to this chapter for details of the rank-order tournament approach.

13. For details of agency relationships, see Ross (1983) and Harris and Raviv (1978, 1979).

14. See Stiglitz (1974) and Harris and Raviv (1978, 1979) for details.

15. See, for example, McAfee and McMillan (1986).

16. See Lazear and Rosen (1981) and Nalebuff and Stiglitz (1983b) for details.

17. In the case of Fig. 20-2, however, it can be easily verified that $x_1^*(x_2)$ is an increasing function of x_2 as long as x_2 is not too large.

VI

Further Problems in the Formulation of
Future Industrial Policy

21

Problems Related to Industrial Adjustment Policies

This book has dealt with a wide range of theoretical topics related to industrial policies. Although a diverse range of topics have been covered, some aspects have received only a cursory treatment. Section VI deals with two such topics deemed to be especially important.

The first of these deals with the declining industries and the problem of industrial adjustment. The problem of industrial adjustment is not peculiar to Japan but has become a serious problem for all the developed economies. The ways and means to deal with this problem have important implications for the prosperity of these countries. The present chapter discusses the nature of industrial policies for industrial adjustment within the framework of economic theory.

The second aspect needing further attention is related to the problems associated with the industrial policy of Japan, a large country now, for maintaining an amicable economic relationship with other foreign countries. The economic interdependence among the nations has increased to unprecedented levels. A large number of economic activities are now conducted across national boundaries and the erstwhile industrial policies, taking nations as the basic unit, are becoming increasingly meaningless. The increased economic frictions with Western Block countries in recent years may also be interpreted as a manifestation of the changes in the economic environment.

The Japanese share in this intricately linked world economy has increased substantially and the Japanese policies can now significantly affect the patterns of world trade and investment. This also explains the need for a reconsideration of industrial policies in an international perspective. Chapter 22 analyzes industrial policy in this perspective.

The two problems mentioned above, in fact, are too important to be treated within the space of one chapter each. The analysis developed in the subsequent pages, therefore, does no more than make some highly simplified comments and puts the main arguments in perspective, leaving a detailed analysis of the problem for a different occasion.

21.1 An Overview of the Problem of Declining Industries

The industrial structure of a country and, for that matter, of the world is in a continuous state of flux. As discussed in Part II as well, for the economy to grow at a rapid pace its industrial structure must change correspondingly. This, however, is accompanied by substantial adjustment pains.

Adjustment of industrial structure involves shifting factors of production, like labor and capital, from declining industries to industries with rising competitiveness. However, the transfer of factors of production is not smooth in most cases. Workers released from the declining industries are not easily absorbed into the other sectors of the economy and the adjustment process usually ends up producing unemployment.

Industrial adjustments in postwar Japan began with a shift of factors of production from the primary to the secondary and tertiary sectors. The primary sector, accounting for nearly 50% of total employment in the early postwar era, declined rapidly to fall below 10% in recent years. A large number of workers, during this period, shifted into secondary and tertiary occupations. However, the increase in secondary sector employment, after rising from 20 to 34%, came to a stop around 1970 and, now, it is the tertiary sector that is the main source of increases in employment. Agricultural employment declined sharply up to the 1960s and a number of adjustment assistance and subsidy policies were directed at this sector. However, since we are interested more in policies toward the manufacturing industries, we do not go into the details of such policies.

Although the manufacturing industry has not shown much change in terms of proportion of total employment, industrial structure within this sector is also undergoing substantial changes. As was seen in Chapter 3, up to 1970 the Japanese industrial structure was shifting from a preponderance of light industries to heavy and chemical industries. A steep rise in imports from the ASEAN countries, as a result, gave rise to many problems, in industries like textiles, that characterize declining industries. The Japanese government undertook a host of policy measures like the purchase and closure of "excess capacity" and structural improvement programs to meet this situation.[1]

The coal industry went into a decline much before the textile industry. As a result of a shift from coal to petroleum as the chief source of energy, and because of a rise in the cheap import of coal, the Japanese coal industry lost its competitive edge. The importance of coal as a source of primary energy declined rapidly from 50% in 1950 to just over 20% in 1960 and down to 20% in 1970. Besides, the proportion of imported coal also rose from 3 to 60%. This resulted in a drastic reduction in the amount of coal mined and gave rise to large-scale personnel shake-ups and mine closures, leading to substantial unemployment among coal miners. It was difficult for the mine workers to utilize their skills in other industries, which has resulted in making the employment problem of coal miners difficult to solve despite the implementation of industrial adjustment policies such as the Coal Mining Industry Rationalization Law in 1954.

The industrial adjustment problems of the 1970s, triggered by the two oil shocks of 1973 and 1978, became more serious. The steep rise in oil prices had a serious impact on the heavy and chemical industry in Japan, heavily dependent on imported oil, and industries like petrochemicals and aluminum smelting quickly lost their competitive edge. The ship-building industry of Japan also lost competitiveness in the face of the stagnating international demand for shipping and the emergence of NICs (newly industrialized countries).

With the advent of the oil shocks, the Japanese industrial structure shifted gradually from heavy and chemical industries to fabrication industries like automobiles, electric and electronic equipment, and machine tools. These changes were made possible by a rise in energy costs concomitant with the oil shock and a rapid increase in productivity in the fabrication industry brought about by improved production and quality control technologies.

Increased productivity in the fabrication industries raises its international competitiveness and causes the yen to appreciate. This, in turn, leads to a decline in competitiveness of the heavy and chemical industries. Thus, even though yen appreciation seems to be responsible for the decline in competitiveness of industries like iron and steel and shipbuilding, the real reason is a shift in comparative advantage toward the fabrication industries.

The problem of adjustment assistance to declining industries, with the steep appreciation of the yen since 1985, has become all the more serious and has become an important policy problem. The rise in the value of the yen in the first half of the 1980s was stopped short by the fiscal policies adopted by the United States, making the exchange rate adjustments since 1985 all the more severe. It is possible that such a rapid rise in the value of the yen has imposed unnecessary and rapid industrial adjustments on Japan.

The industrial adjustment policies are complex and encompass a diverse set of problems. For example, problems of employment, regional (industrial localities) employment and diffusion of economic activity, scrapping of capacity or adjustments in rate of capacity utilization, and retraining of the work force are some of the problems of the adjustment process that need attention. Besides, the nature of problems associated with each declining industry tends to differ. For example, employment is the major problem in shipbuilding and iron and steel industries while it is not as important in the labor-saving aluminum smelting industry. Similarly, while iron and steel and petrochemical industries are composed of large-scale firms, industries like textiles have a preponderance of medium- and small-scale firms.

The available policy measures for adjustment assistance—unemployment benefits, subsidies for retraining the work force, trade controls to eliminate foreign competition in the short run, cartels for scrapping of capacity and production adjustments, assistance to the declining industries to shift abroad (foreign direct investments), regional policies, promoting expansion of new industries—are also quite varied.

In view of such complexity and diversity associated with the industrial adjustment policies, the desirability of a policy measure may be impossible to discuss without undertaking an analysis of individual industries and policy measures. Considering the space limitations, the discussion below is limited to a general view of shifts in industrial structure and the accompanying adjustment policies.

Besides efficiency, considerations of fairness in income distribution are also important for a proper understanding of industrial adjustment policies. The evaluations based on standard economic analysis normally tend to emphasize efficiency in resource allocation. This is because value judgments invariably creep in while discussing the distribution problem, making an objective analysis difficult. Industrial adjustment policies, however, while altering the resource allocation within an economy, also have a significant effect on the distribution of income. In the process of industrial adjustments, the workers in the declining industries bear substantial losses in the form of unemployment and, if industrial adjustment assistance policy takes the form of trade restrictions, consumers lose. Thus, an economic analysis of adjustment policies must deal with the issue of changes in income distribution accompanying the adjustment process and analyze the effect that various policy measures can have on the distribution of income. The subsequent discussion tries to incorporate this aspect to the extent possible.

21.2 INTERINDUSTRY FACTOR MOVEMENTS AND INDUSTRIAL ADJUSTMENT

The discussion in this section uses an extremely simplified two-goods model to analyze the problem of movements in factors of production accompanying the adjustments in industrial structure. Although simple, the two-goods model makes it possible to bring the changes in economic welfare and the manner in which the various adjustment assistance policies affect the movement of factors of production from the declining to nondeclining industries into clear light.

The problem of industrial adjustment involves, basically, dynamic considerations. Adjustments in industrial structure imply intersectoral movement of productive factors and are associated with factors such as the speed with which factors of production move among industries, the distinction between the short- and long-run effects in the process of such movements, the dynamic factors impinging on policy formulation, and the reaction pattern of the private economic agents—factors that can be clarified only with a dynamic analytical framework. Space considerations preclude a rigorous dynamic analysis but the discussion below does take these aspects into account.

First, let us discuss the basic structure of the two-good model employed and the effect of movements of productive factors from the declining to the non-declining industries on economic welfare.[2]

The horizontal axis of Fig. 21-1 measures the production and consumption of good 1 while the vertical axis measures the same for good 2. The country under consideration is a small country and both the goods are traded. *AB* in Fig. 21-1 represents the long-run production frontier of the country and curves represented by u_1, u_2, u_3, and u_4 are the indifference curves of a representative individual. All the factors of production are fully employed such that an optimum interindustry resource allocation results in production to be undertaken at a point lying on the production frontier.

Let us assume that the slope of the straight line q represents the initial terms of trade faced by the country. Assuming the country to be in long-run equilibrium under these terms of trade, the production and consumption points are represented by E and F, respectively. In this situation, the country is exporting good 1 and importing good 2.

Now, let us assume that a decline sets in for the industry producing good 2 (import good). In the subsequent discussion, a gradual decline in the relative price of good 2 in the foreign market implies that the industry producing good 2 is a declining industry. The domestic firms, thus, face increased competition from the foreign firms whose prices are gradually falling.[3]

As a result of a fall in the foreign price of good 2, the terms of trade for the home country improve and are given by the slope of the straight line q'. If all the adjustments, including those of factors of production, are instantaneous, the production and the consumption points shift to E' and F', respectively. It is easily verified from Fig. 21-1 that the economic welfare of the home country rises.

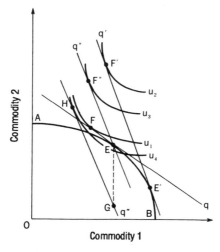

FIG. 21-1

This point can be interpreted as follows. A decline in international prices enables the home country to import good 2 at a lower price. The improved terms of trade generate consumption as well as production gains.[4] The consumption gains refer to the increase in economic welfare as a result of improved terms of trade since, even with initial production levels, it is now possible to import more of good 2 with less exports of good 1. In terms of Fig. 21-1, with production point fixed at E, the consumption point shifts from F to F'' as a result of improved terms of trade and the utility level shifts from u_1 to u_3. The production gains, on the other hand, represent the economic benefits that the home country derives by increased production of good 1 as a result of improved terms of trade. As production shifts from E to E' in Fig. 21-1, the consumption shifts from F'' to F', raising the utility level from u_3 to u_2. In Fig. 21-1, i.e., in case of an improvement in terms of trade, production as well as consumption gains emerge at the same time.[5]

However, the process of industrial adjustment, as discussed above, is seldom smooth. First, a transfer of resources from the industry producing good 1 to the industry producing good 2 may be quite time consuming. Let us consider a situation where movement of productive factors entails costs and a shift in production point from E to E' takes quite a long time.

The economy does not face any unemployment problem, even when the adjustment process is time consuming, as long as it is producing at some point on its production frontier. The economic welfare, especially when terms of trade improve in favor of the home country, i.e., when the import industry becomes a declining industry, cannot fall below the preadjustment level. For example, if a change in terms of trade does not lead to any change in production structure and the economy continues to produce at E, improved terms of trade result in higher economic welfare. In this case, the economy fails to reap production gains but is benefited by gains in consumption. A quick shift in production structure may be desirable but a failure to bring about such a change does not lead to precipitation of the industrial adjustment problems. On the contrary, resource costs of hastening the pace of movement of productive factors above that dictated by market forces are known to exceed the benefits.

The above arguments are important for a proper understanding of the industrial adjustment problem. The preceding discussion indicates that the usually accepted belief, that speed of factor transfers among industries is the most important aspect of industrial adjustments, is not correct. To put the problem of industrial adjustment in a proper perspective, it is imperative to look into factors other than the speed of interindustry factor movements. The factor–price rigidities, considered hereunder, is one such problem.

21.3 WAGE RIGIDITY AND UNEMPLOYMENT

The discussion in Section 21.2 assumed that the production point is always on the production frontier. The industrial adjustment problem, however, becomes severe when the production point moves inside the production frontier. The production point can lie on the production frontier only if the production factors are fully employed. Existence of unemployment brings the production point inside the production frontier and the discussion carried out above no longer stands. Considering the fact that unemployment is invariably a major concern in any discussion of industrial adjustment problems in the real world, this point assumes greater importance.[6]

The existence of some form of rigidities in factor prices can also bring the production point inside the production frontier. This has been made amply clear by the disequilibrium trade theory described by Haberler (1950). Let us briefly explain this point.[7]

Let us assume that the price of and wages in the sector producing good 1 stay unchanged while the price of good 2 falls. The relative wage for a firm producing good 2 rises due to a fall in the price of its product. As a result, a part of workers employed in the production of good 2 lose their jobs. This does not create any problem if workers released by firms producing good 2 are employed by firms engaged in the production of good 1. However, since the price of good 2 and the wage rate in this sector remain unchanged, there is no incentive for the producers of good 2 to increase employment. If unemployment leads to a decline in wages, the producers of good 1 may employ a part of the unemployed work force and the redundancy of workers in the good 1–producing sector may also be small. But this mechanism fails to work in the presence of wage rigidities. As a result it is possible for the production point in Fig. 21-1, in response to a change in terms of trade, to shift from E to a point like G.

An economy, despite an improvement in its terms of trade, may suffer a loss in economic welfare if its production point moves inside the production frontier. Figure 21-1 represents such a case. The straight line q''' passing through point G represents the same relative price as the straight line q' but the utility level u_4 has declined. Thus, industrial adjustment becomes a serious problem for a country when it is faced with production losses due to the emergence of unemployment.

21.4 Industrial Adjustment Assistance Policies: Trade-Restricting Policies

The emergence of serious unemployment accompanying the process of industrial adjustment or of less-than-full employment of other factors of production calls for some form of policy intervention. In the rest of this chapter, we analyze the economic effects of some of the representative policy measures. In this discussion, we assume that wages are sticky downward and, in the absence of some sort of policy intervention, unemployment is bound to occur.

Since in the example discussed above it was an improvement in terms of trade that triggered industrial adjustment, let us consider a policy that mitigates this shock. More concretely, one can consider tariffs or import controls that result in

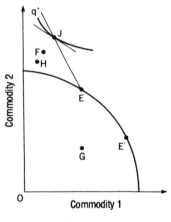

FIG. 21-2

raising the relative prices in the domestic market. Let us consider the impact of such a policy using Fig. 21-2, which is a touched up version of Fig. 21-1 (the notations in Fig. 21-2 correspond to those in Fig. 21-1).

Let us assume that the government imposes a tariff on the import of good 2 that is just enough to nullify the effects of a change in terms of trade. This results in domestic relative price staying at the level obtained before the terms of trade changed and the production remains at E. Since the terms of trade for the country have improved, the consumption level is given by point J in Fig. 21-2. It is clear that economic welfare is higher with policy intervention than in the absence of such a policy, when production falls to G.

The unemployment accompanying industrial adjustment resulted from the changes in relative price facing the producers and a trade-restricting policy to nullify this change in terms of trade was effective in solving the unemployment problem. The above discussion deals only with a tariff policy but a policy imposing import quotas also leads to similar conclusions.

Thus, a trade-restricting policy mitigates the shock arising from a change in terms of trade in the short run. However, the long-run implications of such a policy are problematic. With a change in terms of trade, it is necessary for the factors of production, in the final analysis, to move out of the declining industry into some other industry. Such resource transfers are triggered by the signals provided by the prices faced by producers. Such resource transfers become difficult if trade-restricting policies hinder changes in domestic prices.

The experience with protective policies for declining industries in a number of countries shows that such policies usually end up preserving the declining industry and the required resource transfers never materialize. This points to the existence of a trade-off between avoiding short-run unemployment problems and requirements of long-run industrial adjustment. It is impossible to generalize, with any degree of certainty, about which of the two targets should be given precedence over the other since the priority attached to a target is determined by the rate of time preference (discount rate, interest rate, and so on) of the economy concerned. The short-run unemployment problem may receive greater priority if the rate of time preference is high.

A trade-restricting policy for a limited period may be of some use in dealing with the problems of short-run unemployment and industrial adjustment at the same time. Let us assume that an import-restricting policy valid for a limited period of 5 years is adopted to rescue the declining industry. The understanding that the import controls will be dismantled in 5 years, in this case, can reduce mid- to long-term investment in the declining industry, thereby promoting inter-industry resource transfers. However, there is substantial scope for further theoretical analyses in the context of such time-bound protective policies.[8]

The only problem with time-bound trade-restricting policies is related to the question of whether the time limits imposed on such protective policies can be effectively met or not. This is usually referred to as the problem of "policy credibility." Since this is an important aspect of the problem, we briefly discuss it hereunder.[9]

The government introduces a trade-restricting policy to avoid the unemployment problem. A time limit placed on such a policy is expected to promote inter-industry factor movements. The reason why a time-bound policy promotes inter-industry factor movements is as follows: As long as protection is believed to be temporary, the private economic agents expect the factors of production remaining in the declining industry, once the protection is withdrawn, to generate only losses. As a result, the declining industry does not hire new workers, which are absorbed in other industries. The workers already employed in the declining industry take a cue from this and shift to other industries. Investment funds are withdrawn from the declining industry and invested elsewhere.

The problem, however, is whether the private sector, at the time of introduction of time-bound trade-restricting policies, believes in the time limits imposed or in whether the government can, when the time arrives, dismantle the restrictions or not. Can a government dismantle trade restrictions if it finds the actual interindustry factor movements to be short of initial expectations once the time for such removals arrives?

Removing trade restrictions can lead to a serious unemployment problem if the factor movements have been insufficient. It may be difficult, therefore, for the government to close its eyes to such a problem and remove the trade restrictions. If the private sector anticipates the government's dilemma, it will tend not to carry out the distasteful industrial adjustments, banking on an extension of trade restrictions. As a result, dismantling of time-bound trade restrictions becomes all the more difficult. If the government is in a position to commit to the time limits of the trade restrictions in some manner, the private sector may undertake the required adjustments. It is, however, not clear if such commitment is possible.

In a historical perspective, there is a preponderance of cases where trade-restricting policies introduced as time-bound measures to assist adjustment have tended to continue forever. Looking at the postwar Japan–United States trade relations alone, one can find a number of trade-restricting policies adopted in the name of assisting industrial adjustments. In the 1950s, in the wake of a rapid increase in exports of cotton products, temporary voluntary restraints on Japanese exports to the United States were adopted. These export (import) controls on textile products, however, were gradually formalized and now cover a large number of countries besides Japan and the United States. International trade in textile products is now carried out within the framework of MFA (Multi-Fiber Arrangement), an international arrangement to manage trade. Managed trade has blocked export opportunities for the developing countries and delayed industrial adjustments in the developed countries, the main importers.

Again, managed trade in iron and steel was introduced in the late 1960s in response to a rapid increase in exports from Japan. Although in a changed form, this measure has been in place ever since. Indications of further strengthening and continuation of managed trade are found in the extension of such measures to the automobile and integrated circuits industries. As managed trade spreads to more and more industries, the system of free trade, laboriously built up in the postwar period within the GATT framework, can break down completely. We will come back to a detailed discussion of this point in Chapter 22.

21.5 INDUSTRIAL ADJUSTMENT ASSISTANCE POLICIES: CARTELIZATION POLICIES

The trade-restricting policies, discussed above, sometimes take the form of voluntary export restraints by the partner country. Implementation of voluntary export restraints requires the industry to be oligopolistic to some extent. This is because implementation of export controls requires imposing export quotas on individual producers and the existence of a very large number of firms or the possibility of free entry makes it difficult to allocate such quotas. It may be possible, even if an industry is composed of a large number of firms, to implement export quotas if some form of industry association, like an export association, has a strong guiding power over the industry. But, generally, it may prove to be a difficult task.[10]

The "cartelization effect," discussed below, is strong when voluntary export restraints are implemented in an oligopolistic industry. The space limitations prevent a detailed theoretical analysis of the cartelization effect and we restrict ourselves to an intuitive explanation of the phenomenon.[11]

The United States domestic market price of passenger cars is said to have risen by 30 to 60% as a result of voluntary export restraints introduced on Japanese exports to the United States since the early 1980s. It is interesting to note that the price of the United States–produced passenger cars also rose along with those of the Japanese-produced cars.[12]

The mechanism behind such an increase in prices can be described as follows. Before voluntary export restraints came into effect, the United States producers had to set their prices at a low level since any increase in prices on their part could easily bring about a rapid increase in Japanese exports. However, once export restraints came into effect, the United States producers did not have to fear an increase in exports from Japan even if they posted higher prices. With an upper limit on exports by Japanese producers, any shift in demand away from the United States to Japanese-produced passenger cars resulted in a rise in the Japanese car prices rather than increased exports from Japan.

The Japanese producers also, in a sense, expected the United States producers to raise their prices. An increase in prices posted by the United States makers enabled Japanese producers to raise their own prices. Thus, with voluntary export restraints, both the United States and Japanese makers have a strong incentive to raise their prices, leading to a significantly large increase in prices. It is theoretically possible to show that, even in the absence of a decline in real export volume, prices can shoot up sharply with the imposition of an upper limit on exports. This is nothing but the "cartelization effect." Unless the upper limit on exports is set at an exceptionally low level, the United States and Japanese producers profit from the introduction of voluntary export restraints. It goes without saying that this increase in profits is at the cost of the United States consumers.

Introduction of voluntary export restraints in oligopolistic industries, as discussed above, generates strong incentives for the firms to raise prices and changes the competitive structure significantly. Moreover, since allocation of export quotas is based on noneconomic considerations, it also suppresses new entry and expansion of capacity by the competing firms. As a result, continuation of voluntary export restraints over extended periods can cause the industry to lose its vitality. The effect of capacity adjustment and production adjustment cartels, although not discussed here due to considerations of space, can be similarly evaluated.

21.6 INDUSTRIAL ADJUSTMENT ASSISTANCE POLICIES: EMPLOYMENT SUBSIDY POLICIES

Trade restrictions are not the only way to circumvent the unemployment problem. Employment subsidy policies can also serve the same purpose effectively. Let us explain this point with the help of Fig. 21-3 (drawn under conditions similar to those for Figs. 21-1 and 21-2, with the same notations).

An appropriate wage subsidy to the declining industry, producing good 2, reduces the wage burden of the firms in this industry for continued employment and

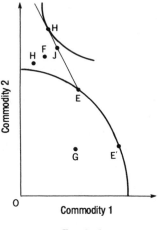

FIG. 21-3

can help maintain production on the production frontier. In terms of Fig. 21-3, the short-run production and consumption are at points E and H, respectively. Comparing this new situation with that in Fig. 21-2, it may be noted that, in the case of a wage subsidy, in contrast to trade restrictions, the consumers stand to gain from improved terms of trade. This is because the consumers can attain point H with a wage subsidy as compared to point J under a tariff.

A direct intervention in the form of a wage subsidy policy is an effective measure since it directly affects the immediate concern—short-run unemployment. Import restrictions, on the other hand, entail side effects in the form of distorted domestic consumer prices and result in correspondingly lower economic welfare.

As in the case of import restrictions, an employment assistance policy can also give rise to a conflict between the short-run unemployment and the long-run industrial adjustment problems. As long as the producers of good 2, the declining industry, are provided with wage subsidies, factor movements away from this industry and into other industries become difficult. A time-bound policy in this case, too, is bound to face the same problems as in the case of import restrictions.

21.7 INDUSTRIAL ADJUSTMENT ASSISTANCE POLICIES:
POLICIES DIRECTED AT BUSINESS SWITCHOVERS

Each of the three policies discussed above was concerned more with finding a solution to the unemployment problem than promoting the outflow of factors of production from the declining industries. It is possible to consider policies that promote the movement of factors of production away from the declining and into other industries. Provisions for technical training to facilitate job switching by the workers, providing incentives to move firms away from areas with a preponderance of declining industries, subsidies for scrapping capacity, etc., are some such policies.

Since, in the long run, withdrawal of productive factors from declining industries to be reemployed in other industries is desirable for the economy, the policies to promote a shift in the industrial structure may be important. A theoretical analysis of such policies, however, reveals that the problem is not as simple as it appears. Space considerations do not allow us to go into a detailed theoretical analysis here and we restrict ourselves to presenting some of the most important points.

1. Deteriorating performance in the declining industries in itself is a signal for the factors of production to move out of the industry. Therefore, sooner or later, the factors of production are bound to move even if the government does not take recourse to any policy to promote structural shifts. The only problem is whether or not the adjustment speed, left to market forces, is desirable from the viewpoint of economic welfare. Policy interventions may be justified if it is desirable to raise the speed of adjustments.

The argument that autonomous adjustments brought about by market forces are slower than is socially desirable lacks solid theoretical foundations. Mussa (1978, 1982) explores this point using a dynamic model, concluding that autonomous adjustments based on market mechanism are sufficient to bring about socially desirable adjustments. The Mussa model, however, is a highly simplified model with no market failures and assumes perfect foresight on the part of private economic agents. It is, however, not clear how the conclusions will be affected once these assumptions are removed. One will have to wait for further research to be able to say more about these aspects. For example, Mussa has nothing to say about wage rigidities, referred to in our earlier discussion, which may be an important form of market failure affecting adjustment speed.

2. Wage stickiness does not necessarily justify policies to promote structural shifts. For example, consider the case of a declining industry which is labor intensive. Furthermore, the wages are sticky and some unemployment already exists.[13] In this case, government intervention can lead to excessive movement of factors of production and may, in fact, end up in increased unemployment. Let us assume that there are only two factors of production, labor and capital, and the government's adjustment assistance policy tries to promote transfer of capital from the declining industry into other sectors. In such a case, while the other industries are unable to absorb the labor force released by the declining industry fully, the policy leads to further outflow of capital from the industry. If labor redundancy accompanies such capital outflow, unemployment is bound to rise.

3. Although the above arguments concentrate exclusively on efficiency considerations, the distribution problem is also extremely important in a discussion of declining industries. This is because the workers employed in the declining

industries, in most cases, are in a weak position and need some form of social protection. Looking at the problem in this perspective, policy intervention in the form of subsidies for job switching by the workers, although unwarranted on efficiency grounds, may be meaningful.

21.8 IN CONCLUSION

The above analysis of declining industries and the related industrial adjustment policies has touched only the surface of the problem. However, even this cursory analysis is enough to show that the industrial adjustment problem is multifaceted with complex interrelationships amongst the various aspects. The economic investigations into the problem of industrial adjustment cannot be considered to have been sufficiently productive. To close the discussion, therefore, we suggest some possible directions for future research.

First, as mentioned earlier in this chapter, investigations incorporating the dynamic aspects of the problem are imperative. The speed with which factors of production move among industries has important implications for the industrial adjustment problem. It is necessary to determine the socially desirable adjustment speed and whether policy intervention is necessary toward this end. And, if policy intervention is deemed necessary, what sort of measures need to be adopted? Works by Mussa do indicate a broad direction for such research but are beset with a number of problems. For example, factors like structure of the industry concerned, labor intensity of the technology employed in the industry, and the structure of the labor markets can significantly affect the speed of adjustment. Mussa's research practically ignores such factors.

Second, it is necessary to conduct deeper research into the process of policy formulation. As discussed briefly in this chapter also, the formulation and implementation of policy measures are governed by the interactions among the private economic agents, market conditions, and government and political considerations. The process of policy formulation, inclusive of the lobbying and rent-seeking activities by the interested parties, can have a significant effect on the content of adjustment assistance policies which, in turn, have serious implications for income distribution.

Third, the industrial adjustment problem needs to be analyzed in an international perspective. The industrial adjustment problem is not a problem of a single country but has implications for international resource allocation as well. Policy coordination required for industrial adjustment in individual countries to proceed smoothly and the necessary changes in the present GATT rules required to attain this objective are some points which demand a much deeper level of analysis.

Fourth, analyses treating the distribution problem in a more explicit manner are needed. The real-world industrial adjustment policies tend to lean strongly toward the opinions of the group with the higher stakes in the problem. In most cases, the industrial adjustment problem gives rise to a small group that stands to lose heavily and a large group whose individual gains are much smaller. Taking Fig. 21-1 as an example, the unemployed workers and the industrialist with falling profits represent the first group, and consumers, who gain from improved terms of trade, the second. More often than not, trade-restricting policies, inappropriate from the viewpoint of total social welfare, are adopted strongly reflecting the opinions of the smaller group with high stakes.

The available analyses of social desirability of policy formulations leave much to be desired. Deardorff (1987) shows that it is possible to justify protective policies on the basis of a conservative standard that calls for reducing the loss of the most affected person to the extent possible. This conclusion may, in fact, be an appropriate reflection of the actual process of policy formulation in the real world. It may be fruitful to develop such an argument further for a detailed discussion of the "problem of second best"—a search for a policy to bring about an efficient resource allocation without causing a significant shift in income distribution.

NOTES

1. For an overview of industrial policy in the context of textile industry, see Yamazawa (1984) and Dore (1986).

2. For details of the argument developed below, see Itoh (1984) and Itoh and Ohyama (1985). Itoh and Negishi (1987) discusses the relationship between unemployment and trade in detail.

3. It is possible to define a declining industry in terms of a shift in production frontier but the basic results do not change.

4. See Chapter 1 of Itoh and Ohyama (1985) on consumption and production gains.

5. A worsening of terms of trade generates production gains but involves consumption losses. It is, therefore, possible for economic welfare after the change in terms of trade to decline.

6. If factor movements among industries entail costs, the production point may move inside the production frontier even when all the factors are fully employed. In this case, however, a move to a production point within the production frontier is an unavoidable cost and one may consider this as a socially desirable state. For details on this point, see Mussa (1984, 1978, 1982) and Mayer (1974).

7. Itoh and Negishi (1987) provide a comprehensive survey of developments in this field.

8. The time-bound protective policies for growth industries, discussed in Chapter 12 of this book, are essentially similar to those under consideration here.

9. For details, see Itoh, Kiyono, and Masuda (1986, 1987).

10. For theoretical underpinnings of these arguments, cf. Okuno, Postlewaite, and Roberts (1980).

11. A theoretical treatment of this point can be found in Itoh and Ono (1982).

12. The rate of increase in the yen prices of Japanese-produced passenger cars may have been higher than dollar prices since the yen was depreciating during this period. Although an exact estimate of the rate of increase in car prices may be difficult due to diversity in options and accessories attached, there is no doubt that prices rose by a large margin.

13. For details, see Neary (1982) and Itoh and Ohyama (1985).

22

Internationalization of the Economy and Industrial Policies

22.1 INTRODUCTION

The postwar international trade is structured around the GATT (General Agreement on Tariffs and Trade). The basic position of the GATT system in the postwar period has been to dismantle the trade restrictions in the form of tariffs and quotas, leaving the domestic industrial policies and other controls to the discretion of individual countries. This system of international trade, although simple, functioned quite effectively. The prosperity that the world economy has enjoyed in the postwar period could not have materialized in the absence of the free trade system based on the GATT. The postwar rapid economic growth of Japan, in particular, has heavily dependent on the expanding international trade. It may not be an exaggeration to state that Japan benefited the most from the free trade system in the postwar period.

The present-day free trade system is at a critical juncture. The repeated occurrence of trade frictions has posed complicated problems and a number of protective policies have been enforced. The trade behavior of Japan—the main beneficiary of the free trade system—has become a major problem in the context of the increasingly complex trade frictions.

The rapid expansion of Japanese exports of products, starting with textiles and continuing in iron and steel, color television, automobiles, and semiconductors, has given rise to a diverse variety of discords with its trading partners. The increase in the Japanese share in the world economy has resulted in increased foreign interest in the domestic markets of Japan and almost all aspects of the Japanese economy—uniquely closed distribution system, strict import restrictions on agricultural products, the form of industrial protection, and other economic regulations—have come under severe criticism from abroad.

The free trade system structured around the GATT proved to be particularly suitable for the conduct of postwar Japanese industrial policies. On the one hand, a gradual dismantling of tariff and nontariff barriers in individual countries favored expansion of exports by Japanese firms. On the other hand it allowed

258

Japan, foreign pressures for dismantling of tariff and quota barriers apart, to have a free hand in adopting independent domestic policies without any foreign interference.

This policy environment is undergoing substantial changes in recent years. The Japanese policies and organizational set-up, since Japan has emerged as a large country, are now in a position to make a serious impact on foreign countries as well as the world economic system. It is impossible for Japan to conduct its industrial policies within the limited perspective of the domestic economy alone. This chapter discusses the significance of changes in the industrial policy environment, as a result of Japan's emergence as a large country and the internationalization of its economy, for policy conduct.

22.2 CHANGES IN JAPANESE INDUSTRIAL STRUCTURE AND TRADE FRICTIONS

A fleeting look at the past figures is enough to bring out the dynamic pattern of Japanese export expansion. Within a decade after the war hostilities ended, Japanese shipbuilding rose to occupy the number one position in terms of orders received. The Japanese steel exports to the United States, standing at 4.5 million T in 1967, were up to about 7.0 million T in 1968. Similarly, exports of color televisions to the United States market rose from 1.0 million units in 1975 to 2.5 million the following year—a 2.5-fold increase in 1 year. A similar phenomenon can be discerned in semiconductors and copying machines as well. Despite the fact that Japan was a latecomer in the United States market, the pace of expansion of the Japanese share of the market in these industries was exceptionally high. The rapid expansion of exports may be a striking phenomenon in itself but one must not ignore the fact that severe competition among the Japanese firms, resulting in a steep fall in prices and improved product quality, was also responsible for the emergence of this phenomenon. Almost all the products mentioned above are produced by a large number of firms competing fiercely amongst themselves. There are about 10 Japanese firms producing automobiles; almost all the major electrical companies are also engaged in the production of semiconductors and computers. Copying machine producers number over 20. These numbers are exceptionally large when compared to those in Western countries.

The cut-throat competition amongst the firms in terms of quality improvements and price cuts produces tremendous results. For example, in the case of integrated products, the prices of new-generation products introduced into the market fell to one-tenth of their original prices within a matter of few years. While the performance of products like calculators, copying machines, and word processors is rapidly improving, the prices show a sharp decline. The fact that falling prices and quality improvements have increased the export competitiveness of the Japanese firms and resulted in a sharp increase in exports is undeniable. However, the rapid increase in Japanese exports has led to serious trade frictions with the other developed industrial countries, especially the United States. A rapid increase in the share taken by Japanese firms in a short period of time has not only adversely affected the business of foreign firms but has also resulted in problems of a more serious nature, like reduced employment in the industry concerned and unemployment for the foreign countries.

No doubt a rapid expansion of exports by Japanese firms adversely affects the foreign economies, particularly the employees and the management in the given industry, but, at the same time, it also results in substantial benefits to consumers in those economies. This is because a sharp increase in Japanese exports is a result of better product quality and higher exports of Japanese products raise the degree of competition in the foreign markets, causing prices to fall.

Falling prices are not the only benefit bestowed by expanded exports of Japanese products to the United States market. More important, perhaps, is the stiffer interfirm competition induced by rising Japanese exports. The United States producers, to counter the Japanese products, not only must reduce prices but also must put in efforts to raise productivity and improve product quality. The rapid expansion of Japanese exports has increased the incentives for the United States firms to undertake such efforts. Especially in industries like the automobile industry, where technological innovations and improvements in production system are important factors, Japanese exports may, in fact, result in raising United States competitiveness.

22.3 PROTECTIONISM AND MANAGED TRADE

The pattern of expanding Japanese exports, followed by adoption of trade-restriction measures by the United States to counter them, is repeatedly seen in a number of industries. The Japanese exports of textile products, mainly cotton products, rose sharply in the immediate postwar period. Accordingly, this was the first Japanese industry, in the postwar period, to be placed under voluntary export restraints in response to United States demands. Similarly, exports of iron and steel rose rapidly in the 1960s and the voluntary export restraints were adopted in the late 1960s. Similar voluntary restraints were imposed on color televisions in the mid-1970s and on automobiles and semiconductors in the 1980s.

Thus, a sharp rise in exports followed by adoption of some form of import or export controls has been the pattern for a large number of industries in the postwar period. The one point that is common to all these restriction measures is that, once adopted, most of them have become a permanent feature in one form or the other. Let us take textiles as a case in point. The trade control measures, adopted initially in the form of voluntary restraints, were gradually formalized. Besides, while the initial measures were intended to be temporary, covering only three countries (Japan, the United States, and the United Kingdom) and only the trade in cotton products, they spread gradually to a large number of countries and all textile products. As a result, trade in textile products, presently, is conducted within an internationally established managed trade system, the MFA (Multifiber Arrangement). The trade in textile products is no longer governed by free trade principles since the managed trade system covers all the developed and most of the major textile-producing countries.

The import controls introduced in industries like those producing iron and steel and household electrical equipment, although changed in form, continue to be operative. A complete dismantling of the restrictive trade measures in the automobile and semiconductor industries is also difficult to visualize in the near future.

Voluntary restraints and other trade-restricting measures adopted in Japan–United States trade relations, moreover, have spread to trade relations between Japan and Europe as well. One of the reasons for the spread of these measures may be found in the need to counter the diversion of Japanese automobile exports, which could not enter the United States market due to voluntary export restraints, to the EC market. The voluntary restraints on automobile exports have also resulted in increased overseas production. This overseas production, however, is predominantly in the form of assembling of Japanese parts—a way to get around the net of voluntary export restraints. Outcry against this fact has resulted in the strengthening of import control measures, not only on automobiles but also on automobile parts.

Thus, voluntary export restraints call forth more voluntary restraints and trade controls require further trade controls.[2] It may, therefore, not be an exaggeration to state that a large proportion of the world trade, as a result, is managed trade.

Managed trade is having diverse adverse effects. First, the consumers in the importing countries are losing an opportunity to buy good-quality imported goods at cheap prices. For example, the prices of Japanese cars in the United States market rose sharply in the first half of the 1980s as a result of voluntary export restraints. It is difficult to precisely measure the extent of the rise in prices but the fact that this rise was substantial is clear if we also take the exchange rate movements in this period into consideration. The prices of the United States–produced cars have also shown a significant increase during the same period. Such a price rise may have resulted from the international cartelization effect brought about by voluntary export restraints.

Second, export expansion by the developing and the newly industrializing countries has run into difficulties and is acting as a factor impeding their economic development. Especially when trade-restriction policies do not follow an internationally accepted rule but are negotiated between two countries, the militarily and economically weak developing countries invariably find themselves at a disadvantage in the negotiating process.

Third, as a result of excessive protection of the declining industries in the developed countries, competition in these industries has weakened. This has not only caused a loss in the vitality of these industries but has also made a transfer of factor of production away from the declining industries to industries with development potential more difficult.

22.4 RAPID INCREASE IN EXPORTS AND
EXCESSIVE COMPETITION AMONG JAPANESE FIRMS

The rapid expansion of Japanese exports coupled with relatively stagnant imports has produced a huge trade surplus. By 1986, the amount of exports was twice as high as that of imports and the trade surplus reached nearly 5% of the GNP. Quite obviously, the main factor behind such a huge trade surplus can be found in the United States fiscal deficit and contractionary fiscal policies adopted by the Japanese government for the fiscal rehabilitation of Japan. Reflecting the recent upsurge in protectionism, however, the problem of trade surplus has come to be treated as a microeconomic problem.

From a microeconomic point of view, current account surplus is linked closely to policy measures in at least three ways. First, one may argue for imposition of export levies to bring down the current account surpluses. Second, it is argued that the behavior of the Japanese firms, their predisposition toward excessive competition in particular, has led to a rapid increase in Japanese current account surplus, especially its exports. Third, there are apprehensions about whether the free trade system can lead to an optimum international trade structure due to the presence of economies of scale and technological innovations. The last of these points is closely related to the discussion in Parts II and V of this book. In this section we take up the first two points, leaving the discussion of the third to the next section.

A policy to bring the international balance of payments into equilibrium through levies on Japanese exports raises the following problems.

According to Lerner's well-known symmetry theorem of international economics, a policy to restrict exports will have the same effect as an import-restriction policy, as is the case with Japanese agriculture and some other industries.

Lerner's symmetry theorem, as discussed in detail in Chapter 7 also, states that a policy to restrict total exports has the same effect as a policy restricting total imports. The reader may find it confusing. Since import restriction and export promotion have similar effects in that both of these measures benefit the Japanese firms, import restrictions and export restrictions should have opposite effects.

To understand Lerner's symmetry theorem, which appears to be paradoxical at first sight, one must consider the effect of import and export restrictions, not only on the industries directly affected by the policies, but on the economy as a whole as well. The significance of economic theory for policy problems lies in the fact that it helps us to grasp the problem in a wider perspective by going beyond the direct effects of a policy and thoroughly investigating into all the possible repercussions on the workings of the economy as a whole.

What are the implications of placing restrictions on total exports from Japan? In particular, how do the restrictions imposed on Japanese exports affect the exchange rate?

Let us first consider the export-restricting policies. Since Japanese exports become difficult, the supply of foreign exchange on the foreign exchange market weakens, resulting in a relative decline in the value of the yen. This decline in the value of the yen mitigates a part of the effect of an export-restricting policy. Imports, on the other hand, are subdued due to a fall in the value of the yen. Thus, not only are the effects of an export-restricting policy canceled out by the changes in exchange rate but it also results in reducing imports.

Similar results can also be obtained by adopting an import-restricting policy. An import-restricting policy lowers the demand for foreign exchange on the foreign exchange market, resulting in exchange rate appreciation. This dampens the effect of the import-restricting policy and, at the same time, reduces exports.

Thus, a policy to restrict total exports has the same effect as a policy to restrict total imports. In other words, if a policy to restrict exports is deemed desirable, a policy to restrict imports must also be desirable. Conversely if an import-restricting policy is undesirable, export-restricting measures cannot be desirable.

The above analysis, however, assumes that the trade balance determines the exchange rate. If the long-run exchange rate is determined by trade balance (or purchasing power parity), the above analysis may be appropriate for the long run. But if short-run balance of payments (or trade balances) are determined by factors other than those related to the real side of the economy, export-restricting policies may not be meaningless in the short run.

Next, let us consider the view that excessive competition among the Japanese firms is the main cause of trade frictions. It is true that the Japanese firm behavior at the time of entering foreign markets is markedly different from that of the firms from other countries. The following factors may be responsible for this difference.

First, the nature of competition in the home market of Japan differs from that in other countries. Specifically, comparing the nature of competition in the Japanese markets to that in the United States market, one may observe that the Japanese firms tend to seek long-run stability of the firm rather than short-run profits such that market share, instead of profits, becomes the driving force of competition. Therefore, as the foreign markets open up a new opportunity, competition among the Japanese firms, trying to expand their share even at the cost of lower profit margins, leads to a rapid increase in exports.

One factor explaining such firm behavior is the importance attached to stability of long-term relationships, like life-time employment and customer relations, in the Japanese economy. The lesson from the trade frictions, however, is that competition among the Japanese firms for a larger share of the foreign markets has negative long-run effects on the Japanese industry and firms.

A second factor affecting the behavior of the Japanese firms may be administrative guidance and controls. Administrative guidance by the government and the concerned ministries, although much reduced in scale as compared to an earlier period, still influences the decision-making process by the Japanese firms by giving them hope that the government will come to their rescue if something happens to go wrong. These hopes generate excessive competition among the Japanese firms. As Schumpeter has pointed out very appropriately, an automobile runs faster precisely due to the fact that it is equipped with breaks.[3]

In this sense, the competition among the Japanese firms in the domestic market is "controlled competition" since it depends on the implicit understanding that the government will intervene to solve a problem if the worst happens. The restraining hand of the Japanese government is no longer effective as the Japanese firms extend their operations into foreign markets. The losers, in this case, being the foreign firms and foreign labor—Japanese government has no administrative power to rescue them.

An attempt to deal with the export drive of Japanese firms through voluntary restraints or trade restrictions is nothing but an extension of the concept of controlled competition to the foreign markets. However, since administrative guidance in itself is the main source of the problem, a lasting solution, perhaps, is to build up a more free competitive environment in the domestic markets.

22.5 CHANGING INDUSTRIAL STRUCTURE AND TRADE FRICTIONS

Our analysis, through Part II of this book, indicates that the traditional trade theory has only limited value in explaining trade and industrial structure in the presence of scale economies (or set-up costs) at the industry level. The traditional understanding, that unfettered free trade maximizes world economic welfare by giving rise to Pareto efficient resource allocation and industrial and trade structures, is decisively dependent on the assumptions of perfect competition and absence of scale economies. In the presence of scale economies at the industry level, the industrial and trade structure of an economy comes to depend on change and the industrial policies followed by individual countries. As a result, a country getting an early start on the industries that generate greater benefits can attain higher levels of economic welfare as compared to other countries. This may be especially important in the case of future growth industries like the high-technology industries.

The development of the major industries, inclusive of the high-technology industries, in the developed industrial countries owes much to accumulated production experience and technology and product development investments. For example, let us consider the accumulation of production experience. The semiconductor industry is believed to be characterized by strong learning curve effects. This effect implies that the higher a firm's cumulative production is, the lower are the production costs. If we take cumulative production on the horizontal axis and unit production costs on the vertical axis, the relationship describes a forward-falling curve.

In industries like that producing semiconductors, production costs fall as various technological problems, encountered in the production process, are gradually solved. This results in the relationship depicted by a learning curve effect. The newly introduced products in the semiconductor industry usually see a decline in prices to one-tenth of their original levels within a few years. This becomes possible mainly due to the learning curve effect. The relationship indicating a decline in production costs as accumulation of production experience proceeds can be observed, to a greater or lesser degree, in almost all the industries.

A similar phenomenon is discernible in the case of R & D investments as well. The costs of R & D investments usually have fixed cost characteristics and the larger the amount of good supplied, the lower is the unit cost of investment. Therefore, the firms engaged in large-scale production invest more in R & D. Thus, in the high-technology industries, where R & D investment plays an important role, the scale of production of individual firms can significantly affect their competitive power.

In industries where experience and R & D are important, the firms having a head start in large-scale production and, thereby, in accumulated production experience, have a competitive edge over the other firms. Since lowering of production costs by exploiting the scale economies is desirable from the viewpoint of allocational efficiency, it is important for a limited number of firms to attain a sufficiently large scale of production and accumulation of production experience. As far as this point is concerned, it does not matter which country is producing the output. Since the future economic development of a country can be significantly affected by whether or not it has indigenous high-technology industries like electronic computers, semiconductors, aircraft, and so on, each country tries to develop these industries. It is here that the reason for the severe conflict of interests can be found.

As already discussed in Part II of this book, the pattern of trade or of comparative advantage in industries characterized by significant scale economies is significantly affected by government policies, controls, or even the historical conditions of the market. For example, let us consider a new industry in which firms of two countries have comparable technological strength. If the economic conditions in the two economies do not differ, the firms of one country cannot be more competitive than those of the other. But if the government of one of the countries adopts a policy favoring the home country firms, the home firms come to occupy an advantageous position. This advantage, once established, shows a snowballing effect due to the presence of scale economies. Even when the countries do not differ in terms of policy, differences between the home and the foreign country firms can arise if the consumers in one country have a strong preference for home goods.

This clash of policy interests among various countries is one factor explaining trade frictions. Especially in the case of high-technology industries, a strong desire to retain such industries in one's own country, not only for the economic benefits it entails but also to maintain military superiority, also escalates these frictions. Again, as discussed in Part V of this book, the discord among various countries over high-technology industries is becoming all the more complex due to the problem of intellectual property rights.

Even in the presence of scale economies, the optimum scale is normally smaller than the scale of the national market and, hence, each country may set up a multiple number of firms. But this does not reduce the difficulties faced in dispersing production at an international level and, even if possible, the resulting dispersion may not necessarily be desirable from the viewpoint of resource allocation.

International agreements to regulate industrial policies to promote indigenous industries by individual countries can be one way to maintain fair international competition. But in the case of industries where accumulation of production experience and R & D investment are important, it is not clear whether an optimum resource allocation can or cannot materialize in the absence of government intervention. In such a case, industrial policies, as a market-supplementing measure, may, in fact, be necessary to bring about the desired resource allocation. Internationally coordinated industrial policy is faced with two difficult problems—the problem of efficiency of the world economy as a whole and the problem of sharing economic welfare among the countries. We come back to these problems once again in Section 22.7. But before we proceed to this aspect, let us briefly touch upon the diversification of international transactions and its consequences.

22.6 DIVERSIFICATION OF INTERNATIONAL TRANSACTIONS AND ITS CONSEQUENCES

As pointed out at the start of this chapter, the structure of the GATT system, the centerpiece of the postwar free trade system, has been, very simply, endeavoring to bring down the barriers enforced at the international borders, like tariffs and import quotas, while leaving the conduct of domestic policies basically at the discretion of each country. Such a system was envisaged in view of the belief that international economic transactions involved, predominantly, simple trade—exports and imports of goods.

The present-day international economic transactions among the developed industrial countries, however, are diverging more and more from such a simple form. Increasingly complex forms of economic transactions—intrafirm trading by multinational firms, direct foreign investment to engage in overseas production, vertical integration, by such industries as steel and petrochemical, of raw materials sectors the international level, internationally diversified marketing operations, joint ventures with overseas firms, and international transactions in technology and brands—are gaining in importance.

Also, the goods produced and consumed by the present-day developed industrial countries have a high services content. For example, technological and after-service are important in the case of products like automobiles, electrical and electronic equipment, machine tools, aircraft, semiconductors, and electronic computers. The importance of R & D and technology development also cannot be underestimated.

Thus, most of the goods produced and transacted in developed industrial countries may be seen to have a high service content (proportion of services). Hence, diversification of international economic activities, mentioned above, may be seen as the result of changing service content of the goods transacted. However, at the same time, one must not lose sight of the fact that factors like development of international communications and transport and increased international awareness of the firms and individuals have also contributed to the diversification of the forms of international transactions, leading to expanding trade in products with high-service content.

This phenomenon is especially evident in trade in services such as international transactions in financial instruments and communications. In the case of services trade, supply of services in the form of direct investment in overseas subsidiaries is far higher than current transactions appearing in the international payments balances. This is quite understandable given the unique nature of services.

In the case of international transactions in products with high-service content, including the trade in services, it is not only the regulations imposed at the international borders, such as tariffs and quota restrictions, that affect the transactions. Factors like domestic regulation of particular industries, the taxation system, business traditions obtaining in individual markets, policies restricting foreign investment and immigration, and regulation of related fields (for example, on communications in the case of financial markets or on financial markets in the case of insurance) also have a significant effect on international transactions. Therefore, efficient international transactions require an international economic system that takes all these factors into account. Such a system must be based on concepts radically different from those underlying the GATT.

The surging interest in trade in services and intellectual property rights, in recent years, reflects the changes taking place in the real-world economy. International negotiations in the field of trade in services focus on national institutions and policies of individual countries. These negotiations, by nature, are not restricted simply to the dismantling of regulations blocking trade at the national borders but must tread into the field of domestic policies of the countries involved. The special features of services industries like finance and telecommunications allow trade in services to take the form not only of the normal trade in goods but also such diversified forms as activities of overseas subsidiaries established through direct investment or international joint ventures. This point is quite clear if one looks at the behavior of the Japanese financial institutions in the overseas markets. A meaningful international system for trade in services cannot emerge unless regulatory measures for foreign investment and immigration, issues related to controls adopted and policy implementation in each country, besides the trade restrictions effect at national borders, are also brought to the negotiating table.

An interesting case in this regard is the regulations imposed by the government on the net worth ratio (ratio of net worth to total loans) in the banking industry. Recently, the United States and the United Kingdom have claimed that Japanese regulations on the net worth ratio are weak. It is claimed that since banks compete in the international markets, weaker regulations in the case of Japan only are unfair from the viewpoint of international competition. It is difficult to check the validity of such a claim by the United States and the United Kingdom as it is impossible to discuss the problem on the basis of a comparison of numbers alone, since the behavior pattern and business traditions of the banks in each country differ. A case in point is the evaluation of hidden assets particularly noticeable in the case of Japanese banks. In any case, this example is interesting since it shows that regulations adopted by individual countries are an important factor determining their comparative advantage.

The problem of intellectual property rights also shows similar features. Technology and product development, in the case of high-technology industries, are significant determinants of the competitive edge held by a firm. It is precisely due to this that implementation of licensing and copyright systems, which protects intellectual property rights, has attracted tremendous international attention. However, the licensing or copyright systems differ among the countries, with some countries refusing to recognize property rights granted by other countries, and are a major source of conflict. Any international agreement on intellectual property rights, by necessity, will have to bring the systems followed by each country to the negotiating table. Obviously, it goes beyond the problem of regulations effective at national borders.

The problem of policy or institutional adjustments is not limited to trade in services or the intellectual property rights systems. Various policies and regulations, such as industrial policy, antimonopoly policy, regulation of distribution sector, tax system, and immigration policy followed by individual countries, have a significant effect on trade and other international economic activity. Adjustments in national systems related to these policies are expected to assume greater importance in the future.

The systems and regulations adopted by each country are intended to serve some particular purpose and have their own rationale. Besides, the sovereignty of each country must be respected. Looking at the hard facts, however, it is clear that, in a number of cases, overemphasis on sovereignty by individual countries has hindered the otherwise desirable flow of trade and investments. At this stage, nothing concrete can be said about how to go about reconciling the systems enforced by individual countries. It is also not clear whether a uniform system for all the countries is a fair solution or not. It may, however, be said that the conduct of industrial policies in the developed industrial countries, including Japan, should not only look at national benefits but must also give more attention to the harmony of the international socioeconomic structure. Otherwise it may be impossible to sustain these policies over the long run until, in fact, they are no longer acceptable internationally.

22.7 INTERNATIONAL COORDINATION OF INDUSTRIAL POLICIES

Finally, let us come back to the problem of international coordination of industrial policies. As seen earlier, the free trade system based on the GATT, although it earns high points for its historical role in bringing about a prosperous world economy in the postwar period, has reached its limits as a framework for international economic transactions. The forms of international economic transactions have diversified extensively beyond the simple structures implicitly presumed by the GATT system (exports and imports of merchandise). Alongside this, the institutional and policy choices, falling within the discretionary limits of individual countries, have gradually become a target of mutual criticism and international adjustments. In this light, there is a clear need for a new frame of reference to govern international economic transactions to replace the present GATT system. An in-depth analysis of such a new framework is beyond the scope of this book. The discussion, here, focuses its attention on pointing out some problems associated with some of the attempts to solve international economic frictions related to diverse aspects of trade, institutions, and policies within the existing frame of reference.

At present, ad hoc solutions to the international economic frictions by way of international agreements, between two or a small number of countries, limited to specific industries, is the standard practice. This method of solving the problem, however, is beset with following problems.

1. As is evident in the case of voluntary restraints in the automobile industry, restraints on exports to the United States market lead to a diversion of Japanese automobile exports to the EC market, inducing import controls by the EC countries. Again, as revealed by the Japan–United States conflict over the semiconductor agreement, regulation of exports to the United States market is rendered ineffective in the absence of comprehensive measures to regulate exports to third countries. Thus, effective regulation through international agreements requires the agreement to bring all the affected countries into the net. But the interests of the individual countries involved are too diverse to allow the formulation and implementation of such global agreements. Besides, monitoring the adherence of individual countries to the agreement involves significant costs.

2. In the context of the complex nature of international economic transactions in recent years, as compared to the simple form of international transactions in the form of merchandise trade of the earlier years, it is not easy even to define the

scope of international agreements. As is clear in the case of voluntary restraints on the automobile industry, the restrictions on exports of finished passenger cars can be easily circumscribed by exporting parts and assembling the finished units overseas. Thus, implementation of effective controls, even if the product or the industry is specified, is not necessarily simple. In the case of trade in services or intellectual property rights, negotiations limited to the industry concerned are meaningless in most cases. An effective agreement in this case must be extensive which, once again, serves to narrow down the possibilities of concluding an agreement.

3. Negotiations between two or among a small number of countries normally come to a conclusion through an opaque political process. Let us consider the voluntary restraints imposed on the automobile industry once again. As discussed earlier, these regulations adversely affected the American consumers. But, since the per capita loss to the individual consumer was very small, opposition by this group could not generate much political pressure. In contrast this, per capita gains, from the voluntary restraints, to the employers and employees in the United States automobile industry were sufficiently large to build up solid political pressures for their demands. Thus, negotiations strongly influenced by the demands of directly affected groups, with consequent localization of the issues, are difficult to rationalize in a wider perspective. Besides, if one group succeeds in obtaining protection by the exercise of its political negotiating power, the rent-seeking behavior can easily spread to other industries trying to benefit from such protection. This erodes industrial vitality and further strengthens protectionist tendencies.

4. In political negotiations limited to a small number of countries, the militarily and economically strong countries tend to have an advantage. However, efficiency of the international economy and fairness of international distribution of welfare require the setting up of rules to govern international agreements that give a just treatment to the small and developing countries as well.

Future international agreements and adjustments, in the light of the above discussion, should take a form that satisfies at least the following three conditions:

a. The agreement helps in the formulation of a comprehensive framework for economic transactions based on international agreements in the true sense of the word, and is not based on negotiations between two or among a limited number of countries.

b. This frame of reference should not be limited simply to transactions in goods and services but should extend to agreements on domestic legislations and regulatory systems of individual countries.

c. The international body charged with administering this framework should conduct itself in a fair manner, following civilized rules.

It goes without saying that the above conditions are only necessary, and not sufficient, conditions for building up a desirable framework for international coordination. This point has also been discussed under problems (1) to (4) above. Of interest, however, is the fact that even the GATT, the system governing the postwar free trade, has also been paying close attention to these necessary conditions. Bilateral or multilateral negotiations, in fact, go against the GATT principles. In groping for a framework to govern international economic transactions to replace the GATT, one must not lose sight of the basic principle of a comprehensive system of international coordination espoused by the GATT.

The expression "groping for a framework to govern international economic transactions" may give an impression that one is espousing managed rather than free trade. It has been repeatedly pointed out in this chapter that market failures seriously undermine the optimality of free trade. Despite this, our faith in the importance of the concept of "freedom" in the context of economic activity is deep rooted. We would like to close our discussion in this chapter by emphasizing this point once again and establishing the significance of the concept of freedom.

The focus here is on the implications of the concept of freedom. Free trade, in the absence of quotas, tariffs, or nontariff barriers, may be referred to as what Berlin (1969) called "negative freedom." [4] According to this concept, a person is said to have (negative) freedom if he or she is free to decide, on matters of a personal nature or those falling within the national jurisdiction, on his or her own without any external pressures or suppression (from the government, traditions, or from abroad). The GATT system aimed at establishing exactly such a free trading system, a system in which each country was free to choose its own institutional and policy framework within its own jurisdiction. The problem, however, arises when pursuit of freedom in the above sense leads to adoption of policies by one country that have serious repercussions on other countries and gives rise to self-contradictory results in the sense that it is no longer possible to guarantee an equitable freedom for all the countries. The reason we call for a system to replace the GATT framework lies precisely in the self-negating characteristic of the concept of freedom.

In contrast to the above, the concept of freedom has another interpretation— what has been termed as "positive freedom" by Berlin. One is said to enjoy (positive) freedom when the right and capacity to decide on and implement one's own behavioral guidelines, without being forced to follow decisions taken by others or without any outside interference in making one's own decisions, is socially guaranteed. An equitable access to all economic opportunities by every economic agent is one of the preconditions necessary to ensure freedom in this sense. The Japanese socioeconomic set-up seems to glaringly lack this precondition for (positive) freedom. The system of inviting tenders only from the predesignated dealers, air administration requiring approval from competent authorities for opening up of new air routes, and refusal to allow imports of cheap and delicious foreign rice are just a few stark examples. Moreover, the Japanese business environment, where the vested interests of senior officials are taken for granted, symbolizes the fact that equality of opportunity is not necessarily ensured. Therefore, the criticism by foreign firms trying to enter the Japanese market, that opportunities for prompt access to economic activity are lost due to opaque and complex business practices of the Japanese firms or that new entry is impeded, is not just unfounded dissatisfaction. Any firm, to whichever country it may belong, must be provided with the same rights as long as it behaves in a fair manner within the framework of a civilized set of rules. This is the essence of the free market system that we are groping for. This may not be a free system as visualized by the free trading system under the GATT, but it does guarantee equitable opportunity to the economic agents of every country to pursue their potentialities in a fair manner. In this sense, it is clearly a free economic system.

NOTES

1. A part of this chapter is a touched up version of Motoshighe Itoh's "Recurring and Increasingly Complicated Trade Frictions and a Desirable Trade System." *Gendai Keizai* (*Economics Today*), No. 7, 1987.

2. The tendency for controls to breed controls and for restrictive measures to trigger further restrictive measures is a vicious circle that invariably accompanies artificial intervention in the market system to bring prices and volume of transactions under policy controls. The observation by the then party secretary of the LDP (Liberal Democratic Party), during the deliberations on introduction of two oil laws (the Crude Demand–Supply Adjustment Law and Law on Emergency Measures for Stabilizing the National Standards of Living) at the time of the oil crisis, that "Once we start regulating we may have to regulate even Ueki tsubo (flower pots)" is a well-known episode.

3. See Schumpeter (1942), p. 88.

4. See Berlin (1969).

References

Arrow, K. J. (1962). Economic welfare and the allocation of resources of invention. In "The Rate and Direction of Inventive Activity," (R. R. Nelson, ed.), pp. 619–622. Princeton University Press, Princeton, New Jersey.

Baldwin, R. E. (1969). The case against infant-industry protection. *J. Pol. Economy* **77**, 295–305.

Baldwin, R. E. (1984). Rent-seeking and trade policy: An industry approach. *Weltwirtschaft. Arch.* **4**, 662–677.

Barzel, Y. (1968). Optimal timing of innovations. *Rev. Econ. Stat.* **50** (August) 348–355.

Baumol, W. J. (1982). Contestable markets: An uprising in the theory of industry structure. *Am. Economic Rev.* **72** (March) 1–15.

Baumol, W. J., and Willig, R. D. (1981). Fixed costs, entry barriers, and sustainability of monopoly. *Quart. J. Econ.* **95**, 405–431.

Baumol, W. J., Panzar, J. C., and Willig, R. D. (1982). "Contestable Markets and the Theory of Industry Structure." Harcourt Brace Jovanovich, San Diego, California.

Benoit, J., and Krishna, V. (1984). Dynamic duopoly: Prices and quantities. *Rev. Economic Stud.* **54**, 23–35.

Berlin, I. (1969). "Four Essays on Liberty." Oxford University Press, London and New York.

Bhagwati, J. N. (1958). Immiserizing growth: A geometric note. *Rev. Economic Stud.* **25**, 201–205.

Bhagwati, J. N. (1965). On the equivalence of tariffs and quotas. *In* "Trade, Growth and the Balance of Payments," (R. E. Caves, H. G. Johnson, and P. B. Kennen, eds.), pp. 53–67. Rand McNally, Chicago, Illinois.

Brander, J. A., and Spencer, B. J. (1981). Tariffs and the extraction of foreign monopoly rent under potential entry. *Can. J. Econ.* **14**, 371–389.

Brander, J. A., and Spencer, B. J. (1983). Strategic commitment with R&D: The symmetric case. *Bell. J. Econ.* **14** (Spring) 225–235.

Brander, J. A., and Spencer, B. J. (1984). Tariff protection and imperfect competition. *In* (H. Kierzkowski, ed.) "Monopolistic Competition in International Trade" (H. Kierzkowski, ed.), pp. 194–206. Oxford University Press, Oxford and New York.

Brander, J. A., and Spencer, B. J. (1985). Export subsidies and international market share rivalry. *J. Int. Econ.* **18**, 83–100.

Bresnahan, T. F. (1981). Duopoly models with consistent conjectures. *Am. Economic Rev.* **71**, 934–945.

Bronfenbrenner, J. (1966). Excessive competition. *Monumenta Nipponica,* **21**, 114–124.

Bulow, J. I., Geanakoplos, J. D., and Klemperer, P. D. (1985). Multimarket oligopoly: Strategic substitutes and complements. *J. Pol. Economy* **93**, 488–511.

Chipman, J. S. (1970). External economies of scale and competitive equilibrium. *Quart. J. Econ.* **84**, 347–385.

Corden, M. W. (1974). "Trade Policy and Economic Welfare." Oxford University Press, Oxford and New York.

Dasgupta, P., and Stiglitz, J. (1980a). Uncertainty, industrial structure and the speed of R&D. *Bell. J. Econ.* **11** (Spring) 1–28.

273

Dasgupta, P., and Stiglitz, J. (1980b). Industrial structure and the nature of innovative activity. *Economic J.* **90**, 266–293.

Deardorff, A. V. (1987). Safeguards policy and the conservative social welfare function. *In* "Protection and Competition in International Trade" (H. Kierzkowski, ed.), pp. 22–40. Blackwell, Oxford.

Demsetz, H. (1969). Information and efficiency: Another viewpoint. *J. Law Econ.* **12** (April) 1–22.

Destler, I. M., Fukui, H., and Sato, H. (1979). "The Textile Wrangle: Conflict in Japanese–American Relations 1969–71." Cornell University Press, Ithaca, New York.

Dixit, A. K. (1979). A model of duopoly suggesting a theory of entry barriers. *Bell. J. Econ.* **10**, 20–32.

Dixit, A. K. (1980). The role of investment in entry deterrence. *Economic J.* **90**, 95–106.

Dixit, A. K. (1982). Recent developments in oligopoly theory. *Am. Economic Rev.* **72** (May) 12–17.

Dixit, A. K. (1985). "The Cutting of International Technological Competition." Mimeograph.

Dixit, A. K., and Grossman, G. M. (1986). Targeted Export Promotion with several oligopolistic industries. *J. Econ.* **21**, 139–152.

Dixit, A. K., and Kyle, A. S. (1985). The use of protection and subsidies, for entry promotion and deterrence. *Am. Economic Rev.* **75**, 139–152.

Dixit, A. K., and Stiglitz, J. E. (1977). Monopolistic competition and optimum product diversity. *Am. Economic Rev.* **67**, 297–308.

Dore, R. (1986). "Flexible Rigidities." Athlone, London.

Dornbusch, R., Fischer, S., and Samuelson, P. A. (1977). Comparative advantage, trade and payments in a Ricardian model with a continuum of goods. *Am. Economic Rev.* **67**, 823–839.

Eaton, C., and Lipsey, R. (1980). Exit barriers are entry barriers: The durability of capital as a barrier to entry. *Bell J. Econ.* **11**, 721–724.

Eaton, C., and Lipsey, R. (1981). Capital, commitment, and entry equilibrium. *Bell J. Econ.* **12** (Autumn), 593–604.

Eaton, J., and Grossman, G. M. (1987). Optimal trade and industrial policy under oligopoly. *Quart. J. Econ.* **101**, 383–406.

Ethier, W. J. (1982). Decreasing costs in international trade and Frank Graham's argument for protection. *Econometrica* **50**, 1243–1268.

Farrell, J., and Saloner, G. (1985). Standardization, compatibility, and innovation. *Rand J. Econ.* **16**, 70–83.

Fox, J. R. (1974). "Arming America: How the U.S. Buys Arms." Harvard University Press, Cambridge, Massachusetts.

Friedman, J. W. (1977). "Oligopoly and the Theory of Games." North-Holland, Amsterdam.

Friedman, J. W. (1986). "Game Theory with Applications to Economics." Oxford University Press, Oxford and New York.

Fudenberg, D., and Tirole, J. (1984). The fat-cat effect, the puppy-dog ploy, and the lean and hungry look. *Am. Economic Rev.: Papers and Proceedings* **74**, 361–366.

Fudenberg, D., and Tirole, J. (1986). "Dynamic Models of Oligopoly." Harwood Academic Publishers, Chur, Switzerland.

Fudenberg, D., and Tirole, J. (1987). Preemption and rent equalization in the adoption of new technology. *Rev. Economic Stud.* **52**, 383–401.

Fudenberg, D., Gilbert, R. J., Stiglitz, J. E., and Tirole, J. (1983). Preemption, leapfrogging and competition in patent races. *Eur. Economic Rev.* **22**, 3–31.

Gilbert, R. J., and Newbery, D. M. G. (1982). Preemptive patenting and the persistence of monopoly. *Am. Economic Rev.* **72**, 514–526.

Grubel, H. G. (1966). The anatomy of classical and modern infant industry arguments. *Weltwirtschaft. Arch.* **97**, 325–342.

Haberler, G. (1950). Some problems in the pure theory of international trade. *Economic J.* **60** (June), 223–240.

Harris, M., and Raviv, A. (1978). Some results on incentive contracts with applications to education and employment, health insurance, and law enforcement. *Am. Economic Rev.* **68**, 20–30.

Harris, M., and Raviv, A. (1979). Optimal incentive contracts with imperfect information. *J. Economic Theory* **20**, 231–259.

Heller, W. P., and Starrett, D. A. (1976) On the nature of externalities. *In* "Theory and Measurement of Economic Externalities" (S. A. Y. Lin, ed.), pp. 9–21. Academic Press, New York.

Herberg, H., and Kemp, M. C. (1969). Some implications of variable returns to scale. *Can. J. Econ.* **2**, 403–415.

Hindley, B. (1984). Empty economics in the case for industrial policy. *World Economy* **7**, 277–294.

Hirshleifer, J. (1971). The private and social value of information and the reward to inventive activity. *Am. Economic Rev.* **61** (September), 561–574.

Houthakker, H. S., and Magee, S. P. (1969). Income and price elasticities in world trade. *Rev. Econ. Stat.* **51**, 111–125.

Imai, K.-I., Uzawa, H., Komiya, R., Negishi, T., and Murakami, Y. (1972). "Kakaku Riron" ("Price Theory"), Vol. 3. Iwanami Shoten, Tokyo, Japan.

Itoh, M. (1978). "A Theory of Imperfect Competition in International Trade and Investment." Ph.D. Dissertation (unpublished). University of Rochester, Rochester, New York.

Itoh, M. (1984). Boeki masatsu to seisaku teki taio (Trade friction and policy response). *Kanzei Chosa Jiho* (*Tariff Study Journal,* Special Issue), vol. 35, Tariff Bureau, Ministry of Finance.

Itoh, M. (1985). Boeki kozo to kawase reto (Trade structure and exchange rate). *Keizai-Gaku Ronshu* **54** (No. 1), 62–75.

Itoh, M. (1987). "Industrial Policy and Corporate Growth in the Automobile Industry—Japan's Postwar Experience." Paper presented at the MITI Conference, Tokyo.

Itoh, M., and Kiyono, K. (1983). "Strategic Export Subsidization Policy and the National Welfare; Lerner's Symmetry Theorem Reconsidered." Discussion paper, 83-F-9, Faculty of Economics, University of Tokyo, Tokyo, Japan.

Itoh, M., and Kiyono, K. (1987). Welfare enhancing export subsidies. *J. Pol. Economy* **95**, No. 1 (February) 115–137.

Itoh, M., and Negishi, T. (1987). Disequilibrium trade theories. *In* "Fundamentals of Pure and Applied Economics." Harwood Academic Publishers, Chur, Switzerland.

Itoh, M., and Ohyama, M. (1985). "Kokusai Boeki" ("International Trade"). Iwanami Shoten, Tokyo, Japan.

Itoh, M., and Ono, Y. (1982). Tariffs, quotas and market structure. *Quart. J. Econ.* **97**, 295–305.

Itoh, M., and Ono, Y. (1984). Tariffs vs. quotas under duopoly of heterogeneous goods. *J. Int. Econ.* **17**, 359–373.

Itoh, M., Okuno, M., Kiyono, K., and Suzumura, K. (1984). Sangyo seisaku no keizai bunseki (Economic analysis of industrial policy). *Kikan Gendai Keizai* [*Contemporary Economy*] **58**, 73–90, **59**, 82–99, **60**, 113–137, **61**, 65–90.

Itoh, M., Kiyono, K., and Honda, T. (1986, 1987). Seisaku kettei to minkan no taio: Boeki seisaku no koka ni tsuite no atarashii shiten (Policy decision and responses: A new view on the effects of trade policies"). *Keizai-gaku Ronshu,* **52** (No. 3), 33–46; (No. 4), 69–79.

Johnson, H. G. (1965). An economic theory of protectionism, tariff bargaining, and the formation of customs unions. *J. Pol. Economy* **73**, 256–283.

Johnson, H. G. (1970). A new view of the infant industry argument. *In* "Studies in International Economics" (I. A. McDougal *et al.,* eds.), pp. 58–76. North-Holland.

Kaizuka, K. (1973). "Keizai Seisaku no Kadai" ("Problems of Economic Policy"). Tokyo Daigaku Shuppan-kai, Tokyo, Japan.

Kamien, M. I., and Schwartz, N. (1982). "Market Structure and Innovation." Cambridge University Press, Cambridge and New York.

Katz, M. L. (1986) An analysis of cooperative research and development. *Rand J. Econ.* **17** (No. 4) (Winter), 527–543.

Katz, M. L., and Shapiro, C. (1985). Network externalities, competition and compatibility. *Am. Economic Rev.* **75**, 424–440.

Kemp, M. C. (1960). The Mill–Bastable infant-industry dogma. *J. Pol. Economy* **8**, 65–67.

Kemp, M. C. (1964). "The Pure Theory of International Trade." Prentice-Hall.

Kemp, M. C. (1974). Learning by doing: Formal tests for intervention in an open economy. *Keio Economic Stud.* **11**, 1–7.

Kemp, M. C., and Negishi, T. (1970). Variable returns to scale, commodity taxes, factor market distortions and their implications for trade gains. *Swed. J. Econ.* **72**, 1–11.

Kirzner, I. M. (1973). "Competition and Entrepreneurship." The University of Chicago Press, Chicago, Illinois.

Kiyono, K. (1986). Fundamental nature of quasi-Cournot oligopoly markets. *Gakushuin Economic Papers* **59**, 133–155.

Kiyono, K. (1987). "Strategic Trade Intervention for International Oligopoly Reconsidered." Mimeograph.

Kiyono, K., and Okuno-Fujiwara, M. (1987). First-mover and second-mover advantage: Innovation and imitation in dynamic oligopoly. *Economic Stud. Quart.* (in press).

Komiya, R. (1975). "Gendai Nihon Keizai Kenkyu" ("Studies of Contemporary Japanese Economy"). Tokyo Daigaku Shuppann-kai, Tokyo, Japan.

Komiya, R., and Amano, A. (1972). "Kokusai Keizai-Gaku" ("International Economics"). Iwanami Shoten, Tokyo, Japan.

Komiya, R., and Itoh, M. (1986). International trade and trade policy of Japan: 1955–1984. *In* "The Political Economy of Japan" (T. Inoguchi and D. I. Okimoto, eds.), Vol. 2: The Changing International Context. Stanford University Press, Stanford, California.

Komiya, R., Okuno, M., and Suzumura, K. (eds.) (1987). "Industrial Policy of Japan." Academic Press, San Diego, California.

Kosai, Y. (1981). "Kodo Seicho no Jidai Gendai Nihon Keizai Shi Noto" ("The Age of Rapid Growth—Notes on Contemporary Economic History of Japan"). Nihon Hyoron-Sha, Tokyo, Japan.

Kreps, D. M., and Spence, A. M. (1983). "Models of Spillovers in R&D." Mimeograph.

Krugman, P. R. (1979). A model of innovation, technology transfer, and the world distribution of income. *J. Pol. Economy* **87**, 253–266.

Krugman, P. R. (1982). Trade in differentiated products and the political economy of trade liberalization. *In* "Import Competition and Response" (J. N. Bhagwati, ed.), pp. 197–208. University of Chicago Press, Chicago, Illinois.

Krugman, P. R. (1983). New theories of trade among industrial countries. *Am. Economic Rev.* **73** (May), 343–348.

Krugman, P. R. (1984). Import protection as export promotion: International competition in the presence of oligopoly and economies of scale. *In* "Monopolistic Competition in International Trade" (H. Kierzkowski, ed.), pp. 180–193. Oxford University Press, Oxford and New York.

Lawrence, R. Z. (1988). "A Depressed View of Policies for Depressed Industries." *In* "Trade and Investment Relations among the United States, Canada, and Japan" (R. M. Stern, ed.), pp. 174–213. University of Chicago Press, Chicago.

Lazear, E., and Rosen, S., (1981). Rank-order tournaments as optimum labor contracts. *J. Pol. Economy* **89**, 841–864.

Lee, T., and Wilde, L. (1980). Market structure and innovation: A reformulation. *Quart. J. Econ.* **94**, 429–436.

Lerner, A. P. (1936). The symmetry between import and export taxes. *Economica* **3**, 306–313.

Linder, S. B. (1961). "An Essay on Trade and Transformation." Almqvist and Wicksell, Stockholm, Sweden.

Loury, G. C. (1979). Market structure and innovation. *Quart. J. Econ.* **93** (August), 395–410.

Malinvaud, E. (1972). The allocation of individual risks in large market. *J. Economic Theory* **4**, 312–328.

Mankiw, N. G., and Whinston, M. D. (1986). Free entry and social inefficiency. *Rand J. Econ.* **17**, 48–58.

Matsuyama, K., and Itoh, M. (1985). "Protection Policy in a Dynamic Oligopoly Market." Discussion Paper Series, Faculty of Economics, University of Tokyo, Tokyo, Japan.

Mayer, W. (1974). Short-run and long-run equilibrium for a small open economy. *J. Pol. Economy* **82** (No. 4), 955–967.

McAfee, R. P., and McMillan, J. (1986). Bidding for contracts: A principal–agent analysis. *Rand J. Econ.* **17** (No. 3) (Autumn), 326–338.

Morozumi, Y. (1966). "Sangyo Seisaku no Riron" ("Theory of Industrial Policy"). Nihon Keizai Shuppan-sha, Tokyo, Japan.

Morozumi, Y. (1973). Sangyo seisaku (Industrial policy). *In* "Sangyo Seisaku no Riron" ("Theory of Industrial Policy") (M. Shinohara and M. Baba, eds.), Vol. 3 of Gendai sangyo-ron (Modern industry). Nihon Keizai Shinbun-sha, Tokyo, Japan.

Mussa, M. (1974). Tariffs and the distribution of income: The importance of factor specificity, substitutability, and intensity in the short and long run. *J. Pol. Economy* **82** (No. 5), 1191–1203.

Mussa, M. (1978). Dynamic adjustment in the Heckscher–Ohlin–Samuelson model. *J. Pol. Economy* **86** (No. 334), 488–510.

Mussa, M. (1982). Government policy and the adjustment process. *In* "Import Competition and Response" (J. Bhagwati, ed.), pp. 73–120. University of Chicago Press, Chicago, Illinois.

Nakamura, T. (1969). Sengo no sangyo seisaku (Postwar industrial policy). *In* "Nihon no Sangyo Soshiki" ("Japan's Industrial Organization") (H. Niida and A. Ono, eds.), pp. 303–315. Iwanami Shoten, Tokyo, Japan.

Nakamura, T. (1974). Nihon ni okeru sangyo seisaku no tokushoku to hyoka (Features and evaluations of Japan's industrial policy). *Tokyo Keizai Rinji Zokan* (*Special Issues on Industrial Policy*) No. 3810, 58–64.

Nakamura, T. (1978). "Nihon Keizai—Sono Seicho to Kozo" ("Japanese Economy: Its Growth and Structure"). Daigaku Shuppann-kai, Tokyo, Japan.

Nalebuff, B. J., and Stiglitz, J. E. (1983a). Information, competition, and markets. *Am. Economic Rev.* **73** (May), 278–283.

Nalebuff, B. J., and Stiglitz, J. E. (1983b). Prizes and incentives: Towards a general theory of compensation and competition. *Bell J. Econ.* **14** (No. 1) (Spring), 21–43.

Neary, J. P. (1982) Intersectoral capital mobility, wage stickiness, and the case for adjustment assistance. *In* "Import Competition and Response" (J. N. Bhagwati, ed.), pp. 39–67. University of Chicago Press, Chicago, Illinois.

Neary, J. P., and Stiglitz, J. E. (1983). Toward a reconstruction of Keynsian economics: Expectations and constrained equilibria. *Quart. J. Econ.* **98** (Supplement), 199–228.

Negishi, T. (1971). "Boeki Rieki to Kokusai Shushi" ("Gains from Trade and Balance of Payments"). Sobun-sha, Tokyo, Japan.

Negishi, T. (1972). "General Equilibrium Theory and International Trade." North-Holland, Amsterdam.

Niki, Y. (1974). Kato kyoso no mekanizumu (On excessive competition). *In* "Sangyo Soshiki" ("Industrial Organization") (M. Shinohara and M. Baba, eds.), Vol. 3 of Gendai sangyo-ron (Contemporary industry). Nihon Keizai Shinbun-sha, Tokyo, Japan.

Novshek, W. (1980). Cournot equilibrium with free entry. *Rev. Economic Stud.* **47**, 473–486.

Ohtaki, S. (1983). Dai-kibo kenkyu kaihatsu purojekuto no manegimento—kogyo gijutsu-ni ogata purojekuto no soshiki bunseki (Management system of large-scale R & D cooperation project—organizational analysis of large-scale R & D project of MITI). *Senshu-Keiei-Gaku Ronshu* **36**, 159–187.

Ohyama, M. (1982). Gekika suru kokusai boeki masatsu (Intensifying trade frictions). *Kikan Gendai Keizai* (*Contemporary Economy*) **48**, 6–20.

Okuguchi, K. (1971). "Kasen no Riron" ("Oligopoly Theory"). Sobun-sha, Tokyo, Japan.

Okuno, M. (1984a). "Scale Economies, Oligopolistic Competition and Effects of Industrial Policies." Mimeograph.

Okuno, M. (1984b). Corporate loyalty and bonus payments: An analysis of work incentives in Japan.
In "The Economic Analysis of the Japanese Firm" (M. Aoki, ed.), pp. 387–411. North-
Holland, Amsterdam.

Okuno, M., and Suzumura, K. (1985). Kasen sangyo he no hojo-kin to keizai kosei (Subsidies on
oligopolistic industries and economic welfare). *Keizai-Gaku Ronshu* **50** (No. 4), 2–15.

Okuno, M., and Suzumura, K. (1986). The economic analysis of industrial policy: A conceptual
framework through the Japanese experience. *In* "Industrial Policies for Pacific Economic
Growth," pp. 24–26. Allen & Unwin, London.

Okuno-Fujiwara, M., and Suzumura, K. (1987). "Strategic Cost-Reduction Investment and Economic Welfare." Discussion paper, 87-F-5, Faculty of Economics, University of Tokyo, Tokyo,
Japan.

Okuno, M., and Suzumura, K. (1988). "Mikuro Keizai-Gaku II" ("Microeconomics, Vol. II").
Iwanami Shoten, Tokyo, Japan.

Okuno, M., Postlewaite, and Roberts, J. (1980). Oligopoly and competition in large markets. *Am.
Economic Rev.* **70**, 22–31.

Okuno-Fujiwara, M. (1988). Interdependence of industries, coordination failure and strategic promotion of an industry. *J. Int. Econ.* **25** (No. 1/2), 25–43.

Ordover, J. A., and Willig, R. D. (1985). Antitrust for high-technology industries: Assessing research joint ventures and mergers. *J. Law Econ.* **28** (May), 311–333.

Panagariya, A. (1981). Variable returns to scale in production and patterns of specialization. *Am.
Economic Rev.* **71**, 221–230.

Perry, M. K. (1982). Oligopoly and consistent conjectural variations. *Bell J. Econ.* **13**, 197–205.

Perry, M. K. (1984). Scale economies, imperfect competition and public policy. *J. Industr. Econ.*
32, 313–333.

Reinganum, J. F. (1983). Uncertain innovation and the persistence of monopoly. *Am. Economic Rev.*
74, 341–348.

Reinganum, J. F. (1984). Practical implications of game theoretic models of R&D. *Am. Economic
Rev.: Papers Proc.* **74**, 61–66.

Ross, S. (1973). The economic theory of agency: The principal's problem. *Am. Economic Rev.* **63**,
134–139.

Salop, S. (1979). Strategic entry deterrence. *Am. Economic Rev.* **69** (May), 335–338.

Schelling, T. C. (1960). "The Strategy of Conflict." Harvard University Press, Cambridge,
Massachusetts.

Scherer, F. M. (1980). "Industrial Market Structure and Economic Performance," 2nd Ed. Rand
McNally, Chicago, Illinois.

Scherer, F. M. (1986). "Innovation and Growth." MIT Press, Cambridge, Massachusetts.

Schmalensee, R. (1982). Product differentiation advantages of pioneering brands. *Am. Economic
Rev.* **82**, 349–365.

Schumpeter, J. A. (1942). "Capitalism, Socialism and Democracy." Allen & Unwin, London.

Schumpeter, J. A. (1950). "Capitalism, Socialism and Democracy," 3rd Ed. Allen & Unwin,
London.

Scitovsky, T. (1954) Two concepts of external economies. *J. Pol. Economy* **63**, 143–151.

Shibagaki, K. (1974). Zaibatsu kaitai to shutyu haijo-ho (Disorganization of zaibatsu-group and anti-
concentration law). *In* "Sengo Kaikaku," Vol. VII. The University of Tokyo Press, Tokyo,
Japan.

Shinohara, M. (1974). 360-Yen reto he no kasetsu (On 360 yen rate hypothesis). *Kikan Riro Keizai-
gaku* **25** (No. 1), 1–9.

Shubik, M. (1982). "Game Theory in the Social Sciences." MIT Press, Cambridge, Massachusetts.

Spence, A. M. (1977). Entry, investment and oligopolistic pricing. *Bell J. Econ.* **8**, 534–544.

Spence, A. M. (1979). Investment strategy and growth in a new market. *Bell J. Econ.* **10**, 1–19.

Spence, A. M. (1981). The learning curve and competition. *Bell J. Econ.* **12**, 49–70.

Spence, A. M. (1984). Cost reduction, competition and industry performance. *Econometrica* **52**, 101–121.

Spencer, B., and Brander, J. (1983). International R & D rivalry and industrial strategy. *Rev. Economic Stud.* **50**, 707–722.

Stewart, M. B. (1983). Noncooperative oligopoly and preemptive innovation without winner-takeall. *Quart. J. Econ.* **98**, 681–694.

Stiglitz, J. E. (1974). Incentives and risk sharing in sharecropping. *Rev. Economic Stud.* **41**, 219–255.

Stiglitz, J. E. (1981). Potential competition may reduce welfare. *Am. Economic Rev.* **71**, 184–189.

Stiglitz, J. E. (1984). "Theory of Competition, Incentives, and Risk." Discussion paper, No. 311. Princeton University, Princeton, New Jersey.

Suzuki, M. (1981). "Gemu Riron" ("Introduction to Game Theory"). Kyoritsu Shuppan, Tokyo, Japan.

Suzumura, K. (1982). "Keizai Keikaku-Ron" ("Theory of Economic Planning"). Chikuma Shobo, Tokyo, Japan.

Suzumara, K. (1983). "Entry in a Cournot Market: Equilibrium versus Optimality." Discussion Paper, No. 94 (November). Institute of Economic Research, Hitotsubashi University, Japan.

Suzumura, K., and Kiyono, K. (1987). Entry barriers and economic welfare. *Rev. Economic Stud.* **177**, 157–167.

Suzumura, K., and Okuno-Fujiwara, M. (1987). Industrial policy in Japan: Overview and evaluation. *In* "Trade Friction and Economic Policy" (R. Sato and P. Wachtel, eds.). Chapter 5, pp. 50–79. Cambridge University Press, Cambridge, Massachusetts.

Takacs, W. E. (1978). The nonequivalence of tariffs, import quotas, and voluntary export restraints. *J. Int. Econ.* **8** (November), 565–573.

Tsuruta, T. (1982). "Sengo Nihon no Sangyo Seisaku" ("Postwar Industrial Policy of Japan"). Nihon Keizai Shinbun-sha, Tokyo, Japan.

Tsusho Sangyo Sho (Ministry of International Trade and Industry) (1975). "Tsusho Sangyo Gyosei Shi Hanseiki no Ayumi" ("A Quarter Century of MITI Administration"). Tsusho Sangyo Chosa-kai, Tokyo, Japan.

Uekusa, M. (1982). "Sangyo Soshiki-Ron" ("Theory of Industrial Organization"). Chikuma Shobo, Tokyo, Japan.

Vernon, R. (1966). International investment and international trade in the product cycle. *Quart. J. Econ.* **80** (May), 190–207.

Vernon, J., and Graham, D. A. (1971). Profitability of monopolization by vertical integration. *J. Pol. Economy* **79**, 924–925.

Von Weizsacker, C. C. (1980a). A welfare analysis of barriers to entry. *Bell J. Econ.* **11**, 399–420.

Von Weizsacker, C. C. (1980b). "Barriers to Entry: A Theoretical Treatment." Springer-Verlag, Berlin and New York.

Wakasugi, R. (1986). "Gijutsu Kakushin to Kenkyu Kaihatsu no Keizai Bunseki—Nihon no Kigyo Kodo to Sangyo Seisaku" ("Economic Analysis of Technical Progress and Research and Development—Japanese Firms' Behavior and Industrial Policy"). Toyo Keizai Shinpo-Sha, Tokyo, Japan.

Wakasugi, R. and Goto, A. (1985). Kyodo kenkyu kaihatsu to gijutsu kakushin (Joint research activities and technological innovation). *In* "Gijutsu Kakushin to Kigyo Kodo" ("Technological Innovation and Firm Behaviors") (Y. Okamoto and T. Wakasugi, eds.), pp. 193–217. Tokyo Daigaku Shuppann-Kai, Tokyo, Japan.

Weitzman, M. L., Newey, W., and Rabin, M. (1981). Sequential R & D strategy for synfuels. *Bell J. Econ.* **12** (Autumn), 574–590.

Williamson, O. (1975). "Markets and Hierarchies: Analysis and Antitrust Implications."

Williamson, O. (1975). "Markets and Hierarchies: Analysis and Antitrust Implications." Free Press, New York.

Wolff, A. (1983). "The Effect of Government Targeting on World Semiconduction Competition." Semiconductor Industry Association.

Yamazawa, I. (1984). Seni sangyo (Textile industry). *In* "Nihon No Sangyo Seisaku" ("Industrial Policy of Japan") (R. Komiya, M. Okuno, and K. Suzumura, eds.). Tokyo Daigaku Shuppankai, Tokyo, Japan, pp. 345–367.

Yanagida, K. (1983). "Nihon ha Moete Irkua" ("Is Japan Burning?"). Bungei Shunju-sha, Tokyo, Japan.

Young, A. A. (1928). Increasing returns and economic progress. *Economic J.* **38,** 527–542.

Index of Names

Subject Index

Economic Theory, Econometrics, and Mathematical Economics

Edited by Karl Shell, *Cornell University*

Previous Volumes in the Series